New Dimensions
in Music Education

by
Lloyd Frederick Sunderman

The Scarecrow Press, Inc.
Metuchen, N.J.   1972

Library of Congress Cataloging in Publication Data

Sunderman, Lloyd Frederick, 1905-
    New dimensions in music education.

    First ed. published in 1965 under title: School
music teaching: its theory and practice.
    Includes bibliographies.
    1.   School music--Instruction and study--U. S.
I.   Title.
MT3.U5S82 1972   780'.72973   73-189289
ISBN 0-8108-0482-4

This is a revised and expanded edition of the
author's School Music Teaching: Its Theory
and Practice, The Scarecrow Press, 1965.

PREFACE

The development of musical culture in America has always been dependent upon the way in which tastes for it have been acquired and nurtured in our schools. Whatever understanding and pleasure an adult experiences with music result largely from his classroom association with functional music during his school days. The keystone in the arch built upon this foundation is, for most individuals, at least 12 years of formal schooling and association with teachers. Just how successfully this teaching is done is the major concern of this book.

This book, revised and expanded from my 1965 work, School Music Teaching: Its Theory and Practice, has been written with a concern for the theoretical and instructional problems confronting elementary and secondary teachers of music in this wholly new musical era of the 1970's. The school music administrator, administrator-teacher, or professional music educator must be trained to develop a vigorous, intelligent music program that helps children to attain musical enjoyment for the full life.

New emphasis has been placed upon philosophical, psychological, instructional and administrative concerns. General and professional music have been given a broad spectrum of discussion. Music education for youth in the inner city, urban, and suburban schools has been discussed in detail. Included are secondary school courses of study from many sections of the United States. They should prove helpful for study and evaluation by the inquiring student. Basically, this book should be of inestimable assistance to all those who are preparing to teach music in the elementary and secondary school.

Lloyd Frederick Sunderman

iii

CONTENTS

v

Part One. Theoretical Considerations

CHAPTER I: EARLY MUSIC EDUCATION

Throughout the 17th and 18th centuries the educational development of the United States was greatly circumscribed by the practical considerations of readin', 'ritin', and 'rithmetic. The early Puritanical desire was to extirpate the objectionable religious dogmas of the Established Church of England, which had eventually caused the Puritans to emigrate to America in revolt.

During this early period of economic, social, and religious struggle for survival, opportunities for music education were lacking. Clearing the frontiers of a new land required a kind of energy more physical than contemplative. With the rise of communal centers there came a demand for social organization--literacy and the significance of the individual citizen became major concerns. Actually, it was not until about 1830 that enlightenment through varied forms of educational opportunity became manifest. This was largely due to the growing emancipation of the individuality of man.

In keeping with the educational philosophy of the period, the champions of education insisted that music should find an important place in the moral and spiritual development of children. Music, like all education, had to demonstrate its worth as a discipline for improving man's moral and intellectual growth. During this early period those enlightened and enterprising citizens who were interested in the welfare of their children championed music because they believed it had a salutary effect upon moral development.

Some Early Concepts. In the history of American school music, the decade 1830-1840 may be considered a period of preparation. An epoch-making speech by William Channing Woodbridge, "On Vocal Music As a Branch of Common Education, " delivered before the American Institute of Instruction on August 24, 1830, stirred the imagination of early educational statesmen to the possibilities of vocal music as a legitimate subject of study. It was so effective that scattered instances of school music teaching were reported almost immediately in New York, Ohio, Pennsylvania, and Connecticut. While these do not prove universal acceptance of the idea of public school music, they do indicate its growth and promise.[1]

Beginning with this significant speech by Woodbridge, there continued through the remainder of the 19th century the development of basic concepts for the teaching of music in American public schools. The earliest comprehensive and positive statement was that vocal music should be a branch of common school education. This concept was basic to the "Magna Charta" of American Music Education signed in Boston in 1838. If vocal music could not become a branch of common education, it could not hope for justification as a school subject. Vocal music for the common education of all the children in a democracy still remains a generally accepted concept in American education.

These early protagonists of school music made claims and advanced concepts which were vigorously championed during this early era of music education. Many writers claimed that "Music had the power to sway the passions of the human heart"[2]--the power to act as a desirable determinant in the excessive desires of the mind. Sometimes referred to as heart action, human passion in the final analysis was considered motivated by intellectual thought processes.[3] It was also asserted that the universality of music was unquestionable. This concept was used to signify its acceptability to all school youth. Other characteristics were attributed to music: it was a mental discipline; it improved one's physical well-being; it improved the discipline of the classroom; it would improve church singing; and it was a socializing force.[4] Many of these claims were exaggerations, but they served to advance the cause of 19th century school music.

Concurrently there appeared many informal and formal organizations designed for the encouragement and promotion of education. Music found its sponsorship through a society known as the Eclectic Academy of Music in Cincinnati. About 1834 the specific aims of the Academy were "to promote the cause of the introduction of vocal music as a branch of school education."[5] A Convention of Teachers held in 1835 at Carthage, Ohio, resolved "that Vocal Music should be made a part of common elementary education, for boys and girls."[6] At the fourth annual meeting of the Western Literary Institute and College of Professional Teachers, held in Cincinnati, October, 1834, Professor Nixon delivered an address "On the Influence of Music."[7] The Convention of Friends of Common Schools, held at Marietta, Ohio, November 7-8, 1836, also appointed a committee to report on the subject of the introduction of vocal music into common schools.

James Mulhern found evidences of music being taught in Pennsylvania high schools as early as 1836. He reported in a study of 48 schools that 12 percent were offering music instruction. In another study of 140 schools, covering the period 1836-1900, fourteen percent offered music instruction. It may be even safe to state that some form of singing instruction was offered in some of these schools prior to 1836. Secondary school music study was in evidence prior to the Civil War, and its importance "as a legitimate high school subject was recognized by the National Educational Association ... by 1875."[8] Thus 1840-1865 may be characterized as the period when there was a determined effort to provide music instruction for grammar and high school students.[9]

Outgrowths of Pre-Civil War School Music. The agitation for school music prior to the Civil War resulted in many music education developments. Among the more important were: (1) the appearance of a host of singing and school-music instructors, (2) almost fanatical devotion to the study of the rudiments of music, (3) formalization of instruction to attain perfection in learning the intellectual-scientific aspects of vocal music study, (4) development of song and note teaching materials to aid music study, (5) consideration given by some school systems to the music qualifications of the regular classroom teacher, (6) incorporation of music into required courses of study, (7) fostering of the cause of school music by teachers' conventions, (8) establishment of school music teaching classes for the in-service classroom teacher, and (9) the acquirement of an important instructional status by the salaried school music educator and supervisor.[10]

As the public school music program expanded, the special music teacher found it impossible to teach each day in each room of the school system. This caused problems in supervision and instruction, of which some of the more important aspects were: (1) dual supervision, (2) the classroom teacher as a teacher of music, (3) optional instruction,

(4) instructional obstacles, (5) the instructional period, (6) examinations, and (7) the need for and the construction of textbooks. [11]

During the period 1830-1870 there was little change in the methods of teaching vocal music. Elam Ives and Lowell Mason were the earliest to formulate methods of teaching elementary vocal music. Early American methodologists of school music were divided into two camps--the "rudimentists" and the "combinationists." After 1870 the breach between the two widened. Music reading became the summum bonum of school music. Luther Whiting Mason represented the "song-singing plan," whereby the child first learned an abundance of fine songs by rote, afterwards learning them by note. Hosea Holt had faith in the "exercise plan" which required the child to be drilled in a host of musical exercises. These were taught independently of the songs, but were later applied to music reading. [12]

Early 19th-century vocal music instruction in institutions of higher learning was offered for two fundamental reasons. Most of the normal schools included music in their courses of study because of increasing demands for teachers who could teach music, and colleges and universities also offered music as a cultural study.

The growth of music education in American normal schools, colleges and universities parallels the development of public school music in primary, elementary and secondary schools. Although the college and university were established earlier than the normal school, they offered music instruction no earlier. They too waited for the appearance of the music education movement which came after 1830. Lowell Mason, Charles Aiken, and Luther Whiting Mason devoted their lives to the early cause. Each was a leader of one or more phases of school music education and are partly responsible for the stature of school music today. [13]

Development. American music education has come a long way during the past century. The various ideas which the protagonists of school music championed during the past century were invariably related to the assertion of the validity of teaching vocal music to children in the public schools. The period 1835-1890 saw a succession of experiments in ascertaining the advisability of teaching music. The successes of these early experiments multiplied with such enormity in the early decades of the present century that whole new vistas of opportunity have opened. The tremendous success of school music has brought with it problems which have often found the teaching profession unprepared for or unsure of. The ramifications of these problems place great responsibility upon the professional music administrator.

The Music Supervisors National Conference was organized early in the 20th century during a meeting in Keokuk, Iowa, April 10-12, 1907. From this early meeting there gradually evolved a closely knit organization which in 1970-71 had 60,246 members. [14]

Out of the social and cultural upheaval of World War II it was natural that new goals were to evolve. Men were demanding an opportunity for the determination of their own destinies. The democratic ideal was dynamic because it provided self-determination for all men. The individual desired to be free to choose those experiences that led to a realization of a better life for him and his fellow men.

This forward surge of man's intellect thus became characterized by the actions of all men rather than of the few. Man indubitably became a greater problem to himself. He became more consciously aware of his insufficiency. Increasingly, every man became compelled to understand his newly found interest--himself. It is hoped and it is believed that education will aid man toward the perfection of himself for purposeful social action. Music from time immemorial has been a convenient and often spontaneous means of self-expression and music will aid man in realizing the potential of his greater self.

Discussion

1. Has vocal music become a branch of common education for elementary school children in the United States?
2. Sketch the development of elementary music education in the United States. Keep in mind population growth and then give your appraisal on the basis of growth percentages.
3. Are we pioneering in American music education or have we attained professional maturity?
4. Have we lost ground in any areas of school music education?
5. Was Lowell Mason the first leader of school music in American schools?

6. Trace the development of instrumental music instruction in our public schools.

7. Name five champions of public school music during the period 1830-1890.

8. How did your own elementary and secondary school
music experience differ from that of the period 1865-1890?

9. Why was instrumental music so slow in entering
the public school curriculum?

10. Compare the growth of music education in the
public schools with the development which attended its appearance and expansion in the normal schools and colleges.
Analyze the philosophical as well as the instructional aspects
of the problem.

Notes

1. Sunderman, Lloyd Frederick. "The Era of Beginnings
    in American Music Education (1830-1840)." Journal
    of Research in Music Education, IV: No. 1 (Spring,
    1956), 33.

2. Ibid., 35.

3. Ibid.

4. Sunderman, Lloyd Frederick. "History of Public School
    Music in the United States, 1830-1890." The Edu-
    cational Record, XXII: No. 2 (April, 1941), 206.

5. Sunderman, "The Era of Beginnings in American Music
    Education (1830-1840)," op. cit., 35.

6. Ibid.

7. Ibid.

8. Dennis, Charles M. "The Dynamics of Music Educa-
    tion," Education. 72: No. 1 (September, 1951), 9.

9. Sunderman, "History of Public School Music in the
    United States, 1830-1890," op. cit., 207.

10. Ibid. 208.

11. Ibid. 209-210.

12. Ibid. 210.

13. Sunderman, "History of Public School Music in the
    United States, 1830-1890," op. cit., 205-211.

14. "MENC Annual Report." Music Educators Journal,
    58: No. 4 (December, 1971) 58.

Bibliography

BOOKS (THESES)

Baynham, Edward G.   The Early Development of Music in
    Pittsburgh. Ph.D., University of Pittsburgh, 1945 (pub-
    lished).

Choate, Robert A.   Music Instruction and Supervision in the
    Oakland Public Schools from 1868 to 1950.   Ph.D., Stan-
    ford University, 1951.

DeJarnette, Reven S.   Hollis Ellsworth Dann.   Ed.D., New
    York University, 1940.

Gary, Charles L.   A History of Music Education in the Cin-
    cinnati Public Schools.   Ph.D., University of Cincinnati,
    1951.

John, Robert W.   A History of Public School Vocal Instruc-
    tion Books in the United States.   Ed.D., Indiana Univer-
    sity, 1953.

Kauffman, Harry M.   A History of the Music Educators Na-
    tional Conference.   Ph.D., George Peabody College for
    Teachers, 1942.

Molnar, John W.   The History of the Music Educators' Na-
    tional Conference.   Ed.D., University of Cincinnati, 1948.

Rich, Arthur L.   Lowell Mason, Music Educator.   Ph.D.,
    New York University, 1940 (published).

Sponseller, Amos N.   The Origin and Development of Public
    School Music in Pennsylvania.   Ed.D., Temple University,
    1941 (published).

Sunderman, Lloyd F.   A History of Public School Music in
    the United States (1830-1890).   Ph.D., University of Min-

nesota, 1939.

Tennant, Donald B. The History of Public School Music in
    Iowa, 1900-1951: A Study Limited to Secondary Schools
    in Selected Cities of Over 15,000 Population. Ph.D.,
    State University of Iowa, 1952.

ARTICLES

Sunderman, Lloyd F. "History of Public School Music in
    the United States, 1830-1890." The Educational Record,
    22: No. 2 (April, 1941), 205-211.

_____. "The Advent of Method in Music Education."
Education, 61: No. 9 (May, 1941), 555-561.

_____. "Early Methods of Popularizing Music Educa-
tion." The Journal of Musicology, 3: No. 1 (Summer,
1941), 60-66.

_____. "The Beginnings of Singing in America." The
Journal of Musicology, 3: No. 2 (Fall, 1941), 101-119.

_____. "Chicago's Centennial of School Music." Music
Educator's Journal, 28: No. 5 (April, 1942), 28-30, 63-
64.

_____. "Sign Posts in the History of American Music
Education." Education, 62: No. 9 (May, 1942), 515-550.

_____. "Lowell Mason--Father of American Music."
The Journal of Musicology, IV: No. 1 (November, 1944),
6-19.

_____. "Sign Posts in the Development of Early Music
Education in New York State." The School Music News
(NY), 9: No. 7 (March, 1946), 23-29.

_____. "Some Early Concepts of the Values of Music
Education." The School Music News (NY), 10: No. 10
(June, 1947), 10, 20-22, 25, 27-28.

_____. "Boston and The Magna Charta of Music Educa-
tion." Education, 69: No. 7 (March, 1949), 425-437.

_____. "Early Music Education in Massachusetts."
Education, 72: No. 1 (September, 1951), 45-67.

_____ . "Music Education--Its Early Development in
Ohio." Ohio Music Club News, XIV: No. 2 (Winter,
1956), 2, 3, 5, 6, 12.

_____ . "The Era of Beginnings in American Music Education (1830-1840)." Journal of Research in Music Education. IV: No. 1 (Spring, 1956). 33-39.

ADDITIONAL READINGS

Ballou, Richard. "Knowledge and the Education of Free Peoples." The Educational Record, 18, No. 4: 389-398
(May, 1954).

Birge, Edward B. "One Hundred Years of School Music."
Music Educators Journal, 22: No. 19 (September, 1935).

Henderson, Algo D. "Balm for a Troubled Conscience,"
The Educational Record, 35, No. 3: 165-177, (July 1954).

Kelley, Earl C. Education For What Is Real. New York:
Harper & Brothers, 1947. 114.

Shaffer, Robert O. "Counseling for Democratic Leadership."
Education, 74: No. 8 (April, 1954), 507-511.

Tead, Ordway. "Four Basic Approaches to Education Administration." Education, 75: No. 4 (1954), 208-213.

Washburne, Carleton. The World's Good. New York: John
Day Co., 1954. 301.

Willis, Benjamin C. "The Stake of Music in Education."
Music Educators Journal, 40: No. 6(June, 1954), 9-12.

CHAPTER II: CONCEPTS AND GOALS IN MUSIC EDUCATION

Any review of the literature of music education reveals the differences of meaning that exist in the ideas, opinions, principles, and purposes expressed by its many writers. Even a cursory review of these writings points up the difficulty in eliminating peripheral notions about what music does to or achieves within the individual. I have therefore striven to isolate and interpret some of the concepts that are fundamental to the philosophical development of music education.

A philosophy of music education does exist, but music educators have often done themselves a disservice by becoming diverted from it by their insistent pursuit of musical specialization. If music is to have a significant cultural value for social living, the education of the few at the expense of the many will never create it. General music education is an objective of high social importance.

There are some concepts of the values of music that we have found to pervade all current music education; these are discussed in the following pages. (No attempt has been made to determine the priority of their importance.)

Feeling and Emotion. An individual responds emotionally to music by the impact of its sound, movement, or structuralisms. Thus, appreciation is a very fundamental concept in music education. Appreciation and enjoyment of music is the perception of a condition, state of feeling, or emotion. There are many feelings that are aroused by music and they have many characteristics of unpredictable intensity.

These emotional states are basic to the initial feelings for music which occur after sound has been uttered. Individuals enjoy music or express themselves through it because it is a convenient vehicle. Beyond the feeling, and the response to that feeling, there is the added element of cognition--the awareness of feeling and emotion. Appreciation and enjoyment are the states that characterize cognition and music education in our schools can aid children in arriving at appreciation through evaluation, discrimination, awareness, acquaintance, and understanding. These concepts must be considered intrinsic if the child is to be assured satisfaction. The collective impact of the remaining philosophical concepts which are to be discussed will play an all important role in attaining musical satisfaction for the child. This impact can be attained by a program that conceives of music education as broadly exploring the cognitions that can be released through rhythmic, song-singing, listening, creative, and re-creative experiences.

Rhythmic Expression and Movement. Rhythm is the life blood of music. Rhythm and movement are the most fundamental physical expressions of music. The cyclic character of impulse or beat in music are an ever-present reality. Pulse is the regulator of movement. Rhythmic movement, like pulse, is expressed in the most basic of all human propelling actions, such as walking or running. Even the beat of the human heart follows a rhythmic pulse pattern.

The early music education of the child is made more interesting and easy by his fondness for any activity that is rhythmic. Rhythm is a medium for the control of duration in musical time and is inseparable from music.

Rhythm is the most powerful medium for aiding children in exploring metre, phrase, form, accent, measure, and the cyclic pulse in music. The creativity that these experiences provide the child is inexhaustible.

Creative Value. Discriminative choices are necessary to the development of discriminative selection, which is basic to the artistic choice of expression, or creativity. The individual must possess these "evaluative" concepts in order to determine his selection of "this or that" music, for the purpose of attaining artistic appreciation.

Musicality (musical intellectual competency) is evidenced by early precocious manifestations of creativity and performance (composing, singing, and playing). Superior musicianship requires intelligence of a high order.

An environment for creativeness must be established whenever instruction takes place. It implies the necessity of creative insight by the instructor as well as by the one to be instructed. The teacher becomes more than a dispenser of musical knowledge; he arouses imaginative thinking during the process.

Song-Singing Value. The human voice is the best instrument that man has for expressing himself. Intelligent
sounding (rhythm, melody, and structuralisms) becomes, with
verbalisms, singing. Song singing is the highest form of
verbal musical expression. It aids the child in expressing
the entire gamut of his feelings and emotions. Singing and
speaking are among the most common activities of man during his waking hours. They completely co-ordinate the action
of body and mind. Of all media of music instruction in our
schools, singing is the most easily initiated and the least expensive.

Such basic elements of music as rhythm, melody,
harmony, pitch, dynamics and tempo are ever-present in
song singing. The individual develops appreciations for tone
quality as well as a broadened understanding of many language acts through song singing.

Song singing in our schools is becoming more imaginative. Especially at the primary school level, children are
being allowed to create their own melodic line and verse.
Music teachers in school rooms are beginning to integrate
song experiences with various subject matter areas in order
to develop appreciation for the cultures of many nationalities.

Participant and Functional Value. Music must be performed to be experienced. A musical experience implies
that the individual has been a participant. But music must
as well become part of the body of the individual--it is a
multiform phenomenon of sound, movement, and structure.
The vibrancy of music's message must pervade his physical,
emotional, intellectual, and spiritual being. The highest
form of music appreciation is creating live music. We have
often counted too heavily on listening--that is too passive.
It is important that how we experience and what we experience be closely allied. If music is to possess a living quality it must aid people in enjoying the functions of daily living; it must harmonize the individual with his philosophical
world.

The participant and functional values of music have
long been recognized. "Music for every child and every
child for music," has long implied the functional partner arrangement that should be every child's experience. Too often curricula have veered from the general educational values
of music and have tended toward specialization and group perfection as set apart from the enriching experiences music

could provide for all men according to their ability to express themselves in and through it. Specialization or limited group experiences must never negate the participative or functional opportunities for every individual. An imaginative music education program can develop these opportunities.

Socializing Value. Undoubtedly one of the most important contributions of musical art to the cultural development of man is the value derived from its power of socialization. During primitive times music was a medium for conveying group emotions. Music has aroused men to march, dance, sing, or to perform individually and in groups on musical instruments. Some vocal response or outburst is usually given to the expression of such emotions as sadness, joy, hatred, and kindness. Evidence of these social reactions can be found in the musical expression of all men. Music is thus a language and a medium for social communication.

Music presents a common denominator for man's inner urge to create and it becomes the medium through which this urge may find expression. Although there is wide variance in individual responses to music, the source of its power as a socializing medium is man's physical, emotional, intellectual, and spiritual capacity to become sensitive to music's sound, movement, and structure. If education results in fulfillment of individuals for social adequacy, it is then easy to accept the concept that music aids in enriching and enlarging horizons for social living.

Spiritual Value. The impact of music upon individuals has from the beginning of civilization been a prime mover of emotional and spiritual expression. The language of music is often described as being an indefinable verbalism. It is difficult to articulate what music does for the spiritual life of the individual.

The spiritual expression of man arises out of his need to sublimate. An overpowering sensation or the experience of divine or supreme authority is often aided by musical experiences. Music becomes an articulate medium for expressing the spiritual goodness of man for which often no verbalism exists. Music gives rise to such emotional and intellectual feeling states as devotion, faith, hope, loyalty, trust, and thus becomes the mosaic of expression from which issues the spiritual goodness of man. The manifest credo of man is stimulated through the expression of those

vocal and instrumental utterances that arise out of his good
self.

Discipline Value. The disciplinary values of music
are manifest in every facet of the school music program.
Singing requires co-ordinated action. The re-creation of a
song or the playing of an instrument requires synchronized
physical and mental action in notated and rhythmic regularity.
Both facets of human action are disciplined in order to a-
chieve the semblance of acceptable performance. Disciplines
exist and are required of the instrumental player in much
the same manner. The mind and body should achieve mastery of instrument technique and performance. The individualized refined disciplines of string quartet players demand
a variety of exactnesses. The young child in the rhythm
band must control his boundless energy in order to become
an effective performer. Choral singing requires young people to duplicate much the same self-discipline for group performance. The preciseness of tonal attack required by the
director demands exactness of response.

Music performance demands discipline which is needed
in a world where unencumbered time is often wanting in constructive employment. Music provides pleasant engagement
of hand and mind.

The Moral Purpose of Music. The associative experiences of music have a moral purpose that commends music study to all individuals, giving them a constructively occupied direction that involves their physical and mental well-
being. Musical creativeness assures each person opportunity
for self-satisfaction and self-fulfillment.

The moral direction of an individual determines the
nature of his conduct in daily living. If music has the power
of sublimating basic human desires, then it is probable that
it becomes part of the ethics of man and exerts impact for
good upon his conduct. Such a salutary effect should help
toward a well-adjusted individual, and we may assume that
music can make a contribution to the moral growth and happiness of man.

Music as a Universal Language. One aspect of the
universality of music is the functional performance that it
initiates and its service to the individual. Music used for a
funeral, marriage, dance, or battle arouses the appropriate
emotional or edifying responses. Church music has long

been used to provide an appropriate setting for religious services. Music has been used for its therapeutic effects in the amelioration of mental tensions.

Music is such a universal expression that it penetrates every area of the individual's social action. From the vocal and instrumental utterances of primitive man to the complex configurations of contrapuntal writing, man has always used music as a medium for expression of the gamut of human emotion. No more effective instrument of self-expression exists for the child, the adult performer, or members of a social group in giving expression to their thoughts. The universality of music provides unlimited opportunities for music educators to aid children in experiencing creativity and enjoyable environment. Schopenhauer emphasizes this point of view when he says

> Music, therefore, if regarded as an expression of the world, is in the highest degree a universal language, which is related indeed to the universality of concepts, much as they are related to the particular things. [1]

School music education is philosophically based on the universality of music. For the child, either as singer or performer on an instrument, music provides spontaneous expression and joyous satisfaction. The modern schoolroom, with its emphasis upon the creative, re-creative, listening, song-singing, and rhythmic aspects of music instruction, can offer a program of such varied music interest that every child will find through proper instruction a medium of expression which is challenging to him.

Summary of the Values of Music. Any concept or function of music education must be experienced significantly --deeply, intensely, personally; it must become an integral part of the individual. It must provide new insights, new attitudes, new skills, new experiences, and new consummations of dispositions toward music. The concepts or functions of music education must eventually furnish insight for a conception of a philosophy of music education. Their final consummation will be the fruition of a significant cultural message.

The individual, if he is to live at a high level of creativity, must feel the overpowering possession that issues to him as he undergoes the many conceptual experiences of mu-

sic. Musical experience, even though it may not be an all-
consuming aesthetic and cultural event, always possesses at-
traction and interest for men. Musical experience by association with music is not enough. There must be "living"
music through which the individual experiences self-satisfaction from its many creative functions. But this is dependent upon insight and insight demands continual experimentation and exploration.

It is quite apparent that there is an inability on the
part of some music educators to employ imagination and insight to provoke life from the philosophical concepts of music presented above. It is unfortunate that the functional aspects of art and music have so often been impoverished in
curricula because of the inability of teachers to visualize
music's manifold opportunities.

Musical experiences for permanent cultural growth
cannot be attained as "hand-me-downs" of educational dogma
and practice. They must be outgrowths of each individual's
creative desires to attain power of musical craftsmanship
and satisfaction of self-expression. This demands continual
experimentation if the subtleties of musical art are to be
real to each individual for his personal enjoyment. There
must be unlimited opportunities for each child to discover
music. The extent of discovery is largely determined by the
growth of a perceptive awareness which will accrue to the
child as he experiences music. Much of this happy discovery
is often destroyed because the music teacher wants to "tell
all"--to interfere with the child's developing insights.

Projected Goals in Music Education.

The basic concepts of the values of music education
have evolved during a century and a quarter. They have oc-
curred as the result of music educators trying to resolve instructional problems in teaching music. Concurrently, there
were the interdependent philosophical and scientific developments involved in the understanding of man. This process
has been slow yet the early champions of American music
education have had faith. The united effort of this leadership is revealed by the monumental achievements of music
education during the period 1907-1957. The reader is referred again to "Mileposts and Stepping Stones"[2] to gain comprehension of the achievements in American music education
during the 50-year history of the Music Educators' National

Conference. During the decade and a half since this milestone, music education has continued to make significant history.

The future of American music education demands that significant leadership must continually be sought out for the task of stabilizing significant gains made in the past and advancing new musical horizons. Some of those concepts of leadership which have a direct bearing upon the future course of music education will, therefore, be discussed.

The Learner-Centered Philosophy. There are two fundamental prerequisites to good school music for youth. First, there must be a philosophy of music education which emphasizes the importance of the learner in the educational process. Second, music must be designed for pleasure; the aesthetic therapeutics which will result from creating such an emotional outlet may promote human happiness.

One difficulty involved in the proper implementation of a learner-centered music program is that music is a curriculum subject which requires an entirely different instructional approach than that suitable for grammar, arithmetic, or history. The average teacher is unable to adjust his teaching techniques to music teaching. Music should be conceived as a need, and the teacher believes he has the proper technique for helping the student realize that need, but many teachers never envision what may be the most important reality to the child--musical enjoyment through participation and experience.

Musical enjoyment is not entirely dependent upon study of the technical aspects of music. Musical understanding rarely results from such study because a child's enjoyment of music is often short-circuited long before he is allowed to experience the joy of music. A music program for children should be constructed solely upon the basis of child interests. No program should be constructed for children which demands a knowledge of the fundamentals of music before they experience its power.

Greater Zeal for Teaching. A passion for individuality is a basic concept in a democracy. Democracy operates in the classroom if techniques are employed which explore the interests of all children. Interests are aroused, if the exploration is based on functional music activities.

Music must be so taught that it will arouse a desire to enjoy its pleasurable, rhythmic, melodic, and harmonic experiences in adult living. The importance of the child's participation cannot be over-estimated. We have just begun to understand what it means to teach music creatively; new media for the dissemination of its cultural message of the past, present, and future must be developed in light of an understanding of child needs. We must understand that an enthusiasm for teaching beautiful music to children will evoke childlike artistic responses which will bring him lasting enjoyment. Love begets love; without it everything may fail.

Just as hatred can be engendered within young children, so it is possible to arouse tendencies toward love and appreciation for the beautiful. Eagerness in learning is dependent upon ability and opportunity. The paramount objective of 20th-century education must be to teach "the child" rather than "the children" and each teacher must dedicate his talents and activities to accomplish this end.

A New Music Education "Magna Charta." Music educators must frame a new Magna Charta. We cannot continue to teach music in our public schools without first evaluating its objectives. We must determine whether or not we are just offering music to school children or whether they are assured opportunities for growth through its inclusion in the curriculum.

The new Magna Charta for music education will need to reevaluate a society that is already struggling with problems of leisure time. Man must learn how to use his waking hours constructively; otherwise, time becomes a liability. The inherent purposiveness of music makes it become a constructive force in the worthy use of leisure time.

The good life should be a happy one; it will become more vital and functional when those authorities responsible for music education have developed a comprehensive program that will provide abundant music activities from infancy through adult living. If music education is to find its place in a full life, it must become a dynamic experience.

The school music program must be geared to its ultimate realization--music for adult living and enjoyment. Professional opera companies, oratorio societies, local bands, community music programs, and radio and television entertainment are but a more or less passive phase of lay

music experiences. There must be encouragement for the
lay musicians. They must have their own choruses, orchestras, instrumental ensembles, bands, and oratorio societies;
music must become a functional and personal experience in
the total adult life of each individual. We must popularize
the idea that mediocre musical performances are as important as are those by professionals. An American school music program is of little value, if we do not see evidences of
music's carry-over into adult living.

During the 1950's and 60's great emphasis was placed
upon quality of performance; many school music programs
overemphasized it. Unfortunately, America is still "winner
conscious." This complex has permeated much of what has
been achieved in athletics and music. Every music teacher
knows that he will be evaluated by his public performances.
Often there is little discernment of what is being done for
the majority of school children. This approach is excellent
for those who intend to become professional musicians but it
does not give consideration to the great mass of our population who desire music for its enjoyment but have no more
than ordinary talent for it.

The prima donna music organizational approach will
not nurture a generation of music lovers. Limited as it is,
because it draws upon the talented few, it is not a program
for the democratic way of life. Music as an art is a great
cultural heritage that can be disseminated in proportion to
man's ability to enjoy it. Creativity is basic to enjoyment.
All men should have the opportunity to participate in the
production of music. The essence of musical enjoyment issues from participation.

Musicians are entrusted with the weighty responsibility
of transmitting much of music's great contribution to man's
aesthetics. As educators, one of their great contributions
should be the dissemination and the interchange of ideas for
educating children in music.

Performance vs. General Education. Music education
since 1900 has made phenomenal strides in many areas of
musical performance. Band and choral performances in elementary and secondary schools have made significant strides.
Often these have resulted in substantial achievement. But
the emphasis upon quality of performances has brought about
an imbalance in many areas of music instruction, notably in
the elementary school, and has hampered equality of music
opportunity.

Prior to 1900 music education stressed the disciplining values of music, and the layman looked upon it as a "frill" unworthy of support. These considerations are for the most part gone from the thinking of modern music educators.

The onus of extra-curricularism has rested on all music educators. The Department of Superintendence of the National Educational Association in 1927 recommended that music be "given equal consideration and support with other basic subjects."[3] Music educators have been remiss in failing to develop programs that apply the all-inclusive nature of music's cultural and educational contribution to the enlightenment of all mankind. Some of the contributing factors have been:

1.   Failure to develop an academically respectable program of music education for all youth.
2.   Undue emphasis upon specialized and individualized performance.
3.   The attitude that performance was the road that led to universal musical enjoyment and participation.
4.   Belief that distinction of musicianship could be achieved by all who studied music. This is impossible, and has undoubtedly turned many from music because, failing to achieve excellence, they have assumed that music was "not for them." Until recently, almost all music study was directed toward the achievement of virtuosity. This was a carry over from the 18th and 19th centuries which emphasized impeccable instrumental and vocal performance.
5.   With the onset of the National School Band, Orchestra, and Vocal Contest Movement during the 1930's, de-emphasis of the elementary school music program started. To be sure, more and better music materials have been made available for elementary school music, but a premium has been put on group public performances. Solid programs of music for every child have not always been encouraged. Leadership in elementary music was gradually usurped by the "men of importance" in music education--leaders of great performing organizations with professional ambitions.

Currently, music education both avocationally and professionally has reached an impasse. At the beginning of the 70's music education in the public schools has arrived at a crossroads. There are evidences that the secondary school music program composed of bands, choirs, and orchestras must increase its emphasis on general music education. The program must be for all people, for whatever enjoyment their training and talent will permit.

We are living in an era of perplexing goals. One of
the major quests of man today is for relaxation--a result
being that we have more uneasy and neurotic people than
ever before. For a quarter of a century we have been emphasizing the leadership principle in our educational institutions and yet today we find the stalwarts of industry stating
that their greatest need is for leadership ability. Leadership for the musical arts demands that a concerted effort
must be made to beget enthusiasm and support for music in
all its forms. We are becoming convinced that there is need
for a reevaluation of all theories and philosophies that determine the course of lay music appreciation. Professionalism
must be deemphasized in favor of amateurism, if the youth
and the adults of America are to become participant members in the enjoyment of the arts. It is important that people try their hands at music. Participation in music leads
naturally to an understanding; great musical culture in America is dependent upon participant experiences.

There also remain the educational and political units
of county, state, and the nation which must be made articulate about the arts. If accreditation means recognition in
courses of study, then legislation must be enacted that will
require all educational groups to recognize music as an educational subject worthy of recognition equal to other academic studies.

International Music Education. A governmental agency
should be created to encourage and promote music; it must
also be able to secure, through certain types of private and
public subsidies, sufficient funds for its work. Its major
function should be the stimulation of cooperative agencies
for effecting intra-continental and world-wide programs of
music education.

Wise planning of a broad program of international
music education might go far to promote understanding and
good will among the citizens of tomorrow. Beginnings have
been made through the International Society for Music Council (ISMC) with its various international member organizations and national committees, and with assistance in many
ways from UNESCO,[4] in Vienna. Since coming into being
in Brussels in 1953, The International Society for Music
Education has had significant leadership from the offices of
the Music Educators National Conference. The following

factors seem essential to future success:

1. Encouragement for UNESCO in all its programs
wherever and whenever it attempts to strengthen and give
encouragement to music education in particular and music in
general.
2. Support for the International Society for Music
Council and the International Society for Music Education
through the Music Educators National Conference.
3. Encouragement for the establishment of an International Institute for Music Education.
4. Encouragement of a spirit of internationalism
which will bring, through cooperative effort and greater resources, a fertility and vigor to all musical art forms.
5. Finally, because music knows no race or creed,
support for the internationalism of all music through education, which may go a long way toward fostering the peaceful
coexistence of all men.

Music education must find its rightful place in the
academic program of every child's education. Currently, in
addition to more than 28,000,000 children of elementary
school age receiving or being exposed to education in music,
there are another 18,000,000[5] who are in secondary schools
and colleges who may find instruction available if they desire
to take advantage of the opportunity. But the education must
be in relation to their needs. The success of tomorrow's
musical culture will be in large part dependent upon the nature of its offerings and the extent to which it enlists the interest of the society it serves.

Discussion

1. Is it possible to conceive of any phase of musical
performance that does not contain some phase of sound and
movement?
2. Are you able to put into words what your "feeling
state" is when reacting to music?
3. What emotions are aroused upon listening to music?
4. Would it be semantically productive to differentiate the meaning of concept, philosophy, and principle?
5. Does the primary school child have the insight
which makes possible choice and discrimination upon listening to music?
6. Suggest social functions that frequently employ

singing.
7. Illustrate music activities that are creative and those that are basically recreative.
8. Differentiate if possible between your concepts of insight and of intelligence. Do not confuse intellectualism with intelligence.
9. What do you discern to be the meaning of the phrase, "I love music"?
10. If you were to tell a child that music has a spiritual value, just exactly what do you expect as a response? What do you mean by such a statement?
11. In what ways does musical study discipline the individual?
12. If music has a moral purpose, would you say that the pursuit of music study has a moralizing effect upon the individual?
13. Enumerate as many instances as possible wherein you feel that the universality of music is expressed.
14. What do we mean by "living" music?
15. How does the implementation of a learner-centered philosophy of music instruction differ from one that is applied to arithmetic, English, or history?
16. Does musical enjoyment always imply participation in order to realize enjoyment?
17. What percentage of your teachers are zealous in the exercise of their instructional responsibilities?
18. Do you believe that school attendance laws should require individuals to remain in school through their 17th year? If not, what year do you suggest?
19. How could aggressive leadership influence the future growth of American music education?
20. How does international music influence the development of American music education?
21. Should school music emphasize the performance concept, or should it stress a strong General Music Program?
22. Discuss: "More people are on the (Music) platform than in the (American) audience."

Notes

1. Schopenhauer, Arthur. "Art and The Art of Music." New York: Readings in Philosophy, Barnes & Noble, 1953, 246-254.

2. "Mileposts and Stepping Stones (1907-1957). MENC

Progress Report from the Records." Music Educator's Journal, 43: No. 5 (April-May, 1957), 40-41.

3. Pierce, Anne E. "Instruction In Music and Art." Bulletin No. 17. Part I. 1932. National Survey of
Secondary Education, Monograph No. 25. Washington, D.C.: United States Government Printing Office,
1933, 1.

4. Kraus, Egon. "The World of Music." Bulletin of The
International Music Council, 3: No. 5 (October, 1961),
115-116. Fourth International Conference of the ISME
in Vienna.

5. The World Almanac. Newspaper Enterprise Association,
Inc., 1972.

Part Two. Instructional Concerns

CHAPTER III: MUSIC TEACHER EDUCATION

Prior to the 20th century our populace was not ready for great art. Up to 1850, music education for the layman was practically non-existent in America. Greater preparation through music education was needed before a market for commercial art could be achieved. This period of preparation includes the teaching of public school music in the Boston public schools in 1838, and the publication in 1870 of a public school music course in which were included a series of song books. There also should be included the organization in 1876 of the Music Teachers' National Association. Luther Whiting Mason was the author of the public-school music course to which we have referred above, and it was he who was largely responsible for summer school and institute movements that did much to focus national attention on the merits of school music education. Thus, Luther Mason's efforts coupled with those of Elam Ives, William Channing Woodbridge, Lowell Mason, and George J. Webb gave early school music in America a good start. The increasing adoption of music into the public school curriculum was certain to become a major instrument for providing musical opportunities for future Americans.

Only through music education in our public schools will the majority of our people come to attain any significant appreciation for music. This emphasizes the importance of the classroom teacher for teaching music.

A recent nationwide poll of American public opinion as to whether or not the man on the street was satisfied with the results of American education indicated that 26 percent said that education was not doing so good a job today as formerly. This is a serious indictment. It must be kept in mind that education has many severe critics. Many educational leaders are not satisfied with the candidates who are available for teacher training, the manner of their selection, and the type of courses being offered for professional preparation.

33

The greatest educational objective is that of providing
a musical education for every child. As previously indicated
that is not being achieved in all of our elementary schools.
This is most unfortunate, because it is at the elementary
school level that music can become a dynamic, all-inclusive,
culturally satisfying experience for children.

Many problems confront the administrator in upgrading
the musical qualifications of the in-service teachers. The
administrator and his staff of music specialists cannot by
themselves provide music training for all the children in an
elementary school. Similarly, the teacher who occupies the
sole school music position, cannot teach music to all the
students in the school and may have to slight the elementary
program. The classroom teacher needs help from the music supervisor and teacher. Practical teacher training
courses in music are an indispensable approach to more effective teaching of music in the schools.

The professional, administrative, and instructional
impediments to development of music programs in our elementary schools are, first, the necessity to educate school
administrators regarding the functional importance of specialists for teaching music to children and, second, an acute
shortage of classroom teachers and elementary school music
supervisors. Elementary school music teaching is not particularly attractive to the professional musician. He feels
that it lacks challenge. There is some evidence that the
professional musician, by personality and interest, is not always qualified to teach young children. The great performing artist is a highly trained specialist, whereas the music
teacher is, by musicianship and training, interested in developing the art in others. Also, music is not the only subject to be taught and the teacher must be evaluated in terms
of his ability to fulfill the total classroom teaching requirement. School administrators, naturally, try to obtain superior elementary school teachers even though they may not be
qualified to teach music.

There has been an increasing number of teachers who
are potentially competent, but who need additional training.
These teachers may be grouped into four classifications:
(1) the teacher who has never taught music but must do so
under emergency conditions; (2) teachers qualified and experienced in some other field who have had to undertake music teaching for which they are inadequately prepared (including teachers of vocal music who are obliged to direct in-

strumental organizations, and vice-versa); (3) teachers who
need additional training for certification; and (4) older teachers who have not continued their formal training. Opportunities for in-service training may take the form of extension
classes, refresher classes, clinics and workshops, radio
projects or county and district music festivals.[1]

From the ranks of highly qualified classroom teachers,
and from the above four categories of provisional, temporary,
substitute, and emergency groups, the school administrator,
together with his music staff, attempts to keep classrooms
operating. But inherent in this problem is the difficulty of
obtaining the quality of teaching which will insure a strong
program of music education for our elementary schools.

A third impediment is that directors of professional
music schools frequently do not have a clear understanding
of their responsibility for the development of adequate music
training programs for the elementary classroom teacher.
Professional music schools and all institutions of higher
learning which prepare elementary classroom teachers must
employ competent teaching staff and must assume responsibility for elementary music training that will be of value to
the individual trainee when he becomes a teacher. The regular classroom teacher should be qualified to teach music because the music specialist cannot always be in every classroom.

Fourth, music supervisors without ability are being
employed to handle grade school vocal programs. The shortage of music specialists has necessitated the hiring of many,
for example, who feel that they are competent to direct instrumental work, but who acknowledge their lack of ability to
carry on a vocal program successfully.

Fifth, there is a tendency to overemphasize "band directing" or "choral directing" as a career. Some school administrators and music teachers in our secondary schools
have a tendency to overemphasize the large music organizations. They can become "showpieces" and thus emphasis is
placed upon their development. Such a false concept of a
good music program tends to deemphasize the development of
elementary music.

Sixth, some classroom teachers are unable or unwilling to teach music. Although not pretending to be musicians,
some of these teachers have good potential musicianship,

while others insist that they would prefer not to teach music.
Whenever a teacher expresses her inability to teach music or
her desire not to do so, the administrator may lend a helping hand. He may employ supervisory music teachers or
specialists to help these people. A teaching exchange arrangement among classroom teachers can serve as a form of
in-service training. Among elementary classroom teachers
there are some who are very proficient as teachers of music.
One classroom teacher who feels inadequate to teach music
may be highly qualified to teach art. Such a teacher may be
encouraged to exchange her music teaching assignment with
another who enjoys teaching music but claims no ability, talent, or interest in teaching art.

These teacher exchanges would not only improve music teaching, but the young, potentially good music teacher
could learn how to teach many aspects of the music program.
Exchange teachers can be of great assistance in finding answers to many vexing music teaching problems. If the exchange plan does not seem feasible, the administrator might
assign special supervisory personnel to certain classrooms.
The difficulty with this suggestion is that most schools are
so inadequately staffed with elementary music supervisors
that even a limited supervisory program is often not possible.
The school system that employs music specialists might use
them more conveniently to serve as teachers for those classrooms that need their professional services. In large school
systems it would be difficult to require these specialists to
be responsible for much regular classroom teaching. The
main purpose for which they were hired would be defeated.

A seventh impediment to a good school music program
is lack of assistance for the in-service teacher through a coordinated training program. Many elementary supervisory
programs fail to assist the teachers in their teaching of music. They are supervisory in nothing but name, because music teaching-administrative personnel responsible for such
supervision are overloaded with direction of large music organizations and they may even be uninterested in children's
music. Then too, highly specialized and professionally
equipped musicians sometimes find it difficult to adjust themselves to elemental music teaching activities. Many in-service music training programs are ordinarily designed for newly appointed classroom teachers. Under this plan the music
supervisor, music specialist, or some qualified music staff
member conducts weekly, bi-weekly, or monthly meetings at
which all newly appointed staff members are made acquainted

with the school system's music teaching program. The classroom teachers are actually instructed in simulated music
class situations. Any teacher in the school system who desires to attend these classes is invited to attend. Sometimes
these classes are continued for the first year of the teacher's
appointment in the school system.[2] The training courses are
designed to teach music and to integrate the efforts of all
teachers toward a common artistic objective. Some educators believe that

> Every good classroom teacher can become a good
> teacher of classroom music. No teacher should
> say that she cannot teach music to her class until
> she has tried honestly after making use of all avail-
> able teaching aids.

> If a teacher is unable to sing, the chances are that
> she can learn. However, if the teacher's ear is
> defective and she finds that she is unable to sing
> the songs accurately in a pleasing tone of voice,
> the school principal should endeavor to have her
> exchange work with some more musical member of
> the faculty for the music period.[3]

Teachers should be encouraged to participate in in-service
training programs, workshops, and seminars designed for the
improvement of instructional services.[4] Among the types of
in-service training for improving the musical qualifications
of the classroom teacher, the following have been found to be
beneficial:

(1) Extension courses in training institutions.
(2) Workshops--under training institution, state or
county supervision, for development of skills and appreciation. These workshops should be taught on the level of the
children the teachers are teaching.
(3) Teacher visitation--under the supervision of a
teacher.
(4) Bulletins.
(5) Institutes.
(6) Teacher singing groups--of songs on the community
singing level, --leading perhaps to county-wide teachers' choruses on a more artistic level.
(7) Visits of helping teachers.
(8) Demonstrations and conferences--by experts from
nearby training institutions, these to be based on the actual
needs of the county or section in which the demonstration
takes place.[5]

An eighth impediment is the lack of appeal of school
music supervisor positions for professional musicians. There
had always been a disparity between the elementary and secondary school teachers' and supervisory salaries. Then too,
the professional musician preparing for elementary school
music supervision, becomes discouraged because he is not sufficiently challenged by the teaching of rote songs, rhythm
bands, and beginning instrumental classes, and by performances of beginning bands and orchestras. The contribution
of the music educator teaching elementary music is exceedingly important, but many brilliant performers believe that
the musical results do not justify the expenditure of their
talents. There is only a limited number of performing musicians who desire to teach elementary music.

And, ninth, there is a need for a greater passion for
teaching music to the child. The classroom offers a mosaic
of abilities. We have neglected the great challenge it offers.
Teachers must want to teach the child as they find him.
Music must be so taught that it will become an abiding interest based upon creative music experiences which children
will demand as adults. The administrator must encourage
creative music teaching through in-service training programs.
He has a great responsibility for selecting classroom teachers who are dedicated to the principle of aiding young children in achieving musical experiences that will help them
live The Full Life.

Characteristics of the Music Educator. The music
educator, as he functions in the American school system,
may be designated by various titles. He may have the name
of administrator, supervisor, consultant, specialist, or
teacher of music. However, by whatever name he may be
known, the professional school music educator is that person
who, by demonstrated musicianship and understanding of educational theory and practice, has developed expertise in imparting musical instruction and learning to the youth in our
public and private schools. While it is necessary that he
possess qualifications that will enable him to perform competently, it is not required that he possess such qualifications to the same extent as the professional musician whose
efforts are confined to one endeavor. However, many music
educators are well qualified as performing musicians.

The typical school music educator is qualified to
teach music in all types of educational institutions. He has
graduated from an accredited college, university, or private

conservatory. He has had four or more years of collegiate training, having pursued a music major consisting of from 40 to 90 semester hours of credit, comprised of both academic and professional music education courses.

Typically, the position occupied by the school music educator provides him with a steady income, tenure and retirement. He often pursues his music avocationally as well as vocationally--he may very likely be earning additional income as a member of a symphony orchestra, or as a choir singer, band director, or choral director. Many music educators maintain private music studios where they may teach music during after-school hours. The music educator is usually more interested in serving the creative needs of many people than he is in promoting the personal performance ambitions of a few.

The successful music teacher is a composite. He must have a blend of personal and musical qualifications that make it possible for him to produce music creatively. If he is to be a leader of musicians he must have the ability to educe desirable musical results from others. This cannot be done unless he has certain qualifications. We have had a great number of specialists in the field of music determine what they believe to be the characteristics of the successful music teacher. They declared these traits to be: a good ear, leadership-personality, musical sensitivity, rhythmical sensitivity, ability to perform adequately on some instrument, evidence of musical stylism, and ability to impart knowledge. It was their belief that a composite of these qualities would provide the foundation necessary for becoming a music educator.

How good should the ear of the prospective music teacher be? This is a difficult question to answer. It is plain that no music teacher should stand before children and attempt to teach unless he has good relative pitch. The ear must have superior acuity. The ear must be highly discriminative of pitch deviations. The teacher of music must be able to discern small pitch deviations or else he will be unable to develop proficient performance. If audiometer or tonoscope readings indicate that the candidate for music teaching is deficient in pitch acuity, it would be better for him to pursue another profession.

The ability to get people to become interested in music for aesthetic enjoyment is of paramount importance in de-

veloping a strong public school program. Every time the
music teacher instructs he is bringing "firsts" into the musical experience of the child. What a challenge! But all
these "firsts" are not easily achieved. Children by their
very immaturity are constantly being required to make beginning overt creative and re-creative responses to new situations. This does not come easily for them. They come
from diverse backgrounds where the arts may or may not be
encouraged. In order for music to become an art, it must
reveal the individual self. This can be done only if instrumental or vocal expression become a creative experience for
each individual. It demands of the music teacher the ability
to get the child to give expression to those more sensitive
beauties which are within him. To get the child to become
a participating creator is a great educational challenge to the
music educator.

A dynamic and enthusiastic personality will arouse
response to music in children more effectively than one who
may feel deeply about the meaning of music yet cannot convey enthusiasm for his art. The musician is always a re-
creator of some art form, but he is constantly creating some
new aspect of the re-created form. Let us consider the
song as an illustration. A singer may sing a song which
was composed long ago, yet in his re-creation of the song
it will be possible for him to reveal new beauties through
imaginative interpretation. His performance will become a
new creation of the work. All beauty is not revealed in one
interpretation. Genius for creation or re-creation does not
exist solely in the mind of one individual. Arousing interest
in music requires that the music teacher possess enthusiasm
for introducing musical experiences to individuals. This in-
fectious nature of the teacher must transcend all initial re-
sistance of individuals to explorations in musical experience.
Instructional techniques should be adequate to meet the learning needs of the students. Finally, the artistic stature of the
teacher should challenge each student to achieve the highest
measure of musical growth of which he is capable.

"She sings beautifully, but her singing sounds like so
much wood; it is expressionless." This comment with its
many implications is very often heard about the performance
of those who lack what is called musical sensitivity.

It is probable that musical sensitivity is dependent upon many other contributory factors. It may be that in the
case of a singer, the individual must have the imagination to

be responsive not only to the meanings of words, but also to
the inherent metre of the text.   But again metre is rhythm,
and this structural component of music must be a natural
ability of the individual.   Music, which consists of combinations of tones, demands a responsiveness to all their component structures which can best be described as a "feeling
for" or a "sensitivity to" them.   Unless an individual possesses this discriminative quality of sensitivity he will be
unmusical to the extent that such deficiencies exist.

Certainly, every person has some degree of rhythmic
sensitivity.   The physical world is full of rhythmical activity.
The human heart beats in a rhythmical pattern.   The keen
observer will note that an individual's gait is characterized
by a definite rhythmic pattern.   The individual listening to
martial music will usually respond to its pulsation by mani-
festing some bodily movement.   There are rhythmic patterns
which require discriminative recognition.   Inability to discern and respond to these rhythmic pulsations is certain to
reflect a lack of good rhythmical sensitivity.   Limited sensitivity to rhythm will not provide an adequate foundation for
meritorious musical performance.

The musician who intends to become a leader of other
musicians must have sensitive rhythmic responses.   Acute
rhythmic response is necessary for musical success, yet our
observation of hundreds of students has been that many talented technicians and performers have encountered difficulty
in mastering rhythmic problems.   It is also our experience
that students who have these problems continue to have difficulty in overcoming them throughout life.   Generally speaking, those people who have rhythmic troubles may do a good
musicianly job, providing they have the other requisites which
we are discussing.   Rhythmic sensitivity is somewhat like
musical sensitivity because its absence can be detected with
little difficulty.   Like musical sensitivity, it too is capable
of development in each individual to the extent to which that
person possesses the inherent capacity to respond.

In teacher-training courses the question of performance
always commands paramount consideration.   At the university
level a common charge frequently hurled at music education
majors is that many of them transferred from vocal and instrumental major programs to music education because they
did not have the necessary skills and musicianship to meet
the demands of concert performance.   But there has been a
great upgrading of the music teaching profession during the

past decade.

The music teacher must be able to perform with distinction on some instrument of his own choosing. Further, he must be acquainted with the playing of many other instruments to become a successful teacher. There is no substitute for knowledge. Respect from his students is impossible if they feel that his performance skills are limited and mediocre. The football coach is assumed to be a player-coach. He must be able to show his players how things are done. Musical knowledge is partially dependent upon experience, and the student obtains that experience through performance supported by skilled example.

The music educator, upon accepting a position in a community, naturally assumes responsibility for leadership of its music. As a public servant he cannot evade the challenge. In assuming music leadership he is confronted with the inevitable comparisons which are made whenever he appears in public performance. Thus, it makes no difference whether he is called upon to demonstrate "the how of playing," or to provide entertainment, he must be able to do either in a manner that will command respect.

Stylism is the essence of all the musical aspects of superior performance. Every performance of a composition should have intelligent treatment. The more mature the musician, the more mature the rendition. Good musical stylism is dependent upon musical maturity.

How does a person attain stylism? How does a person develop an appreciation for color in painting, or gain a comprehension of composition in painting pictures? Both are dependent upon judgments that come from study and experience. This is likewise true of musical stylism. The literature of the people whose music is to be performed must be studied. The traits and traditions of those people whose music the individual wishes to interpret must be learned. Stylism reflects a musician's maturity. A great price is exacted to achieve excellence in this element. The price is effort.

From the musicianly qualifications of the music educator we turn to that requisite which must be considered the most important non-musical qualification--the ability to impart knowledge. To be a competent music technician is not enough. To impart musical techniques effectively is more

important than being a repository for musical knowledge.
The tools of musical understanding to which we have referred
constitute the material aspects of music study used in imparting such knowledge. But musical knowledge cannot be
effectively imparted unless it is welded with the high quality
of the real teacher who in the final analysis determines the
ability to impart knowledge for good teaching.

The genius of musical creativity is fashioned if proper
use is made of the tools of musical understanding. It is the
teacher who brings into perspective the musical creativity of
the past and the re-creativity of the present, and who assumes the responsibility for aiding in its perpetuation for the
future. The music educator must first of all envision his
responsibility as an instrument for molding a culture.

Now do we have a musician? It is a foregone conclusion that the music educator must have a goodly amount
of all the qualities which we have just enumerated. It would
be impossible for anyone to succeed, if he were appreciably
deficient in any of the above traits. The music teacher must
have a good ear for music; he must have a musical sensitivity which reveals his talent; he must have fine rhythmic
sensitivity; there must be evidence of his understanding of
musical stylism; he must be able to perform acceptably; and
he must be able to lead others, so that they will desire to
become participators in and creators of music.

Developing Dedicated Music Educators. We shall
never have strong music education programs unless the educators responsible for such training stress course content
more than course name. The major considerations in developing music education are: (1) greater care in the selection of candidates for teaching music education. Professional
music educators must aid in seeking out and encouraging the
best of our college youth for these careers. Wilson[6] says
that "Music teachers should be willing to sit down and discuss with a student the possibility of his becoming a music
teacher." (2) Teachers who are dedicated to the cause of
education and who, by their high qualifications and professional zeal, raise the standard of music education to new
heights; (3) educators who envision and construct curricular
requirements that will measurably improve the teacher training standards for music educators; (4) greater emphasis on
professional courses to prepare students for the actual job
of teaching music, in order that they in turn may develop
strong programs of general music education; (5) a new con-

cept of the objectives of school music in America. There
must be instilled in music educators and in educators in
general a passion for the enjoyment of music by all. Lay
and professional music will be a natural outgrowth of such a
dynamic philosophy. (6) A new concept of the minima of
course requirements for licensing or certification of music
teachers. The criteria must be based on serious consideration of the question, "Is this candidate qualified for the job
for which he is making application?" The training of tomorrow's music educator must become a program for the professionalization of music education.[7] Bergethon has stated:

> Many teacher education institutions profess to have
> certain minimum pre-requisites for admission. It
> is common knowledge, however, that these require-
> ments are seldom fulfilled by many of the entering
> students. This tends to lower the musical stand-
> ards of music education majors, generally. An-
> other related problem is the student who decided
> to transfer from 'applied music' to 'music educa-
> tion' in his junior or senior year, usually because
> he cannot 'make the grade' in applied music. ...
> The only remedy is selective admission. Selection
> should take place at four crucial periods: admis-
> sion to the institution, admission to teacher edu-
> cation program, admission to student teaching, and
> recommendation for certification. The administra-
> tion of screening is usually the joint responsibility
> of the departments of education and of music edu-
> cation. The music education department must,
> however, be very explicit in formulating the mu-
> sical requirements for each stage in the process,
> and must insist upon their attainment. This in it-
> self would be a great boost to the music education
> program.[8]

Music educators in our public schools are the largest
group of professional musicians in America regularly employed under contract. What is their future? It is believed
that the current imbalance existing between the supply and
demand for competent school music teachers is unlikely to
be appreciably alleviated in the next decade. There are
many unfavorable conditions affecting the decision of young
people who are contemplating music teaching as a career.
Let us review some of the factors which may deter young
people from choosing music as a professional career.

1.   There is a current national emphasis upon the increased need for scientific personnel.   This mushrooming
scientific development has enticed many promising individuals
from entry into the teaching profession.
      2.   There is an insufficient number of teachers enter-
ing the profession because of the high level of employment
and salaries prevailing in many other fields.
      3.   There is considerable teacher turnover which pre-
vents teacher training institutions from making headway a-
gainst prevalent teacher shortages.
      4.   Educational budgets are now strained to provide
minimum instructional and physical plant requirements to
meet the ever-increasing growth in enrollment.   Many educators argue that academic needs must receive first consideration.   This emphasis upon the academic program has had
a tendency to discourage some young people from pursuing
music teaching as a career.
      5.   Not all professionally minded young musicians are
intrigued by teaching youngsters.   Professionals very often
abhor the idea of teaching young musicians struggling with
rudimentary skills.   All musicians do not have the temperament to teach beginners where "middle C may be found."

      Music educators must encourage the selection of in-
dividuals who by training, talent, personality, disposition,
and desire for teaching are most likely to succeed as educators and teachers.   Courageous music leadership is required if the competent are to be trained for professional
music careers; those who are inadequately endowed musically
should be encouraged to train for positions in which they are
more likely to succeed.   Music educators must clearly envision what music education as a profession can contribute
to the culture of all men.

      Vocational guidance for professional musicians is
greatly needed.   Such guidance in institutions of higher education can do much to challenge young people of promise to
achieve success in proportion to their talents.   Effective
guidance will enable educators to discharge their responsibility for screening those students who are inadequately
equipped to pursue music as a career.   It is rank dishonesty
for administrations in conservatories and music schools to
permit people of doubtful talent to matriculate in courses
leading to degrees in music.

      The teacher has infinite opportunities for influencing
the direction of human growth and development.   Thus, the

outcome of music teaching should be of grave concern to him. Instructing a number of musical organizations each week certainly offers ample opportunity for a variety of personal relationships between the teacher and each of its members--so great an interchange of conflicting and varied emotional reactions will probably not be found in any other profession.

One of the great responsibilities thrust upon music educators is the discovery of musical talent. School music is undoubtedly one of the most potent forces for doing this job. But it must be kept in mind that beginning with the young children, the job of arousing their interest in music makes severe demands upon the music educator's musicianship. The discovery of significant music talent is not only made possible through the leadership of a strong music personality which wins confidence, but also through the establishment of a good testing program. If a broadened base of participative music experiences is to be developed for children, the music educator must create a program of activities permitting them opportunities of expression according to their talent and interests.

It must be kept in mind that any music program in our schools which induces participation on the part of the children will encourage our youth to exercise their latent talent. When a child experiences the pleasure that may be derived from participation, he will then be encouraged to extend his musical horizons.

Professional Music Education. Professional education has a responsibility for establishing a teacher training program which will permit the prosecution of a learner-centered type of education. Such a program of education cannot be conceived or achieved if there is a consistent devotion to the status quo. Educators in our educational institutions must develop programs which promote such an end result. A well planned curriculum can become an instrument for achieving such a goal. In order to construct this curriculum, it will be necessary to have a clear conception of the duties and functions of the worker in music education. To build a teacher-training curriculum out of courses in applied music, theory, history, and so forth, patterned on the standard offerings of conservatories and academic departments of music with courses in music pedagogy super-added, is a serious error. This leads to an incoherent and ineffective program because the aims and practices of conservatories and academic music departments are irrelevant in important re-

spects to the training of workers in music education. The
curriculum should be a coherent whole, focused explicitly
upon the type of professional worker considered desirable.

The striking evolution of music in American education
has brought about a demand for what is in effect a new type
of professional worker. Such a worker is called upon to be
something more than, and different from, a teacher of voice,
piano, orchestral instruments, history, or theory, or a director of choral and instrumental ensembles. To be sure,
he needs to be an efficient and versatile teacher, able to get
tangible and creditable results. But in addition to all this
he needs to be an organizer, a promoter, a musical educator in the widest sense. He should be capable of working
resourcefully and adaptably both in the schools and the community to make the art of music a living force. Such social
and educational leadership in the interest of music is indeed
his most essential function.

> Music education has reached a stage of maturity
> where service of this kind is a practical possibility,
> and not a mere utopian dream or idealistic theory.
> In many American communities a worker who un-
> derstands his function in these terms and dis-
> charges it effectively can achieve an outstanding
> success and exercise a most valuable influence.
> He will find that the key to success lies in being
> able to deal with a service situation with initiative,
> resourcefulness, confidence, and good judgment.
> This should be the focus of the training program.[9]

Our newly conceived curriculum for training professional music educators is a challenge and responsibility of
great magnitude. These professional educators in our public
and private schools play an important role in developing desirable attitudes on the part of the general public toward future music education. Their role can be further strengthened
with training. This implies the need for an evaluation of
teacher education training programs. The in-service elementary school teacher, who constructs a foundation for desirable attitudes toward music, must be made cognizant of
her opportunities and must be trained through music courses
designed to aid her in the teaching of classroom music.
Teacher education institutions are best qualified to prepare
teachers for this responsibility. Institutions and accrediting
agencies must develop a professional pattern for certification
that will insure that "the teacher finally certified is a well-

balanced, vigorous, soundly-equipped, and reliable person
who may be expected to grow in service."[10]

Discussion

1. Is there both a professional musician and a public
school musician point of view? Are you able to accept one
standard of performance for both the professional musician
and the public school musician?

2. Among school musicians of your acquaintance,
are you satisfied with their ability as performing musicians?
If not, are they the type of musicians that you want for
teaching American boys and girls in our schools?

3. Is there justification for the professional musicians' criticism of the poor quality of performance standards
in many of our public schools?

4. If you were to adjudicate district choral and band
contests in Ohio, Kentucky, and Indiana, would there by any
reason for you to adjust your ratings to meet local situations,
even though your standard of good performance would be
compromised?

5. Should music contests be supplanted by festivals?

6. What are the opportunities for the professional
musician in your community? Is it possible for him to
maintain a good standard of living from such a livelihood?

7. In keeping with rising costs, is it possible to
raise the piano fee to $6.00?

8. Is the administration and the music staff of your
school interested in a program of music built around winning
One Ratings at state music contests?

9. Do you believe it is possible to put into practice
the motto, "Music for every child and every child for music"?

10. What effect does television have upon the quality
of music performance in our public schools?

11. Generally speaking, does the professional music
critic have an appreciative understanding of what the school
music musician is trying to achieve qualitatively?

12. How would you go about determining a child's
musicality?

13. What do you suggest as a means of improving
the qualitative standards of performance in our schools?

14. How would you go about determining whether or
not a prospective teaching candidate for a position is a good
musician? Would the recipient of a college degree in music
assure qualitative standards?

15. Who is responsible for qualitative music standards in our schools?

Notes

1. Music Education Source Book. Hazel Nohavec Morgan, ed. Chicago: Music Educators' National Conference, 1947, 39.

2. The Ithaca, New York, public school system, under the leadership of Miss Laura Bryant, has employed this in-service training program for many years. This writer has known elementary teachers who have been part of such a training program, and they have nothing but praise for it. It does help teachers learn how to teach music.

3. "Georgia Program for the Improvement of Instruction in the Public Schools: An Introduction to the Use of the State-Adopted Music Books." By M. D. Collins, Georgia State Superintendent of Schools. Atlanta: 1938, 5.

4. Music Education Source Book, 49.

5. Ibid., 49. These selected eight in-service training suggestions were in reference to the in-service training of rural school teachers, and we believe that they are equally applicable to such training for urban classroom teachers.

6. Wilson, A. Verne. "The State of Music Education." Music Educators Journal, 42: No. 3 (January, 1956), 40. (Based on an article by Jack H. Williams in the Oregon Music Educator. November-December, 1955.

7. Note: The reader is urged to peruse Bjornar Bergethon's "Toward improving Music Teacher Education," Education, 76:7 (March, 1956), 431-435.

8. Ibid., 435.

9. Music in American Education. Music Education Source Book Number Two. Ed. by Hazel Nohavec Morgan. Chicago: Music Educators' National Conference,

     1955, 137-138.

10. "The Education of a Teacher," Committee on Teacher
     Education of The Association of Colleges and Univer-
     sities of the State of New York, Edmund E. Day,
     chairman, 15.

CHAPTER IV: CONCERN FOR MUSIC LEARNING

The administrator in a school system must accept responsibility for the musical education of future generations. He must conceive the means to attain those desirable objectives which are likely to create within modern youth an understanding and appreciation for the great art form--music. This tremendous responsibility must be shouldered by the administrator and his staff. Philosophically there are two program-shaping concepts--the means, and the ends. Practically, the means for attaining such a curriculum objective must be crystal clear. Responsible administrators and music educators must be challenged in several ways to achieve this objective.

Achieving the Full Life. The school music administrator must conceive a program of creative and re-creative music experiences which will undergird our school children and assure an aesthetic and cultural development necessary for the full life. What is the full life? It is that experience of living--in this case music--which will assure for the individual the greatest possible satisfactions of which he is capable. This becomes the great challenge to the music educator and administrator.

The music educator cannot possibly achieve a full life musical experience for those for whom he is educationally responsible unless he is able to gather about him competent staff who are able to envision a mutually sympathetic concept of music education. Instruction and learning should not be stereotyped. Those responsible for developing and conducting the program should subscribe to the belief that all individuals should be able to explore those musical experiences which are vital to their cultural development. Thus, the administrator must project a pattern of music learning opportunities which will orient the individual in all the arts.

The basic elements in our music program are so all-inclusive in their appeal to the fundamental emotional and intellectual interests of individuals, that the educator must never cease his effort to provide such opportunities. Aiding

51

people to attain a measure of human happiness through a joyous music experience becomes one of the great administrative and instructional opportunities.

Music Learning and the Child. We have attempted to evolve the thesis that the ends of music education cannot be administratively achieved unless the means for attaining them have been conceived and their instructional content provided for in music curricula. If the following principles of learning are recognized in curriculum content there is greater likelihood that a dynamic program will evolve--dynamic because each individual is employing ever-changing patterns of learning energy.

1) Children of primary school age possess many impulses and energies which are in need of direction. This is a major consideration if children are to be helped in bringing a purposefulness to their innate musical sensitivity. Through the organization of materials and purposes, the teacher must aid the child in perceiving and learning how to give expression to his dominant vocal rhythmic urges.

2) Individual musical talent differences exist irrespective of the intelligence of the child. Statistical evidence indicates that there is a low correlation between intelligence and musical ability; musical talent and achievement are highly specialized traits. Good musical ability is to be found among children of average and below-average intelligence. Such component traits of musicianship as rhythmic sensitivity, aural acuity, phrase sensitivity, and tonal memory may appear singly or collectively as highly developed skills. A child of distinctive talent usually possesses many of these component traits to an unusual degree.

The music educator should accept the challenge that lies before him. The evidence is plausible and even clear that within each classroom the teacher can find sufficient talent to warrant exploration of the dynamic implications of our music program. The ultimate joy is to aid the child in finding his power of musical expression. Creative musical ability not only implies possession of these basic ingredients, but also musical comprehension through insight. Insight brings about discovery and aids musical endowment for functional use.

3) The child is the final determinant in the construction of curriculum content and instructional technique. The

adult is often far removed from childish ways and understandings. His outlook is refined by maturity. Educators
must look to the child for discernment of his motives of action. The administrator must aid the individual in realizing
his expressional needs.

Unless the individual is aided in his desire for musical
expression there will be little aesthetic function. Key curricular understandings will result from a knowledge of the emotional and intellectual cravings and motivations of the child.
Musical creativity thus helps the child in finding his real
self. The child finally reveals himself through his own explorations. He must explore himself and he alone is capable
of doing it so completely. Therefore, the curriculum must
be child-centered.

4) A program of creative activities stemming from a
configuration of learning experiences needs to be organized
for the child. Too often this musical learning environment
is not sufficiently exploratory and the child is not challenged
to assert his intuitive powers. He is not allowed to experience the joy to be derived from the creative opportunities
which participation in music provides. The teacher is too
often interested in the means rather than the function of that
means. The child should have the opportunity of expressing
his own creativity in every learning situation.

5) Every music lesson should be a complete musical
experience. It must reflect many experiences in music.
For the child the lesson must incorporate song-singing,
rhythmic, listening, creative, and re-creative activities. It
must be an integrated effort from which will be fashioned
his early musical understanding. The emphasis should be
upon his exploratory participation in the sound and movement of music. He should be at the center of a whole world
of musical opportunities. The songs he sings must employ
verbalisms which are common to his understanding. There
must exist the relatedness or association of song as part of
daily living. The rhythmic flow or meter of the phrase or
verse must be experienced by him. The re-creativity of a
song-singing experience must create within him a desire for
song performance as a source of personal pleasure. There
may occur the expressed desire to create a verse or melodic line for musical performance. Sheer joy should be derived from listening to others sing. Through musical experience the child is led to activity because of its varied
associations. Art experiences for all children cannot be

fully explored by the mere singing of songs, marching to music, or by the pounding on a drum. The objective should be to explore the artistic mind of the child by ferreting out fundamental emotional and intellectual expressions of his personality.

6) Music is a language of thoughts and feelings, and many forms of varied emotional expression. Many of these emotional expressions are satisfying to the individual. It is easily conceived that the expression of the child's emotions reflects his state of social development. Music for the primary school child should become a way of living for the here and now. Music is an excellent medium of emotional expression for the child.

7) Self-expression is an essential concomitant to learning. Here the child is required to become an active participant in music learning or the experience is not a vital motivating force. Life is an active process. Musical performance is an active rather than a passive act. The major criterion for evaluating musical performance is performance. Performance is always perceptual evidence of successful achievement. It is the fulfillment of each individual's personality. Each new life must be an experiment in creativity. An idea once perceived must be reconceived by the individual or its contributory creative effect to that individual is of little value to him.

8) Creativity is always an individual matter. A given creative musical experience does not exist in the same kind or degree for each individual. These individual differences point up the great challenges that exist in primary school music. Good exploratory activities should result in better learning experiences for the primary school child. The exploratory stage is a developmental stage on the road toward choices for effecting learning. Efficient and effective learning comes from those insights which are derived from self-explorations.

The administrator and music educator must keep in mind that there are two broad considerations in determining the direction of the educative process. One is its basic philosophy and the other, the nature and content of its evolving curriculum. Actually there is almost a one-to-one relationship existing between philosophy and curriculum. The philosophical insights and curricular content of which we have spoken thus become the media for implementing under-

standings which will aid all men in experiencing the creative
and experiential power of music. In man, creativity means
something expressed. If it is creative, it is active; if active,
it implies man's self has been propelled into creativity.

Restructuring New Programs. New music programs
should be conceived for all schools. Students must be at the
heart of the entire music curriculum. Effete music--clas-
sical and romantic--will undoubtedly be a long time coming
in its realizations. The standard of perfection for song and
its performance may be remote and often unacceptable to urban and suburbanite artistic appreciations. In order to reach
every child, his musical experiences must be those that permit him to "cry out, " "laugh out, " and even "sing out" his
innermost moods and feelings. There must prevail a feeling
of enjoyment and emotional release. He must be able to relate to himself and others his innermost desires--the soul of
his being. He must be helped along the road to cultural refinement.

The music teacher must adjust to newer demands involving new curricula needs. The subject, music, is not at
fault if interest lags. Most important is what and how instructional materials are to be presented. Old objectives,
attainments, and logical sequences need drastic reevaluations,
if not in some cases complete discarding.

Singing does not comprise the entire elementary or
secondary school music program. There are many media of
musical experience. Instruments of the orchestra provide
opportunities for interesting music study. More important
is the study of composers, their compositions, and the ethnic
expression and opportunity for appreciation they engender.

New textbooks must include song literature that gives
all ethnic groups opportunity for empathetic feeling and expression for self and mankind. The African lullaby can be
as beautiful as those written by American, German, or
French composers. Songs should be presented for their inherent merits and should not reveal any form of racial bias.
Song literature should be made available that gives expression to the "soul" of man.

The teacher must cast aside much of present-day lecture method. Note-taking and the dry repetition of the lectured or dictated factualism should be relegated to the peda-
gogical "garble-de-gook" of all faltering teaching techniques.

Child involvement should in so far as possible be the con-
summate instructional approach. Music has the power to
communicate to all children, but they must be allowed to enjoy the gamut of their cultural perspectives. Take them
where they are and allow them to expand their horizons.
Music is an ideal medium through which they may find their
identity. Certainly, skills are involved if expression is to
be found. The triumvirate of skills, involvement and communication are powerful tools for positive action.

The teacher does not sit in a seat of authority. Not
anymore! He is simultaneously held in respect and contempt,
he is tolerated and looked upon with incomprehensible indif-
ference. Some students see him as a purveyor of "idiotic
stuff" with almost no practicality. The teacher is subjected
to studied intrigue, discourtesy, and little appreciation; he
must sometimes face arrogance and insults.

Boredom must not enter music programs. Of what
use can the music program be to children? Has fun been
left out of performance or has frustration taken its place?
It is possible that a snobbish minority has left the colossal
majority behind. Should we be interested in impeccable performances by soloists or in large performing groups? Years
ago, it was common to have high school assembly sings as
often as once a week. Community sings could be employed
to get the kids all "gassed up" for a good emotional release.

Boredom could be imbedded in the lack of challenge
at all educational levels. Modern youth demands that things
be achieved "in their time." Many believe that they are going to live but once--they want their experience in the "here
and now."

Educators must start now and give the deprived children their opportunity and not postpone the responsibility to
another generation because it may be too late.

On the plus side are the parents of children. Nearly
all parents have a passion for achieving learning for their
children. But this parental interest cannot function unless
funds and newly conceived programs are articulated. Music
education for all children must become the concept to be
achieved by all Americans. This cannot be achieved by
brick, mortar and steel, but rather by a new concept of ed-
ucation--an ideal--a passion to aid every child beginning
right now!

The Curriculum. The problem in gaining a concept of
the meaning of a dynamic curriculum is that its content and
meaning are derived from the child's multifarious responses
to many media of learning.   There is a classroom situation,
the immediacy of the moment, the act of vocal articulation
and the experience.   All of these are rarely anticipated and
provided for in the curriculum.   Heretofore, it was the
course of study, the course outline, the teachers' guide, or
the teachers' manual, that often guided or initiated experiences to arrive at classroom teacher-guided objectives.   Attainments were seemingly more important than insights.

Thus, the teacher was often circumscribed by inani-
mate outlines and directives beyond which her insights had
not penetrated.   The teacher often protested, "if you don't
write it down, if you don't tell me what to do, how can I
teach anything?"   Such a teacher lacks understanding of the
principles of learning which we have described--does not
know nor understand "what to do," and does not recognize
the existence of a learning situation always present between
the teacher and child.

The curriculum which we conceive should provide for
the dynamic nature of the individual.   Such a condition should
give the individual those insights which will give rise to multiple manifestations of an individual's innate creativity.   Let
us explore the associative experiences that may arise in an
actual learning situation.   The configurations of the learning
situation initiated by the singing of a simple primary school
song, "My Dolly," might appear as follows:

1.   The thought of the "Dolly" as the loveliest object pos-
       sessed by the child.
2.   The associations--its clothes, its size, its beauty,
       the pleasures derived from it.
3.   The desire to discuss other dolls.
4.   The desire for possession--the "belongingness"--gre-
       gariousness--the sense of security--the feeling of
       satisfaction from its possession.
5.   The desire to sing about all the dolls the child owns.
6.   The desire to dance with or for the doll.
7.   The desire to compose a song--even a lullaby.

From the above configurations which might be elicited
by such a song it can be discerned that the teacher must be
sensitive--must have insight into the expansiveness of the
mental urges and drives of the child.   Actually, a whole

world of learning experiences will be lost if the teacher
teaches the song, "My Dolly" as a finite rather than infinite
experience, possessed of many associative understandings
for the child. It is the whole and not a part of the learning
experience that makes for dynamic learning. Obviously, any
curriculum must allow for both teacher and pupil differences
in varied instructional environments. Every classroom is
always composed of a great variety of interests and abilities
on the part of both teacher and pupils.

A determination must be made as to what is to be
achieved. Is the teaching of music the most important end
objective of music education? Is there to be stimulated and
even developed an appreciation for music? Will the curriculum provide for the learning of those skills, appreciations,
expressions, and preferences, and aid the individual in
achieving those insights which should be considered as desirable outcomes of music learning? If so, the curriculum
must become a constructive instrument for aiding in the
achievement of these desired learning outcomes. We have
stated that a good music curriculum should provide for those
functional art experiences which aid in achieving the full life.
It must provide each child a challenge for his awakening
urges.

For a layman a knowledge of musical symbols is of
little value unless they serve these higher purposes. The
dimensions of his mature musical understanding are imbedded
in the growth of his intellectual and musical capacity. Mature dimensions of musical understanding aid the layman in
establishing a basis for reasoned musical judgments and appreciations. A curriculum which is devoid of elements
which will foster this becomes but an organized plan for imitation. A music curriculum patterned according to the dic-
tates of a single mind may lack the beneficial effects of
critical thinking. This is not the type of musical philosophy
that we desire, our curriculum must provide for the opera-
tion of understanding in artistic experiences.

This great potential variation in individual learning
implies greater need for teacher preparation and skills.
Broad learning opportunities demand a dynamic environment
of experiences. The teacher must initiate mind-challenging
activities. The musical experience that started out to be
the learning of songs may become a singing, dancing, rhythmic, listening, verse, and participative narrative activity.
No childlike desire, interest, or insight should be impeded

by insufficient curriculum content. This is why our curriculum must be dynamic.

The development of our primary, elementary, and
secondary music curricula should include eight basic areas
of instruction. They are: 1) vocal expression, 2) listening
program, 3) musical participation, 4) creativity, 5) instrumental expression, 6) rhythmic expression, 7) melodic expression, and 8) theoretical expression. These basic musical experiences can be more fundamentally analyzed as part
of an individual's early tendencies to express himself physically (movement) and vocally. Vocal expression and body
activity are synonomous with response to music. The individual prefers these activities because they are pleasurable.
They are not dependent upon training for their elemental satisfactions. The core units which are now to be discussed in
detail are the framework about which our curriculum will be
constructed.

1. Vocal Expression. We always start with the
most personal gift and possession of all men, the singing
voice. Singing in any form, whether in solo or group, is
always a complete and individual expression. Every note is
an expression of intellectual, emotional, and physical life.
The individual is both instrument and re-creator in one functional act. The first medium of musical expression is the
voice. For the individual, his first music appreciation
comes through this medium.

Even though his singing is learned rotewise until
printed symbolisms have meaning, this vocal utterance is
most satisfying. Too often the teacher prematurely rushes
the learning of musical symbolisms before the child has had
the pleasure to be derived from singing. Symbolisms are
always accessory to understandings. Singing is the important act.

2. The Listening Program. Every musical act is
either an aural or rhythmic experience, or both. Listening
to music is often a passive experience with unbounded opportunity for aesthetic-creative discriminations which are potentially satisfying. Discriminative listening is proportional
to an understanding of music's basic symbolisms. Knowledge
of musical notation, music structure, media for conveying
expression (vocal and instrumental), manner of interpretation,
and musical stylism contribute to the meaningfulness of a listening program. Listening cannot become a significant cre-

ative experience for those who lack the understandings for
these symbolisms. Meaningful listening is always proportional to understanding.

3. Musical Participation. Music is both an individual and a gregarious art experience. Participation in music
is characterized by emotional expressions manifested either
vocally or instrumentally. The learning of vocal and instrumental skills are achieved through such media as individual
and group participation. Group musical participation engen-
ders the spirit of co-operation and during its performance
wipes out social, economic, political, and racial barriers.
Participation is imperative if music is to be enjoyed. Musical performance is always a participative experience for the
individual.

4. Creativity. Music creativity provides those active
learning experiences which give great opportunity for individual expression. Because music offers creative opportunities,
it provides individual needs for aesthetic expression and
keener insight into the life and art of the creator. The
functional nature of music justifies its inclusion in the curriculum because it so completely explores an individual's
creative tendencies. (See p. 113.)

5. Instrumental Expression. The reed, string (mon-
ochord and psaltery), wood, and percussive instruments were
used extensively to express such emotions as fear, hate, an-
ger, or love by earliest man.

Today instrumental expression in music education is
so varied and comprehensive in its employment that it has
become a cornerstone in the development of a strong school
music program. The primary school has many rhythmic
activities which employ percussive instruments in great variety.

Melodic instruments (bells, xylophones, chimes, ma-
rimbas, etc.) find early and happy usefulness. Children in
the elementary grades enjoy playing instruments found in the
modern band or orchestra. The expansion of these instrumental activities has resulted in many thousands of bands
and orchestras in our schools. Instrumental expression apparently appeals to a very fundamental creative desire on
the part of almost everyone.

6. Rhythmic Expression. Bodily rhythmic feeling

and expression are basic to all human movement. Rhythmic
movement (dance-games, etc.) may appear before song. It
is possible that this medium of expression was embodied in
the first music made by man. Human emotion may find its
basic expression in movements ranging from the waving of
the arm or the shaking of a rattle by a baby, to the regular
and measured movement of the body to the accompaniment
of instruments. The rhythmic beat of the heart is reflected
by regular pulsations. Measured cycles of duple or triple
metre in the march or dance are evidences of controlled motion. The stress of any recurring pulsations gives them
measured movement control. Rhythmic metre is present in
all speech, dance, and song, and are media that, if properly
used, will have a profound influence upon the music education of individuals. Finger painting or rhythmical drawing
to the accompaniment of music have found a place of increasing importance in the education of young school children. Their resultant creativity reflects moods of significant importance. Our secondary school marching bands reflect the importance of rhythm in attracting participants for
these organizations. Rhythm is the life blood of musical
movement.

      7. Melodic Experience. A beautiful melodic line is
appealing to the ear. Its appeal is emotional rather than
intellectual. Melodic design--how the notes go--does not
necessarily imply the only form of tonal line that elicits
emotional appeal. The aborigine's monotonous sequence of
notes may not be pleasing to the civilized ear. However,
the aborigine considers it melodic and satisfying. The baby
uttering a repetitious babble of pitch sequences is undoubtedly
responding to pleasing effects on his ear and emotional life.
The organized utterance of a succession of pitches (notes)
results in a melodic design. It does not have to be pleasing
to others. It is an individual matter.

      To the modern school child, melody is inextricably
interwoven with lyrics, rhythm and harmonic and tonal sequences. Melody will never lose its inherent quality of emo-
tional-intellectual appeal. Music has an emotional quality
that does not necessarily require the individual to have an
understanding of its symbols.

      8. Theoretical Experience. The basic symbolisms
of music, the lines, spaces, signatures, notation, and harmonic tonal and atonal structuralisms, must be understood
in order to interpret their meanings. The intensity of this

study for either the child or the adult should be somewhat
proportional to its intended use. In the initial musical education of the elementary school child theoretical study should
be as rudimentary as is required for enjoyable early music
understandings. Many aspects of music may be studied by
all, but the extent of penetrative study is dependent upon individual talent, ability, interest, and the maturation of emotional and intellectual life. Theoretical study is not imperative to musical enjoyment, but it is essential to its discriminative appreciations.

Elementary School Instructional Plans. Music instruction in the elementary schools has had to be adjusted
organizationally to meet some of the inadequacies and exi-
gencies of instruction. Organizational practice designed to
expedite instruction in these classrooms, according to Peterson, [1] follows four plans:

Plan A: All music is taught by a music specialist
with no responsibility for the classroom teacher other
than possible conferences for the purpose of correlating music activities with other areas in the elementary school curriculum.

Plan B: Music is taught in part by the classroom
teacher and in part by a visiting specialist (supervisor, consultant, or co-ordinator) whose major responsibility is to help the classroom teacher in such
matters as organizing the music program, selecting
materials, and introducing new teaching methods.

Plan C: All music is taught by the classroom
teacher with little or no assistance from a music
specialist (supervisor, consultant, or co-ordinator).

Plan D: Music is taught by classroom teachers
who "trade" subjects with one or more teachers in
the school but receive little or no assistance from a
music specialist.

Peterson's study reinforces the conviction of many
music educators and administrators that, for the lower
grades, the music taught by a music specialist or by the
specialist and teacher (Plans A and B) is administratively
most satisfactory and is instructionally necessary because
of the ineptness in music teaching of many teachers in the
primary and intermediate grades. It is also significant that

administrators favor Plan A in grades seven and eight.
There is an apparent interest on the part of administrators
of those grades to include classroom teacher responsibility
for music instruction even though that teacher is assisted by
the music specialist. Peterson concludes by saying that
"Generally speaking, however, there seems to be a tendency
for principals to favor plans involving greater use of the music specialist in the elementary schools."[2]

Recruitment and Enrollment. The elementary school
music program that is imaginatively conceived beyond regular
vocal music instruction truly becomes the foundation upon
which a strong secondary school music program is built. It
is the music educator's responsibility to encourage all types
of ensemble experiences for elementary school children in
order that they will learn the necessary techniques with which
to pursue their musical interests and studies at the secondary school level. We have discussed those broad areas of
musical activity which will provide song-singing, listening,
rhythmic, creative, and re-creative experiences. But the
breadth of the experience within each category becomes an
additional responsibility for the music educator.

Music educators will have to encourage their music
teachers and in-service teachers to experiment further with
creativity in the form of tonette, piano class, instrumental
class, choral and instrumental groups which will utilize the
child's ability to express himself vocally and instrumentally.
A broad program of music experiences for every individual
should be developed in the elementary school. We need recruitment and enrollment methods which will aid in realizing
the dynamic music program which is envisioned.

Among the suggestions and devices proposed, the following have proved effective:

1) Recruitment and enrollment in musical activities
and organizations should take place during the first or second
week of each new school year. It should never be postponed,
as other competing activities are certain to crowd in and
thwart effective organizational plans.
2) The classroom teacher should aid the music teacher in discovering those students who indicate evidence of musical promise, detecting those individuals who have good
singing voices, possess fine rhythmic sensitivity, and have
superior aural acuity. The music educator should aid the
classroom teacher by giving musical aptitude tests for the

purpose of revealing children with fine musical sensitivity.

3) Musical activities and organizational performances can be developed in the intermediate grades (4-5-6) through the co-operative efforts of the various classroom teachers.

4) Special classes in piano and instrumental music should be organized for the specially talented students who could profit from instruction on a semi-private or class lesson basis. Teachers could be drawn from the school and community for instructing these groups.

5) Talented music students should be encouraged through conversations with parents to pursue private music study. The fruition of such an advisory program will be reflected in the musical contribution that these individuals will eventually make to the school and community.

6) Records of especially gifted students should be maintained from grade to grade. These students sometimes drop by the wayside because of the lack of encouragement. Music is fun, but it is also work. Children need to be organized and prodded in their association with musical learning.

7) All teachers should work through the parents in an effort to encourage any child who shows an interest in music. Witness the important work of the Music Parents' Clubs, Band Parents' Clubs, and Music Activities' Clubs in the development of strong music programs in our elementary and secondary schools.

8) Summer band, choral, and orchestral programs do much to maintain a constancy of musical interest among music students. Group musical experiences help greatly in maintaining interest in any activity--the gregarious instinct is a powerful factor in the development of large musical organizations.

9) Finally, no recruitment program will be successful unless the administrator, music educator, his assistants, and the in-service classroom teachers work together to help each child in proportion to his interest and capacity for music and learning. The great satisfaction that may be derived by the child is that there is no more wholesome and individually rewarding experience than that which results from contact with music.

A letter to parents and students of the Independent School District of Boise, Idaho, invites the enrollment of "new students from the fifth and sixth grades" to join instrumental classes. The letter explains who may join the classes, the nature of the classes, the cost of instruction, how an instrument may be obtained, and a blank for the

parent to fill out. Such a letter sent to the home of every
fifth and sixth grade student is certain to aid in the search
for new instrumental players. It is reproduced below.

Independent School District of Boise City[3]
Boise   Idaho

To Parents and Students:

We are now enrolling new students from the fifth and
sixth grades in our instrumental classes in the schools.
Students with previous training will be given the opportunity for ensemble playing and beginners will receive their fundamental training. Students are urged
to enroll immediately so as to avoid conflicts. Classes
are scheduled during school time and will not interfere
with academic work. Instruction is offered on string,
woodwind, brass, and percussion instruments.

All the music stores in the community have convenient
low cost instrument rental-purchase plans. They offer the opportunity to apply the rental paid on the purchase of the instrument.

A demonstration of the band and orchestra instruments will be given by the music instructor at school
on _____, _____ ___, 19___ at
_____.

Parents and students are urged to attend this demonstration in order to see and hear each instrument and
to discuss the choice of an instrument with the music
instructor.

The opportunity to receive free lessons, play in ensembles, do solo playing, and enjoy group participation is one of the educational benefits offered by the
Boise school system. Music plays a very important
part in the complete education of the child. It teaches
appreciation, broadens and improves the mind, provides a wholesome outlet for expression, teaches discipline, teamwork and democracy, improves coordination of thought and action, and provides the opportunity
for those who may later make music a career.

Students who begin their training early have a decided
advantage. By continuing their training through the

schools, they will eventually have the chance to play
in the fine orchestras and bands at the senior high
schools and later the college and civic groups.

Any student interested in taking part in the classes
should fill out the blank below and return it to the
school principal or music teacher. If further information is desired or help needed in the selection of
an instrument, call _____, instrumental music
teacher, at _____. The best time to phone is
between _____ and _____.

****

Name_____Phone_____
                                      Grade &
Address_____School_____Teacher_____

What instrument would you like to play?_____

Do you own an instrument?_____What?_____Rent?___

Would you like further information?_____

_____
Parent's Signature

Discussion

    1. What do you conceive as being the full life?
    2. Should music play an important part in attaining
the full life?
    3. How would you ascertain music talent in a child
of five years? What devices would you use for measuring
his talent?
    4. What is the co-efficient of correlation between
musical talent and intelligence?
    5. Are you basically a hereditarian or an environ-
mentalist? Do you believe that any intelligent person can
become a good musician?
    6. Should the child be the final determinant in cur-
ricular construction?
    7. Who propounded the configuration theory of psy-
chology? How would you tie-in its implications with the experiment of Burt Kofka and the monkeys?
    8. Is it essential to learn music symbols in order
to enjoy music?

9. If you were to construct a music curriculum what would you include in it?

10. How would it be possible for the classroom teacher to discover those who possess a high degree of musicality?

Notes

1. Peterson, Wilbur J. "Organizational Plans Favored by Administrators For Elementary School General Music." Music Educators Journal, 43: No. 3 (January, 1957), 48, 50-51.

2. Ibid., 50-51.

3. Von der Heide, Henry J. Handbook for Music Teachers. Boise, Idaho: Independent School District of Boise City, 1957.

Bibliography

Andrews, Frances M., and Cockerille, Clara E. Your School Music Program. Englewood Cliffs, N.J.: Prentice Hall, 1958.

Broudy, Harry S. A Relatistic Philosophy of Music Education." Basic Concepts in Music Education, National Society for the Study of Education. Fifty-seventh Yearbook, Chicago: 1958. Part I, 62-87.

Broudy, Harry S. Building a Philosophy of Education. Englewood Cliffs, N.J.: Prentice-Hall, 1954.

Davison, Archibald T. Music Education in America. New York: Harper & Brothers, 1926.

Ewen, David. Music Comes to America. New York: Thomas Y. Crowell, 1942.

Kingsley, Howard L. The Nature and Conditions of Learning. 2d ed. Englewood Cliffs, N.J.: Prentice-Hall, 1957.

Lahee, Henry. Annals of Music in America. Boston: Marshall Jones Company, 1922.

Langer, Suzanne K. Feeling and Form. New York: Charles
    Scribner's Sons, 1953.

Meyer, Leonard B. Emotion and Meaning in Music. Chica-
    go: University of Chicago Press, 1956.

Nesbitt, Marion. A Public School for Tomorrow. New
    York: Harper & Brothers, 1955.

Nettl, Bruno. Music in Primitive Culture. Cambridge,
    Mass.: Harvard University Press, 1956.

Perham, Beatrice. Music in the New School. (Park Ridge,
    Ill.: Neil A. Kjos Music Company, 1947).

Squire, Russel N. Introduction to Music Education. New
    York: Ronald Press, 1952.

Part Three: Elementary School Music

CHAPTER V: THE ELEMENTARY SCHOOL MUSIC TEACHER

The attitude of the child toward music is basically
formed while he is in the elementary school. One happy or
one unfortunate musical experience during these formative
years may guide future attitudes toward music.

Many unfortunate experiences connected with music
may and do occur during childhood. There is the child who
was told to sit and listen while the others sang, because he
was unable to sing with good intonation. The disturbing factor in this episode is that, usually the child is able to sing.
All too often, it is the teacher's inability to employ the proper techniques for training the child's voice. At the primary
level it is usually a question of inadequate environment or the
need for maturation, instead of poor aural acuity. In a situation like the one just described a demand for exactitude of
performance as a prerequisite for participation has an unfortunate effect upon the child's mental outlook toward music.
A child may enjoy music intellectually even though he recognizes his inadequate performance. The enjoyment he derives
from musical experiences must always be the paramount criterion. If he enjoys music he must be given every opportunity to continue experiencing it. Innate musical ability is a
determining factor in the child seeking further musical experiences.

An effective teacher will always be a powerful medium
for establishing happy aesthetic experiences for his children.
Usually the hindrance to successful enjoyment is the inadequacy of the teacher and not the ineptness of the pupils. If
the child is to experience the important role that music will
play in his daily life, the teacher must have a depth of intuitive understanding which will enable her to assist the child to
browse emotionally and intellectually among many types of
good music. Through such browsing, the child may come to
have an appreciation of music long before he reaches an understanding of its techniques. In fact, he may never attain

knowledge of its formal elements.

The extent of a child's participation in rhythmic activity may far surpass the extent of his knowledge of metre or the notation which is used to transcribe it onto paper. The lesson must include all aspects of rhythmic movement, if the child is to derive enjoyment. Rhythm may be expressed through bodily movement, the dance, the song, and even in the design of a fine painting. In rhythmic activity, the inherent sensitivity of the child is the determinant of immediate pleasurable responses.

The crux of class participation in rhythm activity is whether the teacher has the intuitive ability to arouse the potential of each student as a participant. The success of the class experience can be evaluated by the total proficiency of the group, as well as by the fullness and completeness of each individual's participation. For too long we have measured classroom and individual success on the basis of the "show off" performance of individuals; let us think instead of a class activity in terms of the individual satisfactions it provides. True, the needs of gifted children are not properly provided for and they are often held back musically as well as academically. Inadequate budgets result in incompetent personnel. All too often specialized teachers are not made available to teach music.

The teacher who is interested in the creative development of children must have courage to pursue the idea of individual expression. Many teachers cannot refrain from telling children what should be done at every juncture. The intuitive child is stifled in such a situation and the less well endowed child, likewise, is not allowed to do other than as he is directed by the teacher. We are not recommending that the teacher should not instruct, but instruction should consist of guided musical experiences for pleasurable enjoyment, always geared to pupil interests.

Another great hindrance to the growth of musical enjoyment is the apparent insistence of teachers in underestimating children's ability to enjoy music. We retard the primary child's musical progress by requiring him to participate in activities which he has outgrown. A teacher cannot present irrelevant and totally unrelated ideas about music and expect children to derive pleasure from the experience. The child is often limited by the teacher's limited knowledge rather than by his capacity to absorb beauty, which needs no language and is often more effective if verbalisms are eliminated.

In the intermediate grades, we often find boys and girls singing songs which are not in keeping with their restive spirits. Physical rather than intellectual activity more nearly characterizes their development during the intermediate grades. The boy or girl of ten, eleven, or possibly twelve years will tolerate songs about "The Daffodils," but he is often required to listen to them in junior high school years.[1] The boys are approaching manhood and must be treated in keeping with their dreams of maturity. On the other hand, boys and girls must never be subjected to musical experiences which they do not have the emotional or intellectual maturity to enjoy.

Music Teacher Qualifications. State departments of education and institutions of higher learning qualify music teachers on the basis of very few music courses. A study revealed in 1947 that of 700 freshman students who entered six New York State Teachers Colleges, 45 percent had no music education in grades one to eight, and 75 percent had no regular music instruction in high school. A Committee on Music in Higher Education made a survey in 1953. The reply to the question, "What percent of your elementary teachers are capable to teaching ... vocal music?"[2] was that more than 50 percent were not able to teach music.[3] The current imbalance in our school tax structure in relation to its financial needs has had a deleterious effect upon the music experiences of graduates from secondary schools. Those pursuing teacher training in elementary education are often not qualified to structure a basis for teaching music; this in spite of the minimum music course requirements prescribed in their training programs. The elementary teacher of the 1970's is no better qualified to teach music than he was in the 1950's.

The teacher training curricula of the State Teachers Colleges in New York State do not differ greatly in their music course requirements from the courses of study in colleges in Minnesota and other states. Teacher training courses in music for elementary teachers usually include either four or six semester hours of music. In some institutions a limited number of elective music courses are offered--rarely more than two--with not more than an additional four or six semester hours required.

Institutions that train teachers must assume greater responsibility for music education than is generally offered today. They must provide opportunities for teachers to broaden their limited musical backgrounds in order to improve their skill in teaching music to children. Morgan has recently stated:

An analysis of the reasons why some elementary teachers are successful in establishing this desirable relationship between the child and music and why others fail in doing so, shows clearly that there are many contributing factors which can be identified.

These factors of success or non-success can be roughly grouped into such major areas as: teacher education, curriculum music content and teaching techniques. Two other items are of tremendous importance, namely: (a) the personal attitude of the grade teacher towards teaching music, and (b) a dedicated belief in the power of music in the lives of everyone.[4] The great tragedy is that at this level where music plays such an important part in the socio-cultural development of the child, the teacher is very often poorly qualified to teach the students effectively. Morgan continues,

> While legitimate criticism can be made of the quality of college teaching of the so-called 'music methods' courses, many schools are doing a very acceptable and adequate job of giving their graduates, (a) a knowledge of what (music curriculum content) should be taught, and (b) a knowledge of how (teaching techniques) to teach the what.

Attitude of the In-Service Teacher. The elementary in-service teacher was asked to evaluate the quality of his or her college preparation in music in a study conducted by Newton, who was attempting to find out from elementary teachers in one hundred towns and cities in different localities in the state, how they felt about their college preparation in music. They expressed themselves as follows:

1. Before we could graduate from college, our music instructor required every student to take and pass a course in voice, piano one and two, music methods, music appreciation, plenty of solfeggio and fundamentals. We had to actually do the music teaching in our classes. We are grateful for adequate experience.

2. More time should be spent on "teaching the teacher how to teach music" to children. Fundamentals are necessary but learning the application of the fundamentals is what a teacher needs and that is what is lacking in teacher training.

3. Students leave with very little or no knowledge of the basic textbooks nor do they know how to use them.

4.   Provide more time and opportunities for practice teaching.

5.   Colleges teach music fundamentals but not methods.   The teacher wants to know how to present elementary music problems to children and to lay a good foundation in an interesting way.   Too much time is spent in singing just for fun.   Little opportunity is given in learning how to present a rote song, a rote note and reading readiness song, and rhythmic problems.   The elementary teacher needs these approaches and wants them. [5]

The musical education of elementary classroom teachers may be improved by: (1) more and better music courses in teacher training institutions, and (2) greater emphasis upon more and better in-training supervision by those colleges and conservatories that offer major courses in music education.

A resolution adopted at the 1955 Division Conventions of the Music Educators National Conference recognizes the inadequate pre-service educational opportunities of the classroom teacher when it states

> ... we recognize it has become the acceptable pattern for the elementary classroom teacher to be responsible for the music experiences of her own group.   Yet pre-service teacher education has not prepared the classroom teacher adequately for this responsibility.   In many cases the preparation period has increased from two years to four, but the requirements in music have remained almost static.   Therefore,
>
> We recommend (1) that college institutions educating elementary teachers take active leadership in providing musical experience which enables the teacher to feel at home in dealing with usual classroom activities; that where credit space is limited they employ the laboratory basis of credit in order to increase musical experience, and that they set up musical organizations for such students to provide and encourage participation throughout their years in college.   (2) that elementary school systems provide more adequate music consultant services and in-service development programs, and (3) that state groups of music educators work to-

ward the improvement of certification requirements
to meet this problem.[7]

The provision for additional music courses in the general elementary field is basic to the partial resolution of the
problem. All of the music teaching that should take place in
the classroom cannot be done by one music specialist. It
has been recommended

> That music in elementary schools be taught, in so
> far as possible, by specially trained and qualified
> teachers, believing that the needs of children will
> be better served, that classroom teachers will be
> relieved of a task which is often frustrating be-
> cause of a limited background of experience and
> training, and that the objectives sought by use of
> the self-contained classroom will not suffer from
> judicious employment of the concept of the 'self-
> contained school' ...[8]

but neither can the music specialist hope to provide sufficient
and satisfactory instruction, if he is overwhelmed with instructional duties.

Training the School Music Teacher. More elementary
music is taught by the regular teacher than by the music
specialist. If this premise is accepted, then a program
must be designed to train these teachers how to teach music. Although suggested course requirements as established
by state departments of education are helpful in outlining
course content and objectives, it remains for the teacher-
training institution to revise their programs so that the teacher will be better equipped to teach music to children.

What does the administrator hiring a teacher for the
primary and elementary grades require? In the primary
grades there must be insistence upon the ability of the candidate to play the piano, handle game and rhythmic activities,
and develop a social music program for children; at the elementary level her ability to teach music effectively will be
of more use than knowledge of German or Statistical Methods.
The future of American musical art is in the hands of these
teachers. Yet, little recognition is given to this fact in the
music course requirements prescribed for their preparation.

If we expect the grade teacher to teach music, let us
prepare her for the job. It is high time that teacher-train-

ing curricula include those music courses that will aid the
elementary teacher in serving the child. Heffernan stresses
the fact that, "The most important outcome of music experience in the elementary school, however, is not the acquisi-
tion of knowledge, or skill, valuable, as these are. The
most important outcome is love of music."[9]

What type of program will enhance the professional
status of the elementary teacher--she who must be completely
qualified, even to the extent of demonstrating competency in
teaching music in her classroom? Morgan asks the question,
"Is it possible for the average elementary classroom teacher
to do a creditable job of teaching music?"[10] She says

> the mere listing of required music courses in the
> curriculum for prospective elementary teachers has
> been proved insufficient. Until the heads of de-
> partments have a realization of the problem and
> see to it that these courses are taught by informed
> and experienced persons, no number of credits in
> music courses however large, will be adequate.
> Any adviser who knows the utility value of music,
> especially in the primary grades, will encourage
> the taking of courses which are designed to actually
> (not theoretically) meet this need. Any student who
> shows talent and interest in music should be defi-
> nitely encouraged to attain a college minor or con-
> centration in music education. The problem of ad-
> equate teacher training will be solved only when
> Deans, Heads of Departments, and Advisors are
> aware of what actually (not theoretically) goes on
> in an elementary classroom.[11]

A Suggested Music Teacher Training Program. There
are many basic areas of music understanding that the elementary teacher in training must study if adequate music
preparation is to be provided. The Oswego Plan, which was
inaugurated by the writer, explores what Morgan calls those

> broad and basic concept(s) of music, which includes
> self-expression, understanding, and the develop-
> ment of skills, (which) will lead to tolerance, per-
> sonal abilities, and an awareness of pattern and
> beauty. A child's happy relationship with music
> as a skill and art will result from a competent
> approach to the teaching of music in the elementary
> grades.[12]

The Oswego Plan was an attempt to increase and strengthen the course requirements in music for the preparation of elementary teachers. The usual one year program (thirty-six weeks) was divided into seven major areas of study: 1) Keyboard experiences, 2) Song-singing, 3) Rudiments of music, 4) Techniques for teaching music, 5) Community and School Music leadership, 6) Music appreciation, and 7) Motivation projects.

Keyboard experiences: a thorough understanding of the keyboard is basic to the training of individuals preparing for elementary school music teaching. [13] By learning to play accompaniments employing chords of the tonic, dominant, sub-dominant, and dominant-seventh, these teachers in-training learn much factual information about music. The in-training teacher learns in one process; rhythm, song-singing, theory, ear-training, and keyboard knowledge, all being done in a pleasurable manner. Most lay teachers are vocally self-conscious and the keyboard approach deemphasizes the personal element. It is a way of getting conscious musical experiences with sub-conscious personality and submerged self-conscious reactions. The keyboard approach is aimed at the development of the ability to play simple chordal accompaniments to children's songs.

Song-singing: the song-singing phase of this course is basic to all music work in the grades. Time during each class period is devoted to vocalization, tone production, breathing, and learning how to sing intelligently all types of songs, and particularly children's songs. All people can learn to sing pleasingly for children. The students are also instructed as to the vocal demands for children, grade by grade. Good song-singing is good ear-training.

Rudiments of music: just how much time should be spent in teaching the rudiments of music? This can be answered by asking what knowledge will be required of the teacher in teaching music in grades one to eight. The properly trained teacher must be able to read the symbols on the music page. She must know them in order to teach new songs. Therefore, teachers in training should become familiar with the various methods of reading music, and the syllable, the numeral, and the visual methods of reading should be demonstrated.

Techniques for teaching: methods and materials for teaching music should be the subjects of a comprehensive sur-

vey--much material should be mimeographed for convenience
of study. There should be classroom discussion and demonstration. A bibliography should be made available which
contains a list of source materials suitable for teaching elementary school music. The curriculum laboratory to which
we shall refer should contain much primary and elementary
vocal instructional material. It is there that the student
studies representative courses of study, song books, listens
to selected recordings, collects community sing suggestions,
and gathers additional aids for music teaching.

During the third 9-week period of the 36-week course,
the class in elementary music is conducted on a schoolroom
basis. The class should be conducted as a first, second,
or third grade, each student being given opportunity for
teaching his fellow students as though a regular teaching situation existed.

Whenever a demonstration school is connected with
the teacher training institution, students should visit regular
classrooms for first-hand study of the musical, disciplinary,
and psychological problems involved in teaching music.

Community leadership: techniques for conducting community singing should be taught for the purpose of helping
each student become better equipped to fill a functional place
in school and community music. The rudiments of conducting as related to classroom, assembly, and community singing need to be studied and practiced. Students derive their
experiences from classroom laboratory work and in their
practice teaching centers. While pursuing this program of
study the students should practice in actual teaching situations.

Music appreciation: this comes from an understanding of music which generates intellectual, physical, emotional, and aesthetic responses. Our enjoyment of music
will be in proportion to the influence of these four factors.
Of course, the non-professional music teacher cannot attain
a complete understanding of music in a single or a double
semester. Much can be learned, however, through proper
instruction. Time should be spent in directed listening. A
music curriculum laboratory should be maintained in order
that students may peruse the materials in related fields of
music. Students should be urged to collect good literature
that may be correlated with music teaching at the elementary
school level. They must have materials of their own when

they start teaching.

Motivation projects: as a culmination to each semester's work, the student should be required to develop a project which is related to primary or elementary music. The
Oswego Plan required each in-training elementary teacher to
learn as many as 50 songs of musical interest for children.
The student should be expected to search out imaginative
songs that will appeal to children in the elementary school.
The proper selection of these songs should be a matter of
much concern to both the student and the instructor. In addition to songs, fifty rhythmic piano pieces were selected
which were attractive musically, and included marches,
waltzes, minutes, and many other representative dance forms.
It is imperative that the student be stimulated to seek out
through keyboard, song-singing, rudiments, techniques for
teaching music, community and school leadership, and music
appreciation, areas of particular music interest which he believes will be of service to him when he becomes a regular
teacher. Throughout the academic year, the student should
be required to rehearse and memorize children's songs with
critical emphasis placed upon musical quality and performance. The elementary teacher must know how to present
song material attractively. An intelligent reception comes
from interesting presentations. Likewise, imaginative music
projects are an outgrowth of the interesting exploratory music experiences that the varied nature of the Oswego Plan is
supposed to initiate.

Outline of the Oswego Plan

I. KEYBOARD EXPERIENCES (Unit on Piano Playing).

   (A) Object.

       1. To develop musicianship with the aid of the key-
           board.

       2. To use the keyboard at the opening of the school
           year so that the instrument will become a func-
           tional instrument during the training period.

       3. To acquaint the students with those chords which
           are commonly used in playing simple accompani-
           ments.

4.   To use the keyboard instrument for teaching rhythm, rudiments of music, and singing. At the keyboard they are simultaneously employed.

5.   To demonstrate how students can learn to accompany children's songs.

6.   To give the students specific week by week assignments. These are made in the piano book which is used.

7.   To demonstrate the necessity for the piano in elementary school teaching.

(B) Assigned Activities for the Students.

1.   Write and play common triads in the major keys.

2.   Write and use common chord inversions.

3.   Write and use tonic, sub-dominant, dominant, and dominant-seventh chords.

4.   Play simple songs in at least three different keys, using chords and inversions: F, G, and C.

5.   Play the piano with their classmates observing. This helps self-consciousness; it's an aid to solo teaching appearances.

6.   Serve as student teachers, helping classmates who have little or no knowledge of the piano. (This activity, of course, is assigned only to students with piano background.)

7.   Study graded piano pieces utilizing regularly written parts for the right and left hand, when the chord work is completed.

II. SONG-SINGING (Unit on the Human Voice).

(A) Object.

1.   To make a thorough study of the child's voice, physiologically, emotionally, and psychologically.

2. To make a study of the various human voice problems and classifications and give special attention to the following topics:

    (a) The voice at mutation.
    (b) Discussion of the boy's voice.
    (c) The changes that take place in the child's voice from its initial flute-like tone to its alto, alto-tenor, tenor, or baritone quality in the seventh and eighth grades.
    (d) The quality (timbre) of the various voices.
    (e) The major voice classifications and sub-divisions.
    (f) The range of the various voices.
    (g) Criteria for judging good, bad, and average voices.

3. To give the students some rudimentary vocal lessons; special attention to vowel and consonant production, emission of tones, the head voice, the chest, and mouth resonances; appropriate vocalizes for elementary school children.

4. To devote a minute or two of nearly every lecture period for the purpose of developing good vocal habits--it's a good way to start a class period.

(B) Assigned Activities for the Students.

1. Listen to recordings in the various voices of the four classifications: soprano, alto, tenor, and bass.

2. Prepare lists of the voices found under (B-1)--contemporary artist names should be used in determining representatives for the four voice classifications.

3. Prepare a class program incorporating one soloist from each classification; conduct open forums for study purposes.

4. Have children from the Training-School come in and have their voices tested, listening carefully for the differences to be found in grades one, five, and eight.

5. Compare human voices of a given classification with those of a comparable instrument voice.

Violin	Soprano
Bass-Violin	Basso-Profundo
Bassoon	Basso
English-Horn	Contralto

6. Specific readings relative to this unit.

III. RUDIMENTS OF MUSIC.
(Unit on Facts about Music.)

(A) Object.

1. To teach all the facts related to placing notation on the staff--the clef, signature, different kinds of notes, names of the lines and the spaces, etc.

2. To enable students to become familiar with the various patterns common to elementary school music.

3. To provide opportunity for students to learn the major and minor scales; recognize the major and minor mode; analyze the structure of scales; and to be able to hear and construct at the keyboard chords built on the tonic, sub-dominant, and dominant-seventh.

4. To aid students to learn and have an understanding of the more common tempo, dynamic, and expression marks used in teaching elementary school music.

(B) Assigned Activities for the Students.

1. Interpretation of the meanings of the various categories of musical facts. (Mimeographed lists are prepared for use of the students in this activity.)

2. Analysis of various elementary school song books for the purpose of detecting the use of various factors taught under (A). A comparative study

is made by grade level.

3. Oral practice of the factual aspects of the music page.

4. Frequent reviews covering the factual aspects of music, this being done by calling for the information whenever a new song is studied.

(Unit on Methods of Reading Music.)

(A) Object.

1. To discuss thoroughly the following methods of reading music:

    Rote method   Singing by repetition
    Syllable method   Using do, re, mi, etc.
    Numeral method   Using 1, 2, 3, 4, etc.

2. To give an explanation of the terms movable do and fixed do.

3. To teach the students how to spell the syllable names, chromatically and diatonically up and down the scale.

4. To provide sufficient opportunity for learning how to read music effectively by employing the three methods suggested under 1.

5. To give the opportunity for learning how to read and sing effectively two-three- and four-part songs.

(B) Assigned Activities for the Students.

1. Sight-reading during part of the class time for a period of at least nine weeks.

2. A good way for students to learn the syllable names and to reproduce them in tempo is to have them write them underneath the notes. This is done outside of class time, and makes a helpful assignment.

3. Participation in workgroups for improvement in reading music. The class can be divided into small committees or groups for this purpose. A pianist should be a member of each group.

4. Practice in part singing. The class should be so divided that each section will have an opportunity to read each part. Likewise, the singing of the parts should be alternated.

IV. TECHNIQUES FOR TEACHING (Unit on Song Literature for Elementary Grades).

(A) Object.

1. To acquaint the student with the non-series song books especially adapted to the singing-range and psychological development of children.

2. To acquaint the student with the various series of singing books designed for the elementary grades. They are:

a. American Singer
b. Birchard Music
c. Growing With Music
d. Hollis Dann
e. Music Education
f. Music For Living
g. Music For Young Americans

h. Music Hour
i. Our Singing World
j. Singing School
k. This Is Music
l. Together-We-Sing
m. World of Music

3. To teach the criteria of a good song.

4. To relate the instructional objectives outlined in the Oswego Plan of study, to those found in Keyboard experiences, Song-singing, Rudiments of music, Techniques for Teaching Music, Community and School Music Leadership, Music Appreciation, and Motivation projects.

(B) Assigned Activities for the Students.

1. A comparative study of the various song books using the following topics as a basis of consideration:

a. The various rhythmic problems and where

they are presented.

b. The various notational values; whether sys-
tematically or heterogeneously presented.

c. The type of song materials that should be
used at various grade levels.

d. Determine whether the various song books
emphasize the relation between music and
social studies, opportunities for participating in many musical activities, the amount
of practical suggestions for teaching, and
if the song-singing or song-reading approach
is used.

2. Development of a bibliography containing comments about each book relative to its suitable-
ness for music in given grades. This material
to be mimeographed so that each student has
the material for practice-teaching.

3. A committee of students might survey the
schools in their area served by the teacher
training center, and attempt to determine the
books most commonly used.

4. The singing of one-, two-, three-, and four-
part songs found in the various song book se-
ries-one should be used as a basic class text
in order that students may become thoroughly
familiar with it.

V. COMMUNITY LEADERSHIP (Unit on a Conductor's
Check List).

(A) Object.

1. To discuss the importance of the following criteria for those who wish to become conductors:

a. Ability to harmonize parts.
b. Ability to play the piano.
c. Acute ear.
d. Leadership qualities.
e. Dramatic ability.

f. Understanding of the physiological basis of singing.

g. Rhythmic sensitivity.

2. To consider the importance of the following personality characteristics:

a. A good story teller.

b. A good sense of humor.

c. A strong vitality.

d. A vivid imagination for doing the original instead of the routine.

3. To teach how to conduct the following measures:

a.	Regular	2	beat	measure	2/4
		3	"	"	3/4
		4	"	"	4/4
		6	"	"	6/4, 6/8

b.	Slow	2	beat	measure	2/4
		3	"	"	3/4
		4	"	"	4/4
		6	"	"	6/8

c.	Fast	2	beat	measure	2/4
		3	"	"	3/4
		4	"	"	4/4
		6	"	"	6/4, 6/8

d.	Regular	9	beat	measure	9/8
		12	"	"	12/8

e.	Fast	9	beat	measure	9/8
		12	"	"	12/8

4. To describe the basic tempo (dynamics) meanings and criteria for their usage.

5. To illustrate what to do in order to arouse people through bodily movements.

a. The use of facial gestures--useful for giving attacks and releases, and for denoting placidity, energy, surprise, etc.

b. The use of the arms for starting, stopping,

and increasing or decreasing the speed of a
song in directing.

c. The use of the hands for indicating dynamic,
tempo, and expressional changes.

d. The use of the voice in giving commands,
giving pitch, projecting tones and commands,
and deliverying good enunciation and pro-
nunciation.

6. To teach the meaning of the following special
terms utilized in conducting and to illustrate
their employment by the director.

a. Accent   f. Pause
b. Cut-off   g. Release.
c. Heavy, yet broad delivery of tone
d. Ritardando and accelerando
e. Starting the unfinished measure

7. To enable the student to become familiar with
some of the following special types of songs.

a. Action   d. Rounds
b. Humorous   e. Stunts.
c. Parodies

8. To show how to employ various techniques for
getting interesting effects in community sing
work. Some of these methods are to:

a. Divide an audience so that the ladies sing a
stanza and then the men.

b. Divide audience by age groups, permitting
various ages to sing different stanzas.

c. Call for soloists from the audience to sing
a stanza while the audience joins in on the
chorus or refrain.

d. Call for groups representing various districts to sing a stanza--groups competing
with each other.

9. To familiarize students with the starting beat

and meter signatures of the following:

Hymns	Folk Songs
Adeste Fideles	All Through the Night
Come, Thou Almighty King	Auld Lang Syne
Crusaders' Hymn	Believe me, If all those En-
Faith of our Fathers	dearing Young Charms
For the Beauty of the Earth	Carry Me Back to Old Vir-
Holy, Holy, Holy	ginny
Lead, Kindly Light	Drink to me Only With Thine
My Faith Looks Up to Thee	Eyes
Onward Christian Soldiers	Home on the Range
	Juanita
	Levee Song
	Long, Long Ago
	My Old Kentucky Home
	Old Black Joe
	Smiles
	Yankee Doodle

National and Patriotic	Christmas Songs
America	Away in the Manger
America, The Beautiful	Deck the Hall
Battle Hymn of the Republic	The First Noel
Dixie	Hark! The Herald Angels
Keep the Home Fires Burning	Sing
Star-Spangled Banner	It Came Upon the Midnight
Yankee Doodle	Clear
	Joy to the World
	Silent Night
	We Three Kings
	While Shepherds Watched
	Their Flocks

(B) Assigned Activities for the Students.

The assigned activities for the students are so man-
ifestly implied in this outline (Object, under Community Leadership), that it seems unwise to expand
their implications further.

VI. MUSIC APPRECIATION.
(Unit on the Folk Song, Composed and Non-Composed.)

(A) Object.

1. To show that the development of the folk song records the development of a race.

2. To discuss the divergence of opinion regarding the meaning of folk song. Some authorities recognize both non-composed and composed songs as true folk songs, while others admit only the former.

3. To discuss the many categories of folk songs. Some are:

   a. Festival   e. Marriage
   b. Funeral   f. Patriotic
   c. Jovial, Convivial   g. Work.
   d. Lullaby

4. To discover the many types of racial characteristics to be found in folk songs. It might be said that to know a people's songs is to know the people and their culture.

5. To study the development of the Indian, Negro, and other typically American folk songs.

6. To enable the students to become more familiar with folk songs of the Central and South American countries.

(B) Assigned Activities for the Students.

1. Produce a Pan-American Musicale for members of the class or the student body.

2. Develop units of work related to Indian, Negro, American, Spanish, Italian, German, French, etc., folk songs.

3. Learn many folk songs; (very advantageous for elementary school teaching).

4. Procure interesting stories about the origins of many folk songs.

5. Develop a series of folk song units which may

be correlated with social studies, literature, the regular music program, and a national art. Selected units should be mimeographed in order that each member of the class may retain them for in-service teaching.

6. Specially qualified students produce the units of work (described in No. 5) in Teachers' College Training Schools. This is excellent practice teaching experience.

(Unit on the Art Song.)

(A) Object.

1. To compare the folk song with the art song.

2. To study representative songs of the famous art song composers.

Brahms	Schumann
Franz	Strauss
Grieg	Wolf
Schubert	MacDowell

3. To demonstrate the importance of the great literary luminaries connected with the art song.

4. To evaluate the importance of using art songs in the elementary school music program.

5. To explain the meaning of:

Strophic
Durch-Componirt
Durch-Componirt-Strophic.

6. To study thoroughly a true representative of each of the types under 5.

(B) Assigned Activities for the Students.

1. Listen to many recordings of art songs by great artists.

2. Study some of the song cycles by Schumann,

Schubert, and Wolf.

3. A committee of students might produce a program incorporating some of the finer art songs.

4. Attend a concert by a Lieder singer.

5. A student assembly committee might be instrumental in bringing a singer of fine songs before the student body.

(Unit on the Cantata, Oratorio, Operetta, Opera, and Music Drama.)

(A) Object.

1. To help the students understand the meaning of the terms employed in this unit.

2. To trace the development of vocal forms from the beginning of the opera and cantata through the era of florid gaudiness, and down through the sincere music-dramatizations of Wagner.

3. To make it possible for students to learn to differentiate the various dramatic and less dramatic forms of vocal expression as exemplified in the oratorio, operetta, cantata, opera, and music drama.

4. To trace the significance of the polyphonic forms in the development of the oratorio.

5. To study the important men associated with the development of the oratorio.

6. To give the students an elementary understanding of French, German, and Italian Opera.

7. To give the students a knowledge of the terms: aria, chorus, florid, libretto, overture, recitative, opera, opera buffa, opera comique, etc.

8. To make the students familiar with the locations of the outstanding opera centers of the World.

(B) <u>Assigned Activities for the Students</u>.

   1. The teacher may play a complete recording of
       some opera: scores should be made available
       for students to follow the music. This activity
       should familiarize them with the movement of
       the music on the printed page in relation to their
       aural impressions.

   2. Study dealing with the development of the can-
       tata, oratorio, opera, etc.

   3. Listen to the Metropolitan Opera Broadcasts;
       class discussions may be held before and after
       listening to the broadcasts.

   4. Trace the development of singing; the develop-
       ment of great vocal forms parallels the evolu-
       tion of the art of singing.

   5. Attend a concert of an oratorio, cantata, etc.;
       reports should be made to the class.

   6. Attend a program by an operatic artist and
       evaluate the performance with that of another
       artist (non-operatic).

   7. Secure interesting stories about children's operas
       for use in the elementary school. They should
       be mimeographed for each student as an aid for
       later in-service teaching.

   8. Report on information found on music pages of
       The New York Times; write-ups of performances
       provide interesting reading and discussion ma-
       terial.

(Unit on Form in Music.)

(A) <u>Object</u>.

   1. To give students a working knowledge of musical
       form as related to school music teaching.

   2. To give students a simplified understanding of
       absolute, romantic, and programmatic music.

3. To give students an understanding of the specific topics related to 1 and 2. They are:

    polyphonic, pure, classic, romantic, sonata, sonata form, concerto, overture, suite, chamber, symphony, opera, concert overture, intermezzo, French suite, etc.

4. To give students an understanding of the influence of the French, German, and Italian schools upon the development of musical form.

5. To enable students to become familiar with each of the following:

    a. Classic symphony   e. Sonata
    b. Romantic symphony   f. String quartet
    c. Symphonic poem   g. Trio.
    d. Overture to a major work

(B) Assigned Activities for the Students.

1. Develop a unit of work comparing classical and romantic symphony writers; phonograph recordings should be used.

2. A small group of students or the class: analyze a movement of some sonata.

3. A small group of students or the class: analyze the structure of a classic symphony.

4. Show the importance of musical form in elementary school music.

(Unit on Instrumental Music.)

(A) Object.

1. To pursue a systematic study of the instruments of the various sections of the symphony orchestra.

2. To study the relationship existing between the various voices of the orchestra (violin, soprano; viola, alto; French horn, tenor; bass violin,

basso) and those of the human voice classification.

3. To develop a more intimate understanding by the students of the keyboard instruments (information pertinent to elementary school music teaching).

4. To trace the development of the symphony orchestra in the United States and to discuss its place in the cultural life of America.

5. To give the students a better understanding of the following:

a. Chamber music   e. Piano groups
b. Concert band   f. String orchestra
c. Marching band   g. String quartet
d. Opera orchestra   h. Woodwind quintet.

6. To familiarize students with many of the compositions used for the performance of instrumental music.

(B) Assigned Activities for the Students.

1. Investigate and evaluate the contributions made by various composers of piano music to the development of piano literature.

2. Trace the development of the various instruments of the string section.

3. Show how the science of sound is related to the construction of musical instruments.

4. Trace the evolution of the keyboard instruments.

5. Make a list of contemporary orchestral conductors, violinists, cellists, etc.

6. Trace the evolution of the symphonic form and the historical development of the woodwind, brass, and percussion instruments.

7. Make a study of the classic, romantic, and modern forms of orchestral composition.

8. Learn the terms associated with the performance of symbols and terms found on the printed score. Some are: pizzicato, vibrato, tremolo, mute, harmonics, tenor clef, arco, alla breve, sonata form, recapitulation, enunciation, rondo, etc.

(Unit on the Symphony Orchestra.)

(A) <u>Object</u>.

1. To trace the development of the symphony orchestra.

2. To investigate, analyze, and synthesize the evidence related to the importance of the conductor to orchestral performance.

3. To assist students to become familiar with conductors who specialize in broadcasting or television.

4. To study orchestral instruments with special emphasis upon structure, tonal timbre, voice quality, and effectiveness as mediums of musical expression.

5. To consider the opportunities for American as against foreign orchestral conductors.

(B) <u>Assigned Activities for the Students</u>.

1. Contrast various symphonic organizations for literature regarding the historical development of their company. This can be done by assigning certain students to specific organizations.

2. Make a survey of the outstanding American symphonic organizations tracing the history of the conductor of each group.

3. Attempt to assay the qualifications necessary to become successful as a conductor.

4. Attempt to determine the influence American conductors have had upon popularizing American symphonic works, comparing the programs con-

ducted by Americans with those conducted by Europeans.

5. Attempt to obtain information on the remuneration of conductors.

6. Attempt to assay the influence of symphony orchestras upon American cultural life.

(Unit on Modern Music.)

(A) Object.

1. To study the relation existing between school music and modern compositions and contributions of each to the other.

2. To study the various types of modern compositions and their particular contributions to the art of music.

3. To study the exponents of modern music either as composers or performers.

4. To study the place radio broadcasts have in popularizing modern compositions.

5. To study modern compositions through representative phonograph recordings.

6. To study the importance of jazz, swing, "hot," blues, calypso, highlife, rhumba, and other forms of dance music as part of the school assembly program. Enlightenment brings new appreciations.

(B) Assigned Activities for the Students.

1. Develop a familiarity with a few compositions and their composers through reading about, listening to, and procuring clippings and facts about them.

2. Sing, listen to, and study various types of modern music during portions of class lecture periods devoted to this activity.

3. Attend local concerts devoted to such music and the presentation of critique reports about them.

4. Develop projects by members of the class who are especially interested in the study of modern music.

(Unit on the Radio and Television in Modern Culture.)

(A) Object.

1. To investigate the cultural contribution that radio and television are making to modern civilization.

2. To discover the magnitude of the use of music in radio and television.

3. To study the various types of music sponsored by American manufacturers for broadcasting purposes.

4. To point out suitable types of musical broadcasts for classroom and home reception.

5. To discover the vast quantities of literature suitable for educational purposes.

6. To bring into the classroom the music and literature arising from these sources.

(B) Assigned Activities for the Students.

1. By perusing newspapers and music periodicals, obtain certain types of programs--operas, symphonies, dance bands, and RCA Transcription programs.

2. Procure a quantity of printed material that could be used educationally in the classroom.

3. Correspond with such organizations as the National Association of Broadcasters, 1771 North Street, N.W., Washington, D.C., to request literature on music which is directly or indirectly tied in with elementary school music teaching. Also investigation of various city

boards of education, closed-circuit television music education programs.

4. Study the various music appreciation broadcasts that are available for classroom use.

5. Find out the influence that radio and television have on music in modern education.

VII. MOTIVATION PROJECTS (Unit on the Creativeness of Children).

(A) Object.

1. To instruct in-training teachers how to construct songs for the elementary school child.

2. To demonstrate the creative music possibilities of water glasses, blocks of wood, butter tubs, tin cans, flower pots, wooden keys, cardboard containers, etc.

3. To emphasize the necessity for developing the creativeness of children.

4. To make blue-prints of diagrams of many unusual music makers.

(B) Assigned Activities for the Students.

1. Develop completed music makers as suggested in Object 2 by appointed individuals and groups.

2. Committees reproduce construction diagrams for the class.

3. Create (each member of the class) five rote songs for children including the composition of words and music.

4. Prepare a bibliography of books dealing with creative activities in the elementary school.

5. Produce a creative unit for the training-school or local elementary schools by specially interested students.

*   *   *   *   *

Source Materials. There are many other important considerations connected with teaching music which should challenge the serious teacher. She must have available or know where to procure the materials mentioned below. In actual preparation for teaching music much time could be devoted to each of the items indicated. Two or three lectures could profitably be devoted to many of them. At the conclusion of this program the teacher should possess or know where to get:

1. An adequate bibliography of courses of study and various methods of teaching music.

2. Piano compositions, vocal scores, songs, orchestral scores, rhythm band suggestions, toy symphony materials, and phonograph recordings suitable for children's education and entertainment.

3. Suitable correlation materials for integration with the song literature used in teaching.

4. Literature pertaining to music appreciation including stories directly related to music literature.

5. Adequate suggestions for creative music projects.

6. Adequate materials and equipment for the teaching of music appreciation.

7. Adequate information about radio and television programs and services which are available to the elementary school teacher.

8. A pitch pipe (know how to use it).

9. A mechanical or electric record player. She should know how to operate it and how to determine various turntable speeds, and to check correctly their RPMs.

In addition, she should know how to make simple instruments used in the rhythm band or toy orchestra; tune simple musical instruments such as musical bottles, bells, bars, etc.; and use a staff liner.

Self-Improvement. What can the teacher do to improve her musicianship? Of paramount importance in her training is a need for a functional understanding of the keyboard. It is impossible for a primary school teacher to be successful unless she has an adequate command of the keyboard. To simplify our discussion of musical improvement, the following check list for achieving self-improvement and mastery is suggested:

1. Learn to play the piano; further improve your skill.

2. Learn to sing artistically; take vocal lessons; do the following:

a. Sing in some church choir.
b. Join in a choral society.
c. Play in a civic band or orchestra.
d. Listen to good phonograph recordings of songs by recognized artists.
e. Attend a concert by vocal artists.
f. Be a lay music specialist in your school and community; assist individuals and groups in musical activities.

3. Learn to dance if you do not dance already; improve your skill in this category; dancing will aid you in developing your rhythmic sensitivity.

4. Take the opportunity should it arise, to organize a group such as: rhythm band, elementary school chorus, quartet, trio, piano duo, or faculty musical group; this will educe all the musicianship you are able to command.

5. Co-operate in supporting community musical undertakings.

6. Offer to conduct community sings for local service organizations, P. T. A., groups, or school assemblies.

7. Offer your services as an accompanist for informal or formal musical presentations.

8. Devote some recreational reading time to the literature of music; increase your knowledge of the musical literature written for children.

Suggestions for Effective Instruction. The classroom teacher must be able to make discriminating judgments if she is to be competent in guiding the musical aspirations of children. Efficient teaching requires that the teacher:

1. Be able to evaluate song materials.

2. Be able to interpret intelligently the children's point of view in song interpretation.

3. Have some interesting stories which will assist in the presentation of the songs.

4. Always be cognizant of rhythm, melody, and harmony while presenting a music lesson. The stress is on melody; secondary attention is usually given to rhythm because it is easily perceived, and harmony receives less attention; attempt to equalize the importance of all three.

5. Know where to procure descriptive literature for music listening lessons.

6. Be familiar with the various state music courses of study. They may be procured gratis or at slight cost from many state departments of education.

Discussion

1. Do you believe that a monetary value has been put on art?

2. To what extent do you believe that school music is responsible for the development of lay music appreciation?

3. Would you assume a teaching position if you were aware of the fact that the chief school administrator was unsympathetic to music?

4. What affect does the teacher shortage have upon the school music program?

5. Are colleges and conservatories more interested in the preparation of teachers as directors of choral, band, and orchestras, rather than as educators developing broad programs of general music education?

6. At what one school level do you believe that a student's appreciation or love for music is established?

7. What in-service training aids would you include if you were administratively responsible for a music program in a school system of 22 teachers?

8. How effective are women as high school band directors?

9. Why is a classroom a rare phenomenon of educational opportunity?

10. How important is the elementary teacher in the

development of a child's musical taste?

11. Is it possible for some children to enjoy music intellectually even though they may not possess good performance skills?

12. Do teachers often underestimate the ability of children?

13. How would you go about improving the musical education of elementary classroom teachers? What improvements do you offer over those suggestions by the author?

14. Musically does the self-contained classroom hold much promise for the development of a child's musical growth?

Notes

1. Loveless, Marian. "Music for the Classroom Teacher," Education, 72: No. 1 (September, 1951), 40.

2. "Music for the Elementary Teacher." Music Educators Journal, 40: No. 1 (September-October, 1953), 67.

3. Ibid., 67.

4. Morgan, Hazel B. "Improvement of Elementary School Music," Education, 76: No. 7 (March, 1956), 423.

5. "Music for the Elementary Teacher." Music Educators Journal. 40: No. 1 (September-October, 1953), 67. (This article, a résumé of a survey Miss Margaret Newton conducted as co-chairman of the Minnesota Committee on Music for the Elementary Teacher, is from the April, 1953, issue of Gopher Music Notes, official magazine of the Minnesota Music Educators Association.)

7. "We Recommend; Excerpts from the Resolutions Adopted at the 1955 Division Conventions of the Music Educators National Conference." Music Educators Journal, 42: No. 1 (September-October, 1955), 21.

8. Ibid.

9. Heffernan, Helen. "Education Through Music," Education, 74: No. 1 (September, 1953), 12.

10. Morgan, Hazel Nohavec. "Music and the Elementary

School Teacher," Education, 72: No. 1 (September, 1951), 29.

11.   Ibid., 29-30.

12.   Morgan, Hazel Nohavec.   "Music and the Elementary
        School Teacher," Education, 72: No. 1 (September,
        1951), 28.

13.   It is estimated that more than 50 percent of incoming
        freshmen students entering elementary teacher train-
        ing have had no previous piano training.

CHAPTER VI: THE ELEMENTARY SCHOOL MUSIC PROGRAM

A Review. Elementary school music lost much significant leadership during the period 1940-1958. The voices of McConathy, Giddings, Earhart, Dann, Dykema, and Gehrkens--great champions of elementary school music of the 1915-1950 period--are some that are no longer heard in eloquent behalf of music for the elementary school child. These men firmly believed that elementary school music was the keystone in sound public school music education, and their contributions to that area bear witness to their convictions. The period 1915-1940 felt the devastating ravages of the depression years of the 1930s. Then, the political, social, and economic developments which were an outgrowth of World War II often created difficult educational problems for the music administrator and educator. There was an increasing need for teachers resulting from population growth. Inadequate teacher salaries often contributed to the loss to industry of competent teaching personnel. Communities found it impossible to finance the increasing cost of instructional facilities and the need for additional classroom facilities. The inability of educational practice to catch-up with theory helped to thwart the growth of the elementary school music program.

Since 1940 some elementary school programs have grown and others have deteriorated. Public education has had to make adjustments in the amount of teaching personnel which its program could have. Some of the detrimental aspects of elementary music education to be observed during the period since 1940 are:

1. Whenever teacher shortages existed, school administrators were often required to employ the most competent individuals available, even though they were not always qualified to teach elementary school music.

2. From 1838 to 1914, the emphasis was upon teaching vocal music to the elementary school child. After World War I, the secondary school music (band, choir, orchestra) program developed very rapidly. Consequently, the secondary school music teaching program very often became more

103

attractive to the professional music teacher.   Qualified teachers of elementary music have always been scarce.

3.   The increased development of secondary school
music has sometimes been adulterated by the concept of the
professionalization of secondary school music at the expense
of its educational values.   Sometimes the importance of winning contests, has had a detrimental effect upon Music For
The Elementary School Child.   This was especially true of
those school systems that had but one or two music teachers
who were responsible for the instruction for the school system.

4.   Over-emphasis upon the secondary school music
program has too often brought about poorly organized intragrade
music programs.   The elementary teachers were frequently
without adequate in-service training programs and professional
advisory and instructional services.   The music lesson was too
often composed of the singing of a few simple folk songs.

5.   Since 1945, there has been an increasing tendency
of government and professional educators to encourage the teaching of the sciences.   A large school system in Ohio curtailed its
music offerings for the 7th and 8th grades for 1960.   Unanimous-
ly, school administrators decided to curtail music instruction in
favor of academic subjects.   Now music will only be taught for
45 minutes per week.

6.   More recently, school tax levies for raising additional funds have been a dismal failure.   The curtailment of
music supervisory services has sometimes been drastic and
music teaching has even been eliminated.

There have been encouraging developments in the same period also:

1.   Since 1940, there has been an ever increasing amount
of instructional materials available for elementary school music
teaching.   The variety and excellent quality of newly released
song books, musical equipment, musical instruments, and mis-
cellaneous instructional materials for the instruction of the elementary school child has increased to such an extent that it is
now possible to offer him a wide variety of interesting musical
experiences.

2.   Teacher training institutions have made some effort to improve their music courses.

3. Since the advent of the single salary schedule, it is now financially as attractive to teach at the elementary school level as it is at the secondary. Therefore, professional music schools are encouraging their graduates to consider teaching music at the elementary school level.

4. Wherever the elementary school child is fortunate enough to have competent classroom teachers who are aided by music consultants and supervisory staff, he is certain to experience a wider variety of musical experiences than did the child prior to 1925.

5. There is increasing recognition that the child has a love for music. Because of the widespread dissemination of music through radio and television, music is a vital part of his daily living. Music study in public schools has ceased to be merely a study of symbolism and vocal expression. The possibilities of vocal and instrumental experience for the elementary school child are still being explored.

The past century has been characterized by the Pestalozzian approach to the teaching of vocal music in our public schools; this is true especially of the teaching that was carried on from the time of the introduction of music into the schools of Massachusetts after 1835 right down to 1900. The "signs and then the sounds, " the "note by rote, " and the "mathematics of music, " had been propounded by Lowell Mason, and so well and so widely accepted were his precepts that their lasting effects can be found in vocal teaching throughout the country. It is only within the last two decades that "the child" instead of the "subject" began to receive moderate consideration in the process of teaching music in our schools.

The singing lesson of the past century has given way to a newer concept of school music. This newer concept conceived song singing and creative, recreative, listening, and fundamental basic rhythmic experiences to be the more complete expression of elementary school music. Whereas, in the past it was believed that the teacher understood what music was best for the child, in the newer approach, the teacher encourages the child to explore all his interests. This is done in the hope that through such exploration the child will find satisfaction through performance, or understanding, or both, and that these achievements will arouse in him the desire for further discoveries in music and the other fine arts.

The last century has seen many changes in both the

philosophy and practice of school music education; the next
50 years will undoubtedly see more, for there are many unsolved problems to challenge our profession. The perplexing question of teaching music reading, or reading readiness
as it is sometimes called, is still with us. Another question
is concerned with how best to begin note reading. Should it
be done by the means of pre-instrument study? Still another
unsolved problem is that of initial instrument study, and
whether or not it should be under the tutelage of a private
instructor, or are we convinced that it is usually better to
use the class method? Music educators need to substantiate
the efficacy of the methods they employ.

        Vocal music teaching in elementary schools is still
characterized by the use of traditional techniques. The approach to this phase of music teaching has changed little
since the 19th century; namely, the teaching of musical symbolisms. Wherever possible the teaching of musical symbolisms should be preceded by emphasizing the enjoyment to
be derived from music. Children in the primary grades are
certain to enjoy the physical response rather than the intellectual study of music. The successful elementary music
program must continually adjust the physical and intellectual
appeal of music to the needs of the child. Any elementary
school music program that emphasizes perfection of performance at the expense of enjoyment of music participation is
certain to fail in its educational mission.

        Elementary school teachers are trained in institutions
offering instruction of varying quality--ranging from inadequate to excellent. Institutions which have improved their
music courses find that there are many factors that tend to
diminish their effectiveness. Individuals who are preparing
to become elementary teachers sometimes lack pitch and
rhythmic sensitivity. A majority has insufficient piano skills
with which to make their music teaching more effective. In
the primary grades the ability to play the piano is an asset.
Finally, there are many who are deeply convinced of their
inadequacy to teach music. Due to current teacher shortages,
there is very little opportunity for selecting candidates on the
basis of innate musical ability. If selection were possible,
the courses now being offered would be more effective. But
as this is unlikely, the music departments in teacher-training
institutions must continue to refine the teacher-training music
courses to effect the best possible music instruction for the
future elementary teacher.

Instructional Handicaps. There are several factors
currently operative in the educational situation which militate
against the success of instruction in music in the elementary
schools: 1) The shortage of qualified elementary school
teachers ever since World War II has become increasingly
more pronounced. In order to staff classrooms, administrators have been forced to employ teachers without regard for
minimum proficiency requirements. Many teachers have
been called into service even though their training has not
included the required professional courses for teaching music. 2) There is great need for professional teacher training courses in music. This can be met by offering improved
courses in collegiate and teacher training institutions. Such
courses should be better adapted to actual classroom needs
and should be designed to develop in elementary teachers
more of the basic music skills. Rudiments and techniques
for teaching music must be emphasized, and instruction in
music appreciation should be accomplished through the use
of subject matter that is commensurate with student understandings. 3) The lack of trained elementary school vocal
and instrumental supervisors and teachers is another hindrance to the successful teaching of music at this level.
Like teachers, trained vocal and instrumental supervisors
are in great demand but are few in number. As many as
one out of every four children in our public schools receives
music instruction but once each week. 4) The lack of in-
service training programs is another reason for ineffective
elementary school music programs. When teachers are employed, they should be provided orientation in the school
system's program of music instruction. If teachers are
found wanting in instructional skills, administrative and supervisory personnel should aid them to become more effective as music teachers. Every teacher can become more
proficient if good music training is provided. 5) The self-
contained classroom of the present (or now gaining acceptance) emphasizes the need for a teacher who is adequately
trained to meet the challenge of teaching all the subjects offered in the grade or grades to which she is assigned. In
such a classroom, music is no longer considered a special
subject and proponents of this type of classroom instruction
hold that music should be integrated with the total education
of the child. However, all teachers in systems where this
philosophy is in effect are not competent for the tasks assigned them. To the degree that they are not, this type of
classroom will exert an adverse effect on music instruction
in the grades. Whether or not a classroom is self-contained,
the teacher must either teach music capably, or adequate

music supervision must be provided in order to give substance
and direction to the program.

Responsibilities of the Elementary School Teacher.

Not only is the in-service teacher charged with the responsibility for giving her children the cultural advantage of a musical education, but she should assume the obligation as a
privilege.   Most in-service teachers possess a sufficient
amount of musical sensitivity to discharge this responsibility.
The objectives of musical training may be more completely
realized if the teacher creates for her pupils favorable conditions for experiencing the following: singing of beautiful
songs composed by the masters; intelligent listening to all
forms of instrumental music; creation of music as a form of
self-expression;[1] and the feeling of the impulse of rhythm.
The teacher must provide the opportunities and create the
situations which will permit the child to enjoy these activities.
The teacher should constantly keep in mind the objective of
instilling in her pupils a lasting love for good music--an at-
tribute that will enrich both their childhood and their adult
life.

In the average classroom the teacher is favored with
a wide range of abilities. She has at her disposal a normal
(or nearly so) distribution of aural, rhythmic, emotional,
creative, and manipulatory sensitivities and capabilities.   It
follows, then, that there will normally be about the same
number of children who possess few of these abilities as
there are those who possess many.   The great majority of
pupils in the average classroom will possess these in average amount and degree.   The teacher must explore and develop each child's potential and propensity for music as in-
tensively and as extensively as her time and ingenuity permit.
In such an environment the elementary school teacher can
make a contribution to the musical growth of children.

Sensing the beautiful is a discriminative act which is
dependent upon intellection.   However, very often a child will
manifest a pleasurable response to a given composition, seemingly devoid of the facts necessary to an objective analysis of
its beauty.   This is possible because a performed composition
may have a particularly appealing rhythmic pattern and melodic outline that invites his interest; the performing medium
(instrument, voice, or both) and the individual making the
music possible give added reason for interest.   We emphasize again, that the listening child may possess practically
no technical information yet may derive much pleasure from

the listening experience. Several years ago, Dr. Marietta Odell, [2] an elementary school critic-teacher, was discussing with her children their reactions to a hearing of "Peter and the Wolf." Dr. Odell in the teaching of this first-, second-, and third-grade class, observed that the children asked, after a few playings of the mentioned composition, "When can we listen to the recordings without the story?" Furthermore, they asked: "Why can't we have more such music?"

It is perfectly obvious that these children did not possess knowledge of the criteria for evaluating the various melodic, harmonic, structural, and instrumental appeals which this recording afforded. More important is the fact that these children had discrimination, and that they were allowed to suggest what they desired. Their desires were the results of interests which were stimulated by their teacher. The children knew what they liked and asked for more. When they asked for another recording without the narrative, they were desirous of an opportunity to challenge further their musical understanding. They had attained new degrees of discrimination and their ever-expanding appreciations were demanding further satisfactions. Odell offered to play other recordings which were inferior in musical merit, but the boys and girls would have none of this. They wanted a listening experience equal in merit to that of "Peter and the Wolf." If a teacher constantly attempts to determine how or what they should think, the children are going to say, "There's no point in our attempting to suggest what we think the music says to us. The teacher wants to tell us what to think." Children are quite capable of such deductions and conclusions. Such musical experiences as these offer a lifetime of meaning for young children, who often retain them permanently in their memories.

Primary School Music Curriculum Objectives. There are four fundamental contributions which music makes to the development of the child's personality: 1) it serves as a medium through which the child may become interested in music. This is accomplished through his exploration of the rhythmic, melodic, and harmonic aspects of music study which are found present in all vocal and instrumental forms. 2) It develops desirable attitudes. Music can be effective in creating attitudes which will contribute to a healthy and satisfying life. 3) It assists in creating and developing emotional stability which will facilitate satisfactory adjustment to the circumstances of life. 4) It provides opportunity for the expression of creativity and to aid in its discovery and

growth. These contributions--and they may be listed as objectives as well--are discussed below in relation to the primary music curriculum. Those responsible for this curriculum and its construction must evaluate it (the curriculum)
in terms of these desired results and effects.

1. Exploration of possible interest areas in music:
exploration is a dominant urge in all children. A music curriculum must provide satisfaction for this interest through
the inclusion of stimulating music activities. The child seeks
to express sensitivity to rhythm. He should be provided opportunities to discover that this response may be made in
many ways. The various dance forms can provide interesting activities for children. Appreciation of melodic line can
be acquired later. The child should be allowed to express
himself freely through such activities as walking, skipping,
swinging, swaying, running, jumping, or marching. Intuitive
discernment may be revealed and exercised in the recognition
of fast and slow tempos. This discrimination may lead to
the use of appropriate bodily responses to these rhythmic activities. Following the use of these bodily movements may
come the use of teacher-guided activities; for instance, the
teacher may encourage the child to participate in an imagi-
nary band. He may pretend that he is a drummer. He may
simulate a trombonist with his left fist at his mouth, moving
his right fist forward and backward. He may appear to be
playing the cymbals by moving his hands up and down and by
sliding the palms against each other. These imaginative activities may also include the rocking horse movement of the
teeter-totter.

Responses may include interpretative movements to
mood in music. Music that has rhythmic patterns for simu-
lating movements such as those of clowns, elephants, ducks,
and turkeys may prove helpful in arousing individual and
group participation. Additional types of discriminative rhythmic response may be manifested through meter sensing.
Compositions such as the march, waltz, minuet, and polka
may be interpreted by using appropriate hand or bodily action. Likewise, the rhythm band provides a creative activity
that permits each child to participate. The child should
eventually be encouraged to offer suggestions for orchestra-
tions of compositions suggested by him or by his teacher.

Early familiarity with percussion instruments in the
rhythm band may stimulate early appreciation for orchestral
and sound-producing mediums. Muscular control of these in-

struments is certain to aid in the harmonious co-ordination
of childhood energies. Additional interest can be engendered
by encouraging the child to choose an instrument.

Another area for exploration would include song singing for those who have not gained control of their singing
voice (so-called monotones) as well as for those who are
non-singers. Through individual and group work the teacher
may help them to explore two-note and three-note patterns.
These may be in the form of octave calls for the reproduc-
tion of phrases taken from interesting songs. The good
singers in the classroom may be called upon to reproduce
given note or phrase patterns for the non-singers. Imitation
is extremely helpful, peers' singing voices more effectively
convey a desired tone. Songs reflect many different melodic
beauties, moods, and rhythms. The teacher should be ever
aware of the opportunity for calling the child's attention to
discriminations among these. Good tone quality, pitch accuracy, feeling for tempo and phrasing, and the use of good
articulation should always be emphasized by the teacher in
her effort to help the child become discriminating. Aiding
the child to employ a light, clear, flute-like tone quality
should bring him much pleasure. During the primary school
years, words and music (songs) should be created by the
child. Some children have a capacity for poetic expression
while others have innate melodic sensitivity. These two
areas permit satisfactory outlets for intellectual and emotional expression. It has often been found that the words come
before the melody. This is as it should be. The ideas for
verse content usually are based on the child's every day experience. Even though the tones produced are incorrect,
each child should be allowed to express himself in singing
one- or two-note patterns, or through the singing of complete
songs. The competitive game idea may aid all children in
attaining greater vocal achievement. The corrective techniques should be as attractive and as effective as possible.
The child should never get the impression that he is being
corrected; rather that he is being guided by the teacher to
significant achievement.

2. Development of desirable attitudes: the music
program should help to create desirable attitudes for living.
For primary school children there should be emphasis on
the artistic pleasures to be derived from music through song
and movement. The child receives musical stimuli through
the ear, affording him aesthetic satisfaction and pleasure.
This may be his total response, or he may sing or engage

in bodily movement, bringing additional satisfactions. If
these latter responses are impromptu, the child will enjoy
the artistic satisfaction of having created these pleasures for
himself.

Those children who are strongly influenced by lovely
songs may experience the emotions of joy, sympathy, religious feeling, and sadness. There is no doubt about the mil-
itant effect of the march, the patriotic urges inspired by a
national anthem, or the spiritual result of appropriate modal
music for the setting of religious words. Children may attain self-confidence, self-control, and a feeling of competence to express themselves through participation in varied
types of musical experiences. These achievements should
aid children in attaining a feeling of emotional well-being and
intellectual stability. The earlier a child experiences the
pleasure to be derived from music participation, the sooner
will he be able to grow into understanding of the power that
music can exert in his own life. Music is a language for
interpreting his emotional life.

3. Music promotes emotional stability: the attitudes
that the music program attempts to develop are certain to
have a salutary effect upon the child's emotional life. The
performance of music provides the child with great opportunities for self-expression. Music provides the child with
intellectual and emotional outlets which had not revealed
themselves until he had experienced them. Thus, music will
provide him satisfaction and a feeling of well-being.

The emotionally unstable child finds it impossible to
express his feelings verbally, and music becomes a medium
for release. The emotionally disturbed child may find direction and a degree of control for his behavior through musical performance. Whenever his behavior can be redirected
so as to give him better group adjustment and improvement
of self-respect his emotional stability is certain to improve.

Music has been seen to produce melancholy, move
people to tears, excite man to martial deeds, or
bring about a state of ecstacy. Thus the inclusion
of music in any curriculum concerned with the personality development of children would seem to be
justified. The use of experiences with music for
developing rapport with young pupils probably has
been used more frequently in the kindergarten-pri-
mary program than in the upper grades, but ap-

parently it can be effective at all educational levels.[3]

Therapy employing music in institutions for the mentally ill has received considerable usage since the 1930's.
The work of Van de Wall[4] as early as 1924, indicated that
many types of children can benefit from functional music experiences which special education can provide for the emotionally unstable child. The mental rehabilitation program
at the Essex County Overbrook Hospital, Cedar Grove, New
Jersey, provides for "the largest third" of their mentally ill
and maladjusted patients a music program for effecting more
rapid rehabilitation.

> Specific assignments are gauged by individual con-
> ditions with a choice of activity in each case de-
> termined by interest and suitability. It may be di-
> versional or used for mood control and associative
> values. Certain activities and kinds of music are
> chosen for mental or physical stimulus, and to
> awaken interest or to pull people into a group feel-
> ing of gaiety and fun. In disturbed groups material
> and instructional techniques are chosen with the in-
> tent of relaxing, untying emotional knots, releasing
> tensions, or in cases of apathy to awaken interest
> and stimulate a desire for creating and purposeful
> doing. In all treatment projects specific music is
> chosen for specific reaction as in the case of elec-
> tro-shock and Hydro-therapy .... Thoughtfully
> planned and with the tools skillfully handled there
> is rarely a life which cannot be touched purpose-
> fully in some way by the medium of our profession,
> this 'universal emotional solvent'--Music.[5]

When individuals attain these qualities and experiences through
music creativity, they are certain to enjoy greater integration
of their personality, because they have been a participant in
their realization.

4. Music provides opportunity for creativity: music
is an expressive art, and as such needs expression in order
to be experienced. Creativity initiates the process of making music. Music opens many avenues of creative opportunity.

> A broader meaning is now being given to the term
> creative activity. Any musical experience at any

and all levels, whether it be (a) sensitive and responsive listening to music, (b) active bodily response to rhythm and mood, (c) creative interpretation of music performed, (d) creative planning
and development of assembly programs, pageants
and operettas as an outgrowth of correlated activities, or (e) the creating of original music, is considered a creative activity inasmuch as it provides
a new and inspiring experience which results in
musical growth and personality development of the
child.[6]

The teacher is all important, because through her rich background of musical experiences, it is she who will be able to
open up new vistas of creative opportunity for the child.   It
is she who will be able to encourage the child to express
his thoughts and feelings through the medium of music.   It
is the teacher who will provide the physical and intellectual
environment for this personal creative expression of the
child.   Music creativity properly initiated into being should
be a constantly expanding experience.

Musical experiences and their meaningfulness vary in
intensity with the age of the child.   A chronological development has dictated the following sequence of activities:

Creative listening and creative response to rhythm
and mood;
Creative use of percussion and simple melody in-
struments;
Creative melody writing--vocal and instrumental;
Creative interpretation of music performed;
Creative harmonic writing and arranging--vocal and
instrumental;

Both the latter two creative activities, interpretation and harmonic writing, may be developed
through the correlation of music with other areas.
This could develop into the pageant or operetta at
various levels.   It should be remembered that each
age level has a mode of expression, which, if properly brought out, can best contribute to the emotional and artistic needs of the particular age.[7]

Through the suggested creative experiences the child
will attain a significant appreciation of the part that they can
play in his life.   The primary curriculum must emphasize

these exploratory aspects of music study. Through the employment of these creative media--whether vocal or instrumental--the child should experience the wholesome and integrative power of music. The diversification of study of the various aspects of music will more surely retain his interest.

Teaching the Primary School Child. The music program of the modern primary school needs to be challenged. A recent survey conducted by the writer indicated that some schools still require children to pursue a mathematical study of the rudiments of music as early as the first and second grade. Who could conceive of a more distasteful experience for the child in the name of the enjoyment of music? The approach to musical enjoyment is not fostered by suppressing the inherent responsiveness of children nor by trying to make musicians of them.

If music education is to serve all the children, it should have as its primary objective the development of the ability to enjoy music. If it seeks only the development of creative musicians, our primary objective will be defeated. We must get rid of insistance on mechanical finesse. When we teach music to all the children we must recognize, above all, that we are dealing primarily with non-musicians. Most children listen to music for pleasure and not for intellectual reasons.

The average child in the lower grades is imaginative. He lives in a sensory world. His intellectual life is in direct relation to imaginative situations. Music to him is enjoyment which is not productive of intellectual concepts beyond the world of his realizations. A child's world of musical meanings is in direct proportion to his musical capacities. If he is highly sensitive rhythmically, he will enjoy the opportunity of experiencing music which emphasizes rhythm. If singing gives him great personal satisfaction, then it is imperative that he has an abundance of opportunities to give expression to this medium of musical expression. Thus a child's musical environment must be so organized as to provide learning situations emotionally and intellectually   ·
graded in such a manner that they will be challenging to him.

The fundamental difficulty with many of the primary music programs is that there is an over-emphasis upon the factual aspects of music. If we were to give young children more opportunity for developing enjoyment-readiness, that is, an appreciation-readiness, it would not be so difficult to give older students the factual aspects. Stifling their interest in music in the primary grades is not going to stimulate it in the upper elementary grades. No demand is created where there is distaste; love for the language of music is not created in the person who is deaf to its message. If children begin school with an inherent interest in music and musical sounds, then it is reasonable to insist that a music program be built around their interests. The child reacts emotionally before he reacts intellectually. Children can experience tremendous enjoyment without knowing a single thing about the factual aspects of music.

The slogan "music for every child and every child for music" has misdirected many music educators. It is just as absurd to state "mathematics for every child and every child for mathematics." Psychological research has indicated that many of the arithmetical skills previously required of primary school children should not be demanded of them until later. Children will learn those facts and skills which are of immediate use either as satisfactions in themselves or as tools for obtaining satisfactions. Thus, if song-singing is a major activity for achieving emotional and intellectual satisfaction of children in the third grade, then they should not be expected to learn musical symbolisms which are irrelevant.

Do children like music? It all depends upon the teacher, the music used, and the method employed in its teaching. In some schools children look forward to the music lesson as a period of joy, relaxation, and emotional release. In others there is a heavy atmosphere of drabness or general dislike which results in distaste for the whole business of participating in music.

How is the teacher to determine whether the child is musical or not? In the average American family it is likely that either the mother or father is sufficiently discerning to recognize manifestations of musical ability when they are present even in a child under six years of age. Still, parents want to know just how to determine musicality so that they will not spend money on the musical training of their children when this is not warranted by natural potential.

The important consideration for the teacher is that she recognize that every child has the inherent ability to respond emotionally and intellectually to music. Neither the music teacher nor the psychologist as yet knows which qualities add up to the negative--no talent for music. Children totally devoid of pitch discrimination, rhythmic sensitivity, and tonal memory are rare. Musical talent is a word covering an aptitude that is, at the present time, relative and not fixed as to quality and quantity.

Rhythmic response is probably the most commonly found of all musical elements. All children of normal intelligence can respond in rhythmic manner. Rhythmic response is a physical component of music; it is also basic to a human action.

If the child is able to carry a tune; if he demonstrates rhythmic co-ordination upon the hearing of a march tune; if he shows interest in picking out two or three note patterns on the piano or some keyboard instrument; if he dances; if he asks for the opportunity to participate in music; then the child is very likely to possess some musical talent. If his interest is strong, it is likely that some inherent appreciation is stimulating his desire to participate. It is obvious that it is impossible for a person to form a musical idea without possessing the necessary musical intelligence to do so.

It is possible, by watching children in a nursery school as they march around the room or by observing them react in the presence of music, to determine some of the characteristics which are indicative of musical ability in children. If the child is able to match vocally little phrases or tunes which are sung either by another child or by the teacher or parent, then it is probable that he has some degree of talent in this art.

The child's initial contact with music is very important. Children bring to their first organized schooling a wide range of different musical impressions. It is obvious that the mother who sings or plays for her child contributes greatly to his preschool musical impressions.

Nursery and kindergarten education: for many children this period of life (ages 4-6) constitutes the first period of organized musical experience. The greater proportion of these early musical experiences will be sensory and expressed recreatively. The importance of the teacher cannot be overemphasized. Why? Because it is the teacher of these young children who can fashion their early musical tastes. Probably there is no other individual, including the parent, who has the child under controlled learning conditions for a greater proportion of his waking hours. These teachers have the children when they are in a very impressionable stage.

The teacher should allow the child many opportunities for exploration. He should be given every chance to participate in music whether it be singing or playing a simple instrument. Early in his schooling he should get "the feel" of the enjoyment to be derived from musical participation. If music has exhilaratory effects for participants, then it is imperative that teachers in our schools concern themselves more with the number of musical experiences the child undergoes rather than with how perfectly he can perform on any instrument or how accurately he carries a tune.

Singing for the fun of it creates an excellent environment in which to attempt to reach the goal of musical instruction, that of getting the child interested in perfecting his musical talents to the point where they will serve him for adult living. Music is something to be enjoyed. If it is labored at, then it becomes tiresome. Perfection is not the objective to be sought during early childhood. The intensity of the child's enjoyment and his native talent will, in large measure, determine the course of his future musical study. The truly talented child will most certainly pursue his interest to a great degree of perfection.

Media of early experiences: allow the child to get his experiences from as many sources as possible. In our schools it will be found that rhythm bands, tonettes, flutophones, rhythmic movement, eurhythmics, singing, and listening to vocal and instrumental renditions are just a few of the many activities or media through which the child may enjoy music. It is important that the child receive opportunities for melodic, rhythmic, and harmonic experiences.

A child who sits and listens to music is not necessarily talented. Music psychologists have coined the word "musicality." It is often used to describe musical intelligence. We do not yet know the exact combination of elements that constitute musical ability, but measurements have been devised and critical observations have resulted in the development of aptitude tests that help in determining the characteristics which distinguish individuals who possess musicality. There are ways of determining the acuity of the ear, rhythmic sensitivity, tonal memory, and various degrees of the less tangible capacities which are common among musicians of ability and distinction.

Common among school music programs is the class method of searching out musical ability and teaching boys and girls how to sing or play an instrument. Each year thousands of children are started upon band or orchestral instruments via the class method. This method has proved extremely helpful to parent and teacher in getting a child to demonstrate his talent and the intensity of his interest in music. How sensible it is too! Instead of purchasing a piano, violin, oboe, or cornet, the child is very often allowed to use school owned instruments. By paying a small rental or class instruction fee, the child may get started on an instrument at a moderate cost. If he does not take readily to the instrument he has chosen he may shift to another without the prohibitive initial cost. In addition to minimizing the cost for the trial period, it stimulates interest because other students are doing the same thing. The class method is the sound approach for the preliminary stages. Who wants to pay five dollars per half hour lesson, particularly at the beginning stages, when the child is learning the names of the lines and spaces, and is being shown where middle C is on the instrument? The author has employed the class method of teaching young and old beginning pianists, and has had excellent results. There is no claim that finished artists result from class instruction, simply that satisfying exploratory musical activity can result from the group method of music study.

Every music lesson can be a successful lesson. There is always some aspect of music the classroom teacher can make intriguing to the children. If she cannot sing she can use phonograph records for teaching songs. Interesting listening lessons can be presented to the children by the so-called non-musical classroom teacher, even though she may not be a performing musician. The availability of a vast storehouse of recordings has enhanced the opportunities for the classroom teacher in effectively presenting some aspect of music.

The "Old School": let us look in upon a music lesson being taught by a teacher of the old formalized school. The teacher in our example may be the classroom teacher, music supervisor, or director of music. It demonstrates the formalized approach to teaching music in the elementary school.

The individual teaching the music is full of enthusiasm and has a brain crammed with logical sequences. At the signal of "two taps," "music pass," or "get out your music books," the children shuffle off to their assigned music seats and proceed as ordered; this they have been doing for two, four, six or more months. They sing the songs which are selected by the teacher. They proceed with a military-like precision through logical sequences in the process of reading songs; they interpret the songs as ordered (possibly suggested) by their teacher; they cease singing at a definite command; they proceed to their regularly assigned seats, and heave a sigh which says in part, "That's over." True, this is somewhat of an exaggeration, but the writer has witnessed this mechanically directed and non-inspired type of lesson taught upon many occasions.

The "New School": against the Old School picture of classroom bliss and apparent teacher-pupil esprit-de-corps, let us visualize the pupil-teacher objectives in a democratic, yet seemingly unlicensed situation. The students and the teacher have been spending four weeks working on a South American Unit. They are making a study of the songs, dances, rhythms, instruments, arts, peoples, and geography of South America. What might be the typical situation as we enter this classroom where the more modern approach is used?

The room is seething with activity; some children are making South American instruments; some are writing songs suitable for their unit; some are working on the continuity for the written section describing the people of Brazil, Argentine, and Chile. The singing part of the lesson had ended before we arrived; the lesson is to last for 45 minutes. Heavens!

We are startled because we see little of the old step by step procedures. Such "chaos"! The children are having fun though, we have to admit that.

The teacher is not telling, she seems to be guiding, advising, and helping the students organize their interests.

We notice the children are doing the things they particularly enjoy. That's right, the old Gaussian curve says that all are not alike in ability.

We have not heard a thing about sight-reading; they tell us that they just sing "songs they like."

There is apparent opportunity for each student to offer suggestions, to accept suggestions, and to use his ingenuity.

The music unit is being studied because of student interests; the teacher is the master craftsman of the group.

There is little said about the fact that the children do not know syllables, key signatures, the lives of composers, the diatonic and chromatic scales, how to sight-read; the children are enjoying music for its immediate values with no other purpose than that they grow in intellectual, emotional, and musical stature.

There is a constant emphasis on positives instead of negatives, because the children are employing and pursuing their talents in concordance with their individual drives, likes, and interests.

The music is child-oriented.

In the New School, music is conceived to be a functional instrument for individual enjoyment. The children are motivated by the functional music experiences in which they participate. Music serves them as an instrument for the better enjoyment of daily living. Music is used to unfold to the children the many interesting aspects of man's culture that are to be found expressed through choral and instrumental music. They are permitted and encouraged to view music as a source of enjoyment in itself, and to concern themselves with its fundamentals only when the need for such knowledge is demonstrated. The new school allows children to experience the joy of music long before all its factual aspects are understood. Learning experiences are greatly reinforced by full participation in the learning process.

Objectives of the Elementary School Curriculum. A program of elementary school music should challenge a child's quest for satisfaction in the musical arts. It is not enough to teach him music; it is more important to provide him opportunities for experiencing music in order that his innate aptitude will find expression because of his newly found understanding.

First. Song-Singing. The child should increase
his musical enjoyment through song-singing. It should
be an expression of his inherent musicality; both creative and re-creative song-singing should be permitted.
The teacher is a good guide.

Second. Listening. There should be aural development making for discriminative listening, tonal,
and melodic reproductions. This development should
be the constant concern of the teacher.

Third. Rhythmic Development. The development
of the child's sense of rhythm provides great opportunity for interesting classroom activity and experience. The child should be alert to the various pulsations of music.

Fourth. Creativity. There should be opportunities for the child to engage in creative activities such
as writing songs, originating dance patterns, finger
painting stimulated by music, originating accompaniments, and similar overt responses to music that are
manifest as first or original expressions of music.

Fifth. Re-creativity. Re-creativity demonstrates
the ability to produce previously created music with
understanding and imagination. To sing, to dance, to
play a musical instrument are manifest re-creations
of previously created musical activities.

Conclusion. Music in the elementary schools should
be taught in such a way as to give sheer enjoyment to all
children. From earliest childhood their musical experiences
should be continuous exploratory opportunities. Their experiences should be pleasing to them. Our program purports
to explore the whole emotional and intellectual life of the
child.

After exploration a period of intensified interest should
develop. Thus, the child may desire to learn how to perform or create music on some music-producing instrument.
He may only desire to sing; then too, he may have no interest, but to listen to music. Whatever form of creative
thinking or performance he may express, the music teacher
and the public schools should furnish the child with an appropriate musical environment. Every child should achieve
both self-satisfaction and opportunity for artistic expression

through music participation.

The administrator should envision music as a study experience which will develop a happy, creative, intellectually and emotionally well-balanced child who in adulthood will share his cultural interests with society. Music training for more satisfying living should be the objective.

Discussion

1. What was the Pestalozzian method of teaching music to young children? Who was Pestalozzi?
2. Is modern elementary music primarily a singing class?
3. What are some of the more recent developments that have had a salutary effect upon present day music education?
4. What are some of the mitigating forces in our social order that have had a deleterious effect upon music education since 1945?
5. What phase of elementary music education was stressed during the period 1838-1914?
6. Name five 20th-century musicians who have made a distinguished contribution to elementary education? Give a biographical sketch of each music educator.
7. What are some of the unresolved problems of elementary music education?
8. What are some of the economic, social, and educational obstructions impeding the progress of elementary music?
9. Do the objectives of primary music differ from those of intermediate school music?
10. How would you help the child develop desirable attitudes toward music?
11. Were you fortunate enough to experience music creativity as a child in the elementary school?
12. When should children be required to pursue a mathematical study of the rudiments of music?
13. What is the earliest year that a child should study music? How do you know? Justify your statements.
14. How would you provide a child with exploratory experiences in music?
15. What are the advantages of class music instruction for ferreting out musical ability?
16. How would you go about introducing the child to the keyboard?

17.   Why are piano classes a natural development of the keyboard experience activities in pre-school and kindergarten?

18.   Discuss the statement: The average boy does not experience a change in his voice.

19.   What is meant by reading readiness?

20.   How does music education differ from the exact sciences?

21.   What are the advantages to be derived from using the recorder?

22.   What portable equipment convenience does the teacher need in a self-contained schoolroom?

23.   Why are audio-visual aids so valuable as teaching aids?

24.   What are the essential differences in the music program of the first, third, fifth, and seventh grades?

25.   In what grade or grades will be found:
    a.   Memory songs
    b.   Song books in the children's hands
    c.   Rhythm Band
    d.   Curing of Monotones
    e.   Music Appreciation
    f.   Two-part singing
    g.   The study of the evenly-divided beat
    h.   Three-part singing.

26.   Why do we start two-part singing in the grade(s) you have indicated above?

27.   Does two-part music work mean that we have sopranos and altos?

28.   How would you characterize the boy's voice during the adolescent period?

29.   How would you teach singing with the aid of the phonograph--should it always be done with the piano? Under what circumstances would you alter your method of instruction?

Notes

1.   See page 113.

2.   Dr. Marietta Odell was Assistant Professor of Elementary Teacher Education, Oswego State Teachers College, Oswego, New York.

3.   Thorpe, Louis P. and Schmuller. Allen M. Personality; an Interdisciplinary Approach, New York: D. Van

Nostrand Company, 1958, 205.

4. See W. Van de Wall, Utilization of Music in Prisons
   and Mental Hospitals, New York: National Bureau
   for the Advancement of Music, 1924.

5. Thompson, Myrtle Fish. "Music Therapy At Work,"
   Education, 72: No. 1 (September, 1951), 44.

6. Music Education Source Book. Edited by Hazel Nohavec
   Morgan. Music Educators National Conference, Chicago, 1947. (Chapter XXII, 131.)

7. Ibid., 132.

Bibliography

PRIMARY: SONG BOOKS AND RELATED MUSIC

Bradford, Margaret. Keep Singing, Keep Humming. New
   York: Wm. R. Scott, 1946.

Coleman, Satis N. Dancing Time. New York: John Day
   Co., 1952.

Coleman, Satis N. and Thorn, Alice G. Another Singing
   Time. New York: John Day Co., 1937.

_____. A New Singing Time. New York: John Day
   Co., 1952.

Coit, Lottie E. and Bampton, Ruth. Follow the Music.
   Boston: C. C. Birchard & Co., 1948.

Crowninshield, Ethel. Stories That Sing. Boston: Boston
   Music Co., 1945.

Landeck, Beatrice. Songs to Grow On. New York: Marks
   and Sloane, 1952.

_____. More Songs to Grow On. New York: Marks
   and Sloane, 1954.

Nelson, Mary Jarman. Fun with Music. Chicago: Albert
   Whitman & Co., 1941.

Seeger, Ruth Crawford. American Folk Songs for Children. New York: Doubleday, 1948.

PRIMARY: RHYTHM BAND ACTIVITIES

Diller, Angela and Page, Kate Stearns. How to Teach the Rhythm Band. New York: G. Schirmer, 1930.

Slind, Lloyd H. Melody, Rhythm and Harmony. New York: Mills Music Inc., 1953.

Synnberg, Margaret J. Standard Rhythm Band Instructor. Chicago: M. M. Cole Pub. Co., 1937.

Vandevere, J. Lillian. On the Beat for Rhythm Band. Boston: C. C. Birchard & Co., 1941.

Vandevere, J. Lillian. The Instructor Rhythm Band Book. Dansville, New York: F. A. Owen Pub. Co., 1939.

Votaw, Lyravine. Rhythm Band Direction. Elkhart, Ind.: C. G. Conn, Ltd., 1951.

PRIMARY: READINGS ON TEACHING MUSIC

Barrett, Mary. Living Music With Children. Kingston, R.I.: National Association for Nursery Education, 1951.

Glenn, Mabelle, Chapter 7, "Singing," in National Society for the Study of Education, Music Education, 35th Yearbook, Part II. Bloomington, Ill.: Public School Pub. Co., 1936.

Hood, Marguerite V. and Schultz, E. J. Learning Music Through Rhythm. Boston: Ginn and Co., 1949.

Krone, Beatrice and Krone, Max. Musical Participation in the Elementary School. Park Ridge, Ill.: Neil A. Kjos Music Co., 1952.

Landeck, Beatrice. Children and Music. New York: William Sloane Assoc., 1952.

Mathews, Paul W. You Can Teach Music. New York: E. P. Dutton, 1953.

Morgan, Hazel Nohavec, ed. Music in American Education.

Music Education Source Book Number Two, Washington,
D.C.: Music Educators National Conference, 1955.
Chapter 29.

Mursell, James L. Music and the Classroom Teacher.
Morristown, N.J.: Silver Burdett Co., 1951. Chapter 6.

Myers, Louise Kifer. Teaching Children Music in the Elementary School. 2nd ed. Englewood Cliffs, N.J.: Prentice-Hall, 1956. Chapter 3.

Sheehy, Emma Dickson. Children Discover Music and Dance.
New York: Henry Holt and Co., 1959. Chapter 4.

Sheehy, Emma Dickson. There's Music in Children. New
York: Henry Holt and Co., 1952.

Sunderman, Lloyd F. "The Cherub Choir." Educational Music Magazine, XXXIV: No. 3 (January-February, 1955),
16-17; 40-42.

_____. "Children Need Music." The Indiana Teacher,
92: No. 7 (March, 1948), 220-221.

_____. "Dynamic Music Program for the Modern Ele-
mentary School." Educational Music Magazine, XXVIII:
No. 1 (September-October, 1948), 24-25; 27-28.

_____. "This Child of Mine Should He Study Music?"
The Southwestern Musician, XV: No. 3 (November, 1948),
21-22; 46-47.

Thorn, Alice G. Music for Children. New York: Scribner's,
1929.

Thorne, Margaret. The Young Child and His Music. New
York: Arts Co-operative Service, 1950.

Timmerman, Maurine. Let's Teach Music. Evanston, Ill.:
Summy-Birchard Pub. Co., 1958.

ELEMENTARY: CREATIVE CONCEPT IN MUSIC

[Books and Articles: Dealing with the Creative Concept in
Music Education]

Fox, Lillian Mohr and Hopkins, L. Thomas. Creative

School Music. New York: Silver Burdett Co., 1936.

Heffernan, Helen. "Education Through Music." Education,
74: No. 1 (September, 1953), 11-16.

Loveless, Marian. "Music for the Classroom Teacher."
Education, 72: No. 1 (September, 1951), 39-41.

Murray, Josephine and Bathurst, Effie. Creative Ways for
Children's Programs. New York: Silver Burdett Co.,
1938. 124-142; 216-248 for pictorial summary.

Ohio Elementary Music Guide. Columbus: Department of
Education, 1949. Chapter II, 24-27: Creative Music Experiences."

Perham, Beatrice. Music in the New School. Chicago:
Neil A. Kjos, 1941, 61-90.

Sunderman, Lloyd F. "Children Need Music." The Indiana
Teacher, 92: No. 7 (March, 1948), 220-221.

_____. "Creative Music." Educational Music Maga-
zine, 33: No. 3 (January-February, 1954), 22-23; 52.

_____. "Dynamic Music Program for the Modern Ele-
mentary School." Educational Music Magazine, 28: No.
1 (September-October, 1948), 24, 25, 27, 28.

_____. "Music in the Primary Grades." Educational
Music Magazine, 28: No. 4 (March-April, 1949), 25, 47-
51.

Tipton, Gladys. "Creative Music." Education, 72: No. 1
(September, 1951), 35-37.

ELEMENTARY: BOOKS CONTAINING SONGS

Armitage, Theresa. Folk and Art Songs, Books I-II. Boston: C. C. Birchard & Co., 1924.

Armitage, Theresa, et al., eds. Our First Music: A Singing School Series. Boston: C. C. Birchard & Co., 1941.

Bailey, C. Old English Carols for Christmas. Cambridge,
Eng.: Washburn and Thomas, 1929.

Briggs, Dorothy Bell. Kindergarten Book. Philadelphia:
    Oliver Ditson Co., 1940.

Burnett, Elizabeth and Martin, Florence. Rime, Rhythm,
    and Song. Chicago: Hall & McCreary, 1942.

Bryant, Laura. Songs For Children. New York: American
    Book Co., 1927.

Buszin, Walter E. Motets and Chorales for Treble Choirs.
    Chicago: Hall & McCreary, 1938.

Coleman, Satis. Songs for Kindergarten and Nursery School.
    New York: John Day & Co., 1937.

Cross, Donzella. Music Stories for Boys and Girls. Chi-
    cago: Ginn & Co., 1926.

Crowninshield, Ethel. The Sing and Play Book. Boston:
    The Boston Music Co., 1938.

Crowe, Edgar; Lawton, Annie, and Whittaker, W. Gillies.
    Folk Song Sight Singing Series. Books I-V. London:
    Oxford University Press, 1933.

Dalcroze, Jacques Emile. Rhythm Music and Education.
    New York: G. P. Putnam, 1921.

De Nancrede, Edith and Smith, Gertrude Madeira. Mother
    Goose Dances. Chicago: H. T. FitzSimons Co., 1940.

Diller, Angela and Page, Kate Stearns. A Pre-School Music
    Book. New York: G. Schirmer, 1936.

Diller, Angela and Page, Kate Stearns. The Diller-Page
    Song Book. New York: G. Schirmer, 1939.

Doniach, Shula. Children's Hour; Songs and Action Songs
    for Nursery and Infant Schools. New York: Boosey &
    Co., 1939.

Foresman, Robert. Fourth Book of Songs. New York:
    American Book Co., 1923.

Fox, Lilliam M. Autoharp Accompaniments to Old Favorite
    Songs. Boston: C. C. Birchard & Co., 1947.

Fuller, Esther Mary, and Lewis, Lucy S. A Child's Book of Anthems. Bryn Mawr, Penn.: Theodore Presser Co., 1955.

Fullerton, Charles A. A One Book Course in Elementary Music and Selected Songs for Schools. Chicago: Follett Pub. Co., 1933.

Gag, Floria. Sing a Song of Seasons. New York: Coward-McCann and Co., 1936.

Gaynor, Jessie L. and Blake, Dorothy Gaynor. Gaynor's Songs for Little Children. Cincinnati: The Willis Music Co., 1906.

Glassmacker, W. J., ed. Songs For Children. New York: Amsco Music Pub. Co., 1934.

Hall and McCreary Choral Collection No. 6: Christmas Carols and Choruses. Chicago: Hall & McCreary, 1931.

Heller, Ruth. Father, Hear Thy Children Sing. Chicago: Hall & McCreary, 1953.

Heller, Ruth. Christmas, Its Carols, Customs and Legends. Chicago: Hall & McCreary, 1948.

Horn and Chapman. The Education of Children in the Primary Grades. New York: Farrar and Rinehart, 1935.

Houghton, Winifred E. Thirty Songs for the Nursery and Infant School. London: Boosey & Hawkes, 1943.

Licht, Myrtha B. Let Children Sing. New York: Harold Flammer, 1955.

MacCarteney, Laura P. Songs for the Nursery School. Cincinnati: Willis Music Co., 1942.

Malone, Kathleen. Another Kathleen Malone Book for Home and Kindergarten. New York: G. Schirmer, 1929.

Malone, Kathleen. Book for Home and Kindergarten. New York: G. Schirmer, 1925.

Martin, Florence M. Songs Children Sing. Chicago: Hall & McCreary, 1943.

Palmer, W. American Songs for Children. New York:
Macmillan, 1931.

Reinecke, Carol. Fifty Children's Songs. New York: G.
Schirmer, 1901.

Rowen, Ruth, and Simon, Bill. Jolly Come Sing and Play.
New York: Carl Fischer, 1956.

Rutenbeck, Mabel Nelson. The Cherub Choir Book for
Church and Home. New York: Harold Flammer, 1959.

Siebold, Meta. Happy Songs for Happy Children. New York:
G. Schirmer, 1928.

Siebold, Meta. More Happy Songs for Happy Children. New
York: G. Schirmer, 1928.

Sunderman, Lloyd F. The Primary Choir. Evanston, Ill.:
Summy Pub. Co., 1957.

Wheeler, Opal. Sing for America. New York: E. P. Dutton, 1944.

Wheeler, Opal. Sing Mother Goose. New York: E. P.
Dutton, 1945.

Whelan, Florence O'Keane. All Through the Year, Songs,
Singing Games, Verses, Rhythmic Activities. Chicago:
Hall & McCreary, 1951.

Wilson, Harry Robert, and Hunt, Beatrice A. Sing and
Dance. Chicago: Hall & McCreary, 1945.

Whitmer, Mary Elizabeth. Joyous Carols. New York: Carl
Fischer, 1956.

ELEMENTARY: RHYTHMICAL EXPERIENCES

Amor, Florence L. Activity Singing Games. London:
Boosey & Co., 1936.

Arnold, F. M., Editor. Arnold's Collection of Rhythms for
The Home. Kindergarten and Primary. Cincinnati: Willis Music Co., 1909.

Axtens, Florence. Rhythmic Designs for Songs. London:

Boosey & Co., 1936.

Axtens, Florence. The Teaching of Music Through Movement. New York: Boosey-Hawkes-Belwin, 1936.

Coit, Lottie E., and Bampton, Ruth. Follow the Music.
Boston: C. C. Birchard & Co., 1948.

Crawford, C. Folk Dances and Games. New York: Barnes
and Co., 1923.

Crowninshield, Ethel. New Songs and Games. Boston: The
Boston Music Co., 1941.

Crowninshield, Ethel. Walk the World Together. Boston:
Boston Music Co., 1951.

Dalcroze, Jacques Emile. Rhythm Music and Education.
New York: G. P. Putnam, 1921.

Dixon, Clarice M. The Power of Dance: The Dance and
Related Arts for Children. New York: John Day Co.,
1939.

Driver, Ethel. A Pathway to Dalcroze Eurythmics. London:
T. Nelson, 1951.

Holt, Gwendoline E. Movement Songs for Infact Classes.
New York: Boosey & Co., 1939.

Hood, Marguerite V., and Schultz, E. J. Learning Music
Through Rhythm. Boston: Ginn and Co., 1949.

Hughes, Dorothy. Rhythmic Games and Dances; Basic Activities for Elementary Grades. New York: American
Book Co., 1942.

Hunt, Beatrice, and Wilson, Harry R. Sing and Dance;
Folk Songs and Dances Including American Play Party
Games. Chicago: Hall & McCreary, 1945.

LaSalle, Dorothy. Rhythms and Dances for Elementary
Schools, Grades One to Eight. New York: A. S. Barnes,
1939.

Neilson, N. P., and Van Hagen, Winifred. Physical Education for Elementary School. New York: A. S. Barnes,

1930-32.

Ryan, Helen Chandler, et al. The Spanish American Song and Game Book. New York: A. S. Barnes, 1945.

Shafer, Mary S. and Mosher, Mary M. Rhythms for Children. New York: A. S. Barnes, 1938.

Sutton, Rhoda Reynolds. Creative Rhythms. New York: A. S. Barnes, 1941.

Vesper, Ruth Catherine. Rhythmic Sketches. (For Kindergarten). Cincinnati: The Willis Co., 1937.

Waterman, Elizabeth. The Rhythm Book. New York: A. S. Barnes, 1936.

Whitlock, Virginia. Come and Caper; Creative Rhythms, Pantomimes and Plays with Music by Various Composers. New York: G. Schirmer, 1932.

ELEMENTARY: TEACHING MUSIC

Christianson, Helen. Music and the Young Child. Washington, D.C.: Association for Childhood Education, 1936.

Dann, Hollis. Hollis Dann Song Series; Conductor's Book. New York: American Book Co., 1936.

Dykema, Peter W., and Hannah M. Cundiff. School Music Handbook. Evanston, Ill.: Summy-Birchard Pub., Co., 1955.

Elliott, Raymond. Learning Music. Columbus, Ohio: Charles E. Merrill Books, 1960.

Elliott, Raymond. Teaching Music. Columbus, Ohio: Charles E. Merrill Books, 1960.

Earhart, Will. The Meaning and Teaching of Music. New York: M. Witmark and Sons, 1935.

Fox, Lillian and Hopkins, L. Thomas. Creative School Music. New York: Silver, Burdett and Co., 1923.

Gehrkens, Karl. Introduction to School Music Teaching. Boston: C. C. Birchard & Co., 1919.

Gehrkens, Karl. Music in the Grade Schools. Boston: C.
C. Birchard & Co., 1934.

Giddings, T. P. Grade School Music Teaching. Chicago:
C. H. Congdon, 1922.

Glenn, Leavitt, Baker, Rebman. Music Teaching in the Intermediate Grades. New York: Ginn and Co., 1936.

Glenn, Leavitt, Baker, Rebman. Music Teaching in Kindergarten and the Primary Grades. New York: Ginn and
Co., 1936.

Grant, Parks. Music for Elementary Teachers. New York:
Appleton-Century-Crofts, 1951.

Hubbard, George E. Music Teaching in the Elementary
Grades. New York: American Book Co., 1934.

Krevit, William. Music for Your Child. New York: Dodd,
Mead, 1946.

Krone, Beatrice Perham. Music in the New School. Rev.
ed. Chicago: Neil A. Kjos Music Co., 1950.

Krone, Max and Krone, Beatrice Perham. Music Participation in the Elementary School. Chicago: Neil A. Kjos
Music Co., 1952.

Kwalwasser, Jacob. Problems in Public School Music. New
York: M. Witmark and Sons, 1932.

Mathews, Paul W. You Can Teach Music. New York: E.
P. Dutton, 1953.

McConathy, et al. The Music Hour Elementary Teacher's
Book. New York: Silver, Burdett & Co., 1936.

McConathy, et al. The Music Hour Intermediate Teacher's
Book. New York: Silver, Burdett & Co., 1931.

McConathy, et al. The Teacher's Guide for the Fifth Book.
New York: Silver, Burdett & Co., 1931.

McMillan, L. Eileen. Guiding Children's Growth Through
Music. New York: Ginn and Company, 1959.

Morgan, Russell V. and Morgan, Hazel B. Music Education in Action. Chicago: Neil A. Kjos Music Co., 1954.

Mursell, James L. Music and the Classroom Teacher. New York: Silver, Burdett Co., 1951.

Music in the Elementary School. Board of Education of the City of New York. Curriculum Bulletin, No. 3, 1945-46. Brooklyn: Board of Education of the City of New York, 1945-46.

Myers, Louis Kifer. Teaching Children Music in the Elementary School. New York: Prentice-Hall, 1950.

Nordholm, Harriet and Thompson, Carl. Keys to Teaching Elementary School Music. Minneapolis: Paul A. Schmitt Music Co., 1949.

Pace, Robert. Music Essentials for Classroom Teachers. San Francisco: Wadsworth Pub. Co., 1961.

Nye, Robert and Bergethon, Bjornar. Basic Music for Classroom Teachers. New York: Prentice-Hall, 1954.

Perham, Beatrice. Music in the New School. Chicago: Neil A. Kjos Music Co., 1941.

Perkins, Clella Lester. How to Teach Music to Children. Chicago: Hall & McCreary, 1936.

Pierce, Anne E. Teaching Music in the Elementary School. New York: Henry Holt, 1959.

Pitts, Lilla Belle. The Development Approach to Music Reading. Boston: Ginn and Co., 1950.

Pomeroy, Marie. Foresman's Our Music in Story and Song Manual. New York: American Book Co., 1936.

Sheehy, Emma Dickson. Children Discover Music and Dance. New York: Henry Holt, 1959.

Sheehy, Emma Dickson. There's Music in Children. Rev. ed. New York: Henry Holt, 1952.

Stinson, Ethelyn Monroe. How to Teach Children Music. New York: Harper & Brothers, 1941.

Swanson, Bessie R. Music in the Education of Children.
San Francisco: Wadsworth Pub. Co., 1961.

Thorn, Alice G. Music for Young Children. New York:
Scribner's, 1929.

Wilson, M. Emett. How to Help Your Child With Music.
New York: Schumann, 1952.

ARTICLES

Sunderman, Lloyd F. "A Music Program for Elementary
School Teachers in Training." The Elementary School
Journal, 42: No. 3 (November, 1941), 207-211.

_____ . "The Elementary Teacher Education Program
and the Piano." Educational Music Magazine, 24: No. 2
(November-December, 1944), 27; 53-54.

_____ . "The Music Education Program for the Elementary School Teacher," The Harp, (November, 1947),
1-5.

_____ . "Music in the Primary Grades." Educational
Music Magazine, 28: No. 4 (March-April, 1949).

Part Four.   Secondary School Music

CHAPTER VII: THE JUNIOR HIGH SCHOOL

Leadership for the musical arts demands that a concerted effort must be made to beget enthusiasm and support
for a music program in all of its forms.   In secondary
schools there must be deemphasized even a limited professionalism in favor of amateurism, if the youth of today are
to become participants in the enjoyment of the arts.   The
more widespread the musical participation, the greater the
likelihood that there will be understanding.   This is the
great challenge to secondary music.

The successful music teacher is a blend of personal
and musical qualifications that makes it possible for him to
produce music creatively.   If he is to be a leader of young
musicians he must have the ability to produce desirable musical results.   He must have the ability to arouse enthusiasm
and a desire within secondary school youth to participate in
those media of musical expression that will aid them in finding personal satisfaction.   Teachers must be dedicated in
their efforts to give students a good music education.   This
becomes the great challenge to the school music educator.

There must be a dynamic professional idealism existing between superintendent, principal, and their co-workers.
This may be achieved through dynamic administrative organization, delegation of authority, critical evaluation, and definition of responsibility.   There must be instructional organization by departments where faculty members are able through
democratic processes to refine instructional goals and evaluate achievements.   There must be projection as to where
the academic goal is headed.   There should be horizontal
and vertical articulation of authority and responsibility.   We
have seen "buddy" orientation help given to newly appointed
staff members; cooperative faculty concern for fellow staff
members is bound to better articulate the instructional program.   There could be an administrative "music task force"
which would anticipate and attempt to solve social problems

of the future related to music education. The administration
should be concerned about understanding the problems of secondary youth in order to aid them in becoming better citizens.

Changes That Have Taken Place. Throughout the
period of the last four decades, there have been cataclysmic
changes in student behavior, academic standards, teaching
methodology, instructional programs, curriculum designs,
and newly conceived governmental thought. All of these have
impinged their newly designed thinking upon education in general and school teaching in particular.

The four decades have provided for the writer observation and adjudication of more than 325,000 singers in choral organizations and an opportunity to personally adjudicate
more than 3,500 soloists. These have all taken place at the
junior-senior high school and collegiate levels.

Students representative of more than 1,000 school
systems have passed in review. The changes that have tran-
spired have fallen into many categories with such infinitisimal
variation that their narration should be food for the reader's
imagination: 1) quality and quantity of musical performance
has greatly improved; 2) the music training available and its
general quality has shown immeasurable improvement during
each succeeding decade--teachers are better trained; 3) students have become more perceptive, discriminative, more
knowledgeable and more analytically critical of their needs,
rights and desires for living here and now--they desire to
enjoy their hereafter now; 4) the generation gap is not new,
it is just now being recognized and articulated. Youth are
challenging their peers; there is a demand to measure
up to their preachments. Identification, involvement, and
all enunciated truisms are being challenged on a parity for
youth and adults alike. No double standard can exist simultaneously for youth and for adults. As Shakespeare has said:
"Were I anything else but what I am I would wish me only as
I am." Integrity, honesty, and challenging frankness have
become more and more denuded of those shams that may
exist within either adult or youthful thought. The incarcer-
ated integrity of the past half century is raising its voice.
5) The emancipation of man has thrown akilter many past
acceptances. The honest voice searching for expression has
revolted and has chosen radical means of expression. Adult
or youth often plunge headlong when they are unsure of their
speculations for the future. Much has been ascertained as

arrogant and even rebellious.   6) Parental responsibility must be assumed for youthful laxity and waywardness.   Youth under 21 years of age who are in educational institutions have a righteous expectancy to parental guidance and surveillance. Parental influence must assume responsibility for freedom of expression and any resultant societal chaos.   In reality, parts of these seeming expressions of youthful abandon are attempts to find identification and relevancy, and an honest desire to attain a purposefulness for meaningful living.   Impounded in all youth will be found the cynicism of adulthood and a breeding ground for rabble rousers, revolutionaries, and even the anarchist.   7) Educational administrators have often been remiss in carrying forth significant programs of communication for bridging areas of misunderstanding.   Each individual must be able to articulate his needs in approaching vital living problems.

Below 18 years of age, family surveillance is somewhat taken for granted in matters of financial responsibility and those disciplines connected with home and living.   This thesis does partially pinpoint some significant responsibility for young adults and their behavior.   It goes without saying that there must be guilt connected with behavioral action patterns.   Young adults living under the "parental roof" reflect home learnings.   Parents and society must share and assume great responsibility for student conduct.

Traditionalism in music education still pervades much educational practice.   The practices of the past have been the crucible for the programs for tomorrow's child.   The accumulation of information, although often totally unrelated to any function in the life of the child, is frequently held to be educationally worthwhile.   There are some teachers who have revolted against the stultifying effects of such practice and have achieved significant results with individuals; involvement for these teachers has meant that the child became a creator of music through singing or performing on some musical instrument.   Curricula uniformity implies that all boys and girls are expected to achieve comparable music attainments.   More important a curriculum should be evaluated as to how effectively it eventually functions in the life of children.

The teachers who are prepared to teach in junior high schools are trained in institutions offering varied types of programs.   Many of these training institutions have improved the content of their music programs, but there remain obstacles mitigating effectiveness.

Very often the teacher has been required to conform
to traditional and unimaginative instructional techniques and
procedures. Another deterrent is the appalling yearly turnover of junior high school music teachers. This in spite of
increased salary inducements, tenure, and fringe benefits.
Due to a great scarcity of these teachers, music is often
not even seriously attempted. Finally, the severity of the
situation is emphasized due to the lack of music supervision
and instruction in many elementary schools. A number of
schools do not provide adequate supervision or consultant
services. Among the course requirements established by
state departments of education, music is among those subjects receiving the least emphasis in the curriculum.

There is probably no subject in the curriculum comparable to music for socializing and satisfying the gregarious
tendencies of man. This aspect of music's motivating power
has been pretty well demonstrated in our schools by the increase in the number of bands, choirs, orchestras, and
small instrumental and vocal ensembles. Unfortunately this
expansion has not taken root in the ghetto schools. There
is a need for a revitalization of tomorrow's concept of general music programs so that children at all educational levels will have an opportunity to pursue music as a study.
This presents a two-fold problem. First, in the ghetto
schools the children are the victims of their pathetic environment. The deprivation of the disadvantaged child
wherever he may be is a disgrace to all humanitarian de-
cency. There is a lack of home and often parental continuity, school is boring, music does not relate to their culture,
children do not have a concept of what classical music is all
about, thousands are on a subsistance food program with no
private music instruction or teacher availability, frustration
and prejudice border on apathy and defeatism, teachers are
discouraged and incompetent to handle individual problems,
and budgets are curtailed in many school systems--many
inner-city schools and borderline urban schools are almost
totally without proper physical plant and music equipment
needs. The situation has bred moral depravity, sexual li-
cense, discipline problems of seemingly impossible resolution, disrespect for law and order, and vicious hostility and
militancy.

Second, urban and suburban school problems are often related to those of the inner-city schools. Bi-racial

conditions are reflected in many urban schools. Any minority group might present problems that could be consonant
with the Afro-American situation. Again physical plant, music equipment, instructional competency, and inadequacy of
personnel are major administrative and instructional problems.

Institutions of higher learning have a dispositional in-
clination to offer music programs which prepare musicians
to attain competency in musical performance skills. They
also offer courses in teaching music; these, sometimes under
the guise of music education. There is no legerdemain approach to the teaching of elementary and secondary music.
The teachers are trained as performers, but frequently they
find teaching music in our schools financially more remuner-
ative and more secure than pursuing a professional performance career. There may be some evidence to support the
thesis that the more superior the technician the more likely
may he become dissatisfied with teaching neophytes. Too often these excellent musicians leave the teaching profession.
It must be recognized that there is a greater difference between the artistic performer who is frustrated by being associated with so-called mediocrity and the competently trained
musician who is capable of teaching. This latter group sometimes includes individuals who are borderline competency individuals who are non-imaginative, and unquestionably cannot
challenge the unexplored musical creativity of children. Those
bordering on incompetency faced with teaching in ghetto
schools have an almost impossibly difficult task. Keep in
mind that subject matter is not the crux of the problem, although there has been increasingly a diffusion of philosophical
concept of what is the general music program.

Music offers a multiplicity of interesting activities for
young children. Music education for tomorrow's children
must be constructed about a broad concept of general music.
There is no excuse for not developing a program of enriched
music experiences for each child. The general music program needs change. Such a program properly conceived
would include music for all children. There is available
enough educational organizational ability, instructional material, and equipment to effect a music education program that
would meet the needs of every boy and girl.

Our thesis is that our two-pronged philosophy of music education in the United States often over-emphasizes development of the performing artist at the expense of recog-

nizing the need for providing good music instruction for every
child in our schools. We should adjust the envisioned program to meet the needs of all schools, but the music opportunities for all children should be the same.

All types of music and media for performing music
should be studied. Permanent music appreciation will be derived from vocal and instrumental performance. Rudiments
of music, theory, musical style, rhythmic sensitivity, and
sight-reading can become a more personal involvement if the
child is required to employ these aspects of music study in
the performance of instruments. From the earliest grades,
some form of instrument study should be available to every
child in all grades. Beyond instrumental study there should
be study of all "out" music such as rock, blues, gospel,
jazz, and all other forms of music that each individual can
relate to on a cultural basis. Afro-American, Mexican-
American, Puerto Rican, Japanese, and Chinese-American
require a music and culture comprehensive in scope; all music is an intellectual challenge.

Administratively, the question, "Why a general music
program?" must be resolved if there is to be an intelligent
development of a music curriculum designed for the cultural
benefit of all individuals. General music means exactly what
is implied--music for everybody. A proper general music
program would be so conceived that it would appeal to children in all schools, inner-city as well as urban and suburban. The traditional program where there is considerable
uniformity of objective and procedural suggestion from school
to school should be overhauled.

Formalized methods of teaching music to children are
passé. Forcing a child's thinking into any unnatural situation
immediately creates a mental hazard. This situation which
characterized the teaching of early music methods was even
more greatly reinforced by the failure of many educators to
be fully sensitive to the purposes of general music education.
Historical studies of past methods of music teaching prove
that most music instruction was taught as a science. Music
should be taught for its personalized values; it is being increasingly suggested that early child experiences should be
both emotional and cultural. These realizations will be possible during the years ahead if lay and music teachers recognize a new slogan for elementary music education: Let
music become a recreative experience for every child and
let the music lesson become a fulfillment of such a purpose.

Let us consider for a moment the manner in which the piano in bygone days had been first introduced to the child. The instrument was purchased and then the child was told that he was to begin practice. Available research strengthens our belief that music ability is inherited. Again research and empirical evidence have indicated that a great range of musical ability is to be found among individuals; the greater proportion of this talent is average. Irrespective of the amount of possessed musicality, each child's talent should be utilized.

Our youth have the capacity for becoming appreciators with discriminative tastes. Singing intelligently should be a challenge to the junior high music teacher. They must be taught how to dial in music of quality. The demand for quality of musical performance usually increases in direct proportion to the improved tastes of those who are its producers and consumers.

Passive listening courses pawned off as general music courses are hopeless and have proven to be so for the children in our American schools. A listening course is a poor substitute for a general music program, because it can and should serve as an educational medium around which the entire music curriculum is constructed. General music education courses should not emphasize isolated or specialized areas of music learning. The program should be active rather than passive. In all the schools there must be more "doing about" than "reading about" and "note taking." There must be more total involvement and ethnic identification, rather than listening to lectures. There should be music "making."

Need for General Music. Why develop a general music program in the secondary school? Prominent among many considerations are the following:

1) there is no subject in the curriculum like music for socializing the gregarious nature of man;

2) there is no greater medium for finding the common denominator of man's intellectual-emotional life; music forges a common expressional creed for all men;

3) the kaleidoscopic nature of music is so replete with experiences that no youth should experience difficulty in finding enjoyment through singing, rhythm, listening, playing, and creating;

4) music provides great carryover values into adult living;

5) music educators have not caught a vision of the potential possibilities of a general music program;

6) there is a woeful lack of qualified staff to implement general music programs;

7) teacher-training programs need to provide more imaginative in-service training opportunities which will come to the aid of music teachers in implementing a strong general music program;

8) junior and senior high school music teachers devote inordinate amounts of time to performing organizations at the expense of general music programs;

9) music teachers fail in their attempt to secure public approval for general music: the result is that general music is often deemphasized in favor of the showy-entertainment aspects of music education;

10) there is evidence that our philosophy of general education condones and encourages the commercialized rather than the contributive values of the art for the cultural development of the individual; and

11) music is probably one of the most basic creative manifestations of man's inner well-being.

General music education should be designed for all students who want to enjoy the benefits of music study. Each music educator should provide for each child great opportunity for finding his artistic relevancy in society. Derived from this concept is our program of general education, which encompasses learnings of such magnitude as to aid individuals in understanding music as a culture to be shared and experienced by all. Such understandings bring about satisfactions which give poise to man's emotional, spiritual, and aspirational drives.

Where general music education has been imaginatively tried out it has been proven that children have an inherent disposition to respond to many aspects of musical art. The general music teacher must be well prepared in psychological understandings and the sociological sciences in order to understand children of the ghetto and urban schools. First, the teacher who expects to teach in the inner city schools should be bi-lingual in competency. Without such facility he would be greatly hampered in establishing student-parent acceptance. Students preparing to teach in the inner city should have pertinent courses in ethnomusicology.

Second, vocal and rhythmic experiences in music are undoubtedly more basic to man than many of the more commonly accepted literate means of intellectual communications, such as speech and literary creativity. Vocal and rhythmic responses can be enhanced for the child through accompaniments provided by drums, guitar, recorders, resonator bells, piano, and even the simple tonette and flutophone.

Third, they must have a broad comprehension of various types of music--jazz, rock, ethnic, electronic, pop, and other kinds of white and black music; let's not forget the Mexican-American children and their culture.

Fourth, they must be purveyors of musical media who need to reevaluate music programs for all children. Such developments as television, radio, and electronic recording media have developed to the extent that they can increasingly influence school music education.

The Enjoyment of Music. It is most important to give every child the opportunity to enjoy music. It is not enough to teach him music; it is more important to create within him a desire for experiencing it.

Do junior high school students like music? Success of the music program depends upon the teacher's ability to provide students with the opportunity and environment to enjoy it. In some schools music lessons are looked upon as periods of joy, relaxation, and emotional release. In others it will be noticed that there exists an atmosphere of heavy air drabness or general dislike for music which eventually accumulates into a definite distaste for the entire experience. This is unfortunate, as experience with both children and mature groups reveals that everybody loves singing. In many situations you will hear people say, "Why not just let them enjoy music?"

Every lesson should be an experience in learning how to respond intelligently to music. Physical strain acquired from daily living can be greatly relieved during a music lesson by allowing children to relax and enjoy. Do not always analyze! Do some things just for fun and no subject is better adapted for this experience than is music. Students should hear and see instruments, develop a singing and listening familiarity with the music of man's creativeness and begin to understand why they appreciate some music and are indifferent to others. Dynamic musical experiences must be constructed for junior high school students. A music program must have a definite course to pursue or effort will be aimless.

Structural Organization Concept. There must be a
pyramidical concept of general music education for all Americans. Its reasonableness should be self-revealing.

FOURTH LEVEL (The Base). The base would include
approximately two-thirds of the entire population (Society).
It would include those groups of people who would enjoy music through freely dispensed channels--the radio, television,
recordings, church, and congregational and community singing. There must be those who receive music at the elementary and secondary level; individuals who enjoy cultural music opportunities in institutions of higher education. The
people in GROUP IV would enjoy functional music programs
that stress the cultural non-professional approach to music.

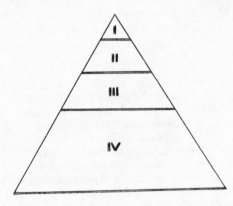

THIRD LEVEL.
This would include am-
ateurs and lay people
who because of oppor-
tunities in private study
achieve some participa-
tive-functional knowledge
of music. There would
also be those who en-
tertain in their local
communities, and find
local opportunities as
soloists. From this
group would come a
preponderance of those
who are willing purchasers of tickets for professional concerts. It would include those whose interests in professional
music are found in more than chance acquaintance with music.

SECOND LEVEL. Included would be professional music educators and musicians, college students majoring and
minoring in music and possibly desiring to become teachers
of music. This group has excellent musicianship and meritorious performing skills. The musicians teach others. They
are all involved in helping promising artists on the road toward ultimate success. At this level should be found some
very good future music teachers. Why? They will have
sufficient knowledge about music and enough technical mastery to aid the student. This group probably would not produce a future Horowitz or a Heifetz.

FIRST LEVEL (Top). The apex of our philosophical pyramid will include a minuscule percentage of the population--those who create and recreate art for the other three levels. This is the elite of America's musicians; they lead the way.

Good music programs should be available to offer continuing growth opportunities for children. This should be the major concern in developing a music program for tomorrow's children.

America must give more serious consideration to the development of a broader base of music activities for involving the child. No program will be complete unless it provides opportunities befitting every child's ability. The extent of the music privileges for Group IV will eventually determine who will occupy the other areas of our stratified concepts. Consumers of music will be found in all groups, but the preponderance of them will be found at the levels III and IV.

Present Program Weaknesses. Subject to criticism are the following:
1) the vise-like grip that academic traditions have retained upon curricular construction--rarely is an appreciable amount of time left for music course offerings for the general college student;
2) the long established extra-curricular onus on music activities that has done much at all educational levels to thwart participation--it is a common practice not to grant sufficient academic credit for some music courses;
3) the pedantic type of memoriter instructional course work offered leading the child to reproduce musical functionalisms which are totally irrelevant to identification, involvement, and group solidarity;
4) present programs for children and young adults that have not been thoroughly reappraised--elementary and secondary schools do not initiate programs that give children personal identification with self and group action; if they sing music it must incorporate meaningful identifications consistent with their heritage;
5) the showmanship complex of the average American, which does much to militate against the universal music education of the child;
6) the fact that college programs rarely initiate beginning experiences for those who have little music talent;
7) the limited way in which community music programs

have been developed;

8) the fact that children are lectured to and are not given the "power" to perform on instruments--this is a grave mistake;

9) the consistent presentation of the same musical information from grade to grade which causes children to get surfeited with similar material with only slight variations;

10) insufficient instruction provided children on instruments such as banjo, guitar, accordion, drums, and in class piano--they should be permitted to play for personal enjoyment;

11) the early mortality of students participating in music--this reaches incomprehensible proportions by the ninth grade;

12) the small number of semi-private and class piano and instrument instruction given at all grade levels: Function and not concert artistry should be emphasized, the latter being a developmental consideration;

13) insufficient testing programs to determine those children who could profit from vocal and instrument study--those who have the ability should be provided the opportunity;

14) lack of opportunity for racial groups other than white, and to some extent blacks, to study and participate in music that relates to their culture;

15) the great number of general music programs that as presently conceived are a rank waste of time and are abhorrent to study--classes in general music have a high mortality of registrants;

16) the fact that the music that is studied is not always authentic--pleasurable identification comes from complete relation and identification with the various expressions of given cultures;

17) the inability of college music programs to aid individuals in preparing for "inner city" and "urban" school music teaching--music programs in our schools must help all youth become involved;

18) the programs of classical music that may stifle participation in music: in baseball, the initial experience is that we give the child a mitt and a ball and we tell him to play--he may have a good coach, but the important consideration is that he plays without the constant inhibiting caution, "don't make a mistake"; the child plays and enjoys the activity because the frustration of "perfection" is not uppermost in his mind--then too, he will perfect as he plays;

19) children being required to sing much literature that they do not like!--many songs selected for bi- or multiracial groups are such that the children "don't dig them";

20) boredom entering into general music classes because the music program is not as challenging as it was in
the intermediate grades--the oft-heard expression, "When
there is nothing else to do we can sing" must not prevail;

21) incomplete understanding of the influence on boys'
vocal satisfaction of the change of voice;

22) the lack of music literature for boys that gives
them a masculine identification--the song literature is too
often geared to feminine interests;

23) song literature that is not chosen with suitable
voice ranges for the boys--they are often unable to reproduce
a satisfyingly virile tenor part and have even more trouble
with mature bass parts; insipid song literature is not able to
arrest the attention of growing boys;

24) lack of understanding that girls are often interested in singing lower parts rather than the high soprano or
first soprano;

25) frequent changes of music teachers, which has a
deleterious effect upon the continuity of music programs;
(and, 26), the resulting discipline problems that are often
difficult to resolve);

27) general music program offerings that are undeni-
ably lacking in their ability to challenge students--because
the programs are not "in the know" they very often do not
appeal to teen-agers;

28) teaching loads frequently filled by assigning any
available faculty member to teach one or more courses in
general music;

29) the evidence that educational philosophy often encourages the commercialized rather than the contributive
values of art for the development of the child;

30) inadequate class preparation and presentation of
instructional materials;

31) almost entire lack of student class preparation--
the requirement of it is down to a minimum;

32) and the fact that many general music programs
are merely music listening lessons.

Projected General Music Program. Will it be a general music program? Would such a program provide the
type of integrated music program that will more nearly
meet student interests for tomorrow? There should be integrated learning situations--an omnibus coordinated music
program containing song-singing, listening, creative, rhythmic, and recreative aspects; and instrument-playing. Integrating all these areas of musical experience should be
the concern of the imaginative teacher. It is he or she who

should provide youth with dynamic music opportunities.

The first and last requisite for projecting a dynamic
music program is the need for a superior teacher-musician.
The individual must be conversant in the humanities, ro-
mance languages, and the fine arts. He should have good
keyboard proficiency to effectively conduct music in the classroom.

A general music program does not imply generality.
Too frequently the program is so generalized, and lacking in
organization, instructional content and imagination, that it
results in disinterested aimlessness on the part of the students. Very often the students are lectured to the point of
vapidity. A general music course should not be a place for
a disc jockey where there is a complete lack of instructional
content. The general music class should never become a
haven for taking care of those slow learners who have failed
to benefit from academic instruction.

Song-singing: the individual should increase his musical enjoyment through much song-singing. This objective
undoubtedly should receive the greatest emphasis. It should
be an expression of his inherent musicality. Both creative
and recreative song-singing should be permitted; the teacher
is the guide. In the junior high school program, song-singing should receive great emphasis for arousing spontaneous
response. Frequently the students should accompany their
singing by playing instruments. Instrumental accompaniment
enhances song-singing performance.

Listening: this phase of our program has been widely explored. From the early contests of the 1920s and 30s,
music has been employed for every activity envisioned by
the teacher. So often, when the music teacher can think of
nothing constructive, she "hauls out a few records" for the
children. Music listening must become a more profitable
venture than just pure absorption of sound.

Methods of teaching music to children should include
more aural development producing accurate melodic reproductions; this should be of constant concern to the teacher.
Good pitch discrimination will be keenly sensed if the teacher is cognizant of good intonation. Individuals should be
taught how to listen to music. Intelligent listening is derived from intelligently directed music experiences. All
music experiences are aural. There are many interpreta-

tions as to how music listening should be presented. Many music teachers are convinced that every music lesson should be an appreciation lesson, consequently there is no necessity for teaching appreciation or the listening act separately. Other teachers conceive of the music listening activity as one where additional opportunities are offered for musical growth. It should offer children a chance to listen, to create, and recreate. True, many children may derive an aesthetic satisfaction from listening to sound, but discrimination of what is being heard beyond the mere production of tone will make for more intelligent listening.

The general music class should emphasize the importance of listening activities. Of great import should be the development of discriminative listening. Singleton has stated the objectives of the entire listening experience as follows:

1) To develop the capacity for enjoying many different types of music experience.
2) To increase the ability to focus aural attention upon music and to perceive the elements which combine to create its beauty.
3) To teach the fundamentals of music language and skill.
4) To explore the vast resources of music literature.
5) To impart knowledge of music's historical progress and social relationships.
6) To show and utilize the relation of music to other school subjects.
7) To encourage use of many community resources.
8) To develop discriminating music tastes.

To be sure these objectives may be realized through many instructional media, the important consideration is that the student be imaginatively taught how to listen and become functionally involved through music participation.

Creative music: this has in the last decade received some attention, but it is still far removed from what self-expression may become for junior high school students. All music, like life, is dependent upon creation; without it nothing is born. All children have the power of creation; they are creative to the extent that their ability permits. Creativeness may be the medium for the children to express their emotional and intellectual dynamism which may lie dormant until the teacher points the way. Closeted in every child's consciousness are ideas needing activation; the teacher should see them through to fruition; they become satisfactions to teacher and pupil alike. The child's imagination plus the teacher's inspiration and leadership can find a wide field of interests through the creation of songs, melodies, interpretive programs, and instrument construction. An individual who creates a verse for a song may find it to be the ultimate of his contribution. He will be proud of the metric beauty which he created. If the teacher will help her children see the relationship existing between what they achieve in their music lesson and what they become actively interested in musically, he will have made a distinct contribution to their appreciation. There is dominant need for teachers who are sufficiently courageous to permit children to become participators in creative learning, instead of being tools of a cause. Intelligence implies the ability to react intelligently in situations with which the individual has had little familiarity. Creative music allows the inquisitiveness of a child to become a vibrant reality. Whatever the child learns through exploration should become realistic when he is again exposed to new situations or explorations in learning. Creative music is justified by the degree to which it best helps the individual realize the function of music in his life. The important consideration is the individual is expressing self and finding satisfaction. Expression should be freely offered. There must be a wanting to do so.

Rhythmic music: rhythmic experiences are now being more fully emphasized in the elementary school. They provide great opportunity for interesting classroom activity. Individuals should become alert to the various pulsations of music. From the beginning of kindergarten music, much rhythm work is devoted to such movements as marching, running, skipping, and clapping. Very often the child is directed as to what he should express. He may be allowed to express himself as he feels rhythmic pulsations. Interpretative eurhythmics may be differentiated from directed rhythmic work, in that the former borders on the more aesthetic rhythmic development of the individual. It is more purposeful in that it uses the entire body for expressing a message. Eurhythmics is the physical interpretation of beautiful music.

Rhythmic work is too frequently confined to directed activities which are teacher initiated. Basically, we must ask the student, "What does the music express to you rhythmically?" Very little is done to give the child opportunity for rhythmic self-expression. We are convinced that in all musical experiences the child must have time to think over,

"Just what does this music say to me?"

Rhythmic self-expression must be thought of as being a creative opportunity for each child. Let each individual reveal what expressiveness the rhythm connotes. The teacher should think in terms of the joy that rhythm might bring toward the self-fulfillment of individual responses. In addition to marking out notational patterns, (marching, for example) let the individual explore rhythmic design, drawing, and bodily interpretation. The structural forms of rhythm as found in the dances of many nationalities may draw from the child a responsiveness which may not be forthcoming in the more formalized treatment which has been commonly used. Participative folk dances may elicit from the child a self-expressiveness which may not be manifest if we continue to "march around the room."

Recreative experiences: these include the performance of music which has been previously created. Many phases of recreativity need more development and exploration for the child: first, there must be continuing emphasis upon self-performance as a means for greater depth of enjoyment. Second, a greater variety of musical literature must be used for developing a broadening contact with all types of music. Third, there must be greater emphasis upon the self-artistic performance aspect of music. And fourth, through the greater exploratory nature of the creative, song-singing, listening, and rhythmic aspects of our new program, there will be developed an ever broadening acquaintance with music. It will become a comprehensive area of artistic expression which will plumb the self-expressive interests of every child in junior high school.

Instrumental playing: the manipulatory activity involved in instrumental playing employs the aural-visual to an extent which is very satisfying. Whereas the voice employs an individualized instrument, the instrumental approach has a wide variety of sound-producers which elicit an individualized response often more variegated tonally.

There is an individualized appeal to those instruments which may be classified in the "blower" and "non-blower" categories. This provides a variety of possible difference of demands in playing the violin, chording on the piano, drumming, and blowing upon a flute. The acuity demands upon an individual and the nature of his reflexes, and the all-encompassing requirements of reconstructing each tone varies from one musical instrument to another.

Excellence of performance by an individual on a violin may accompany mediocrity in pianistic achievement. Individual talents and interests vary widely. Playing the piano for amusement may be the excellence which an individual desires to achieve. Actually, it may even represent his maximum proficiency based upon his "inherent talent." Irrespective of these factors the important consideration is giving the child an opportunity for an instrumental "feelingness." He must not be denied this exploratory experience during his elementary and junior high school education. Those who are responsive to instrumental music must not be denied its aesthetic contribution, enjoyments and empathetic opportunities. The foregoing instructional areas provide core learnings of great potential magnitude. If properly conceived they will become a structurized basis for broad junior and senior high school music explorations in music learning.

Bibliography

1.   Andrews, Frances and Leeder, Andrew A.   Guiding Junior High School Pupils In Music Education, New York: Prentice-Hall, 1954.

2.   Cooper, Irwin and Kuersteiner, Karl.   Teaching Junior High School Music, Boston: Allyn and Bacon, 1965.

3.   Cuban, Larry.   To Make A Difference: Teaching in the Inner City. New York: The Free Press, 1969.

4.   Glenn, Neal E., et al. School Music, Philosophy, Theory, and Practice. Englewood Cliffs, N.J.: Prentice-Hall, 1970. Chapter 9: "General Music," p. 101-159.

5.   Hartsell, O. M. "Preparing the General Music Teacher," from Perspectives in Education, (Source Book III), Bonnie E. Kowall, ed. Washington, D.C.: Music Educators National Conference, 1966, 276-282.

6.   Nordholm, Harriet and Bakewell, R. V. Keys to Teaching Junior High School Music. Minneapolis: Paul A. Schmitt Music Co., 1953.

7.   Singleton, Ira C. and Anderson, Simon V. Music In

Secondary Schools. 2nd ed. Boston: Allyn and
Bacon, 1969.

8. Sur, William R. and Schuller, C. F. Music Education
    for Teen-Agers. New York: Harper & Brothers,
    1966. Chapter 3: "General Music Class," p. 45-70.

CHAPTER VIII: THE GENERAL MUSIC PROGRAM

General music courses are fundamentally non-specialized. Their intelligent conception should provide every individual with some participative experience through his association with music. These courses should provide a broadened base of musical experiences for our school children. Of necessity, therefore, we must emphasize the non-specialized general-interest nature of music courses.

This concept of a general music education program would not delimit the breadth and depth of its content, but would encourage musical experiences of whatever degree that are consistent with the ability of the children to learn. The key to the success of any such program is the understandings that it brings about--enlightenment and appreciation are its function. Furthermore, it provides for greater carry-over values into adult living.

Probably no program in music education has simultaneously received so much vitriolic criticism and so much encouragement for "better things" to be achieved as has the general music program. There are probably two attributable reasons for so many patent failures and oftentimes singular successes: the need for general music oriented specialists to teach general music, and the concept of the program's organizational structure.

General music courses are undoubtedly a partial solution to the administrative desire to conduct junior and senior high school music on a regularly scheduled class basis. They should meet a minimum of three and preferably five times a week. Credit should be proportional to the number of meetings each week and the amount of outside preparation. This course well taught deserves credit as an award for successful accomplishment. There is no reason why daily classes could not be maintained. Class size should be consistent with other academic classes.

Success is more likely to attend the instructor's efforts if a carefully organized course of study is used and an

imaginative and broadly trained musician conducts the class.
Top-notch teacher-musicians should be assigned to teach
these courses.   The inquiring mind is essential to the success of the general music program.

We have emphasized the fact that professional music
education implies dealing with the specialization of the individual, or "oneness," whereas general education implies that
the program must be implemented for the many.   A general
music course must become the core music course from which
effuse manifold musical experiences and activities.

Knuth 15 years ago pointed up problems connected
with implementing the general music program.   His vision
for the program was circumscribed by an expanding traditionalism during the 1950's.   However, the socio-economic con-
vulsions taking place in our society since the above period
has added a new dimension to the general music course concept.   Characteristic of music educators is their inability to
get beyond the sights of their passion for teaching performers
rather than pursuing music education for people.   The explo-
sion of the racial problem has pointed up the great lack of
response of educators to the great music disparity existing
in the inner-city schools.   The general music program in all
inner-city, urban, and suburban schools has been a curricular orphan.   In spite of these circumstances, school administrators should not be lead into believing that the job is impossible.

Secondary school music programs could not possibly
challenge the gamut of youthful interests if they were composed of just song-singing experiences and some listening.
First, no sound philosophy of music education could possibly
advocate song-singing as a complete musical diet.   Second,
song-singing does not contain all the necessary avenues for
musical expression which will induce all children to find
their personal music expression in that manner.   Every individual is a complex organism who reacts in as varied a
manner as there are individuals.   In order to be successful
the teacher must ask, "Does this musical experience meet
this particular individual's needs?"   If so, that music program is on the right track toward eliciting self-expression.
Third, no program of junior high school music education can
possibly be sensitized to individual needs unless it incorpo-
rates instrumental music experiences.   For some children
instrumental sensitivity is stronger than their "feelingness"
for vocal expression.   Then too, for the singer who is mu-

sically sensitive, the proper instrumental activities hold an
even greater allure. Very often there is the complete turn-
about, where the original exploratory acts may find greater
expression through manipulatory or "digital" activities and
later find expression through the vocal medium. Obviously,
the vocal utterances of man come as first aural experiences,
yet the instrumental may be of greater satisfaction through
their expression. Most important is that there is total exploration of the child's sensitivity. This is the job of achieving an early approach to experiencing music.

General Music Instructional Planning. There must be
instructional planning. Too many lessons have no present
and future design. A program should have two distinct instructional targets: general music for the beginner, and general music which is specifically designed for students who
have been in band, choir, or orchestra. In the former group
will be found individuals who have varying degrees of musical
talent. They are students who are there because they have
had little or no contact with music. A general music class
should not present isolated bits of information about music
theory, history of music, keyboard instruments, band, vocal,
or orchestral music.

Does the program which we are now to discuss challenge each individual? Information revealing the dispositional
tendencies of children must be studied. Not only must it be
kept in mind that we may have scientific evidence, but also
that our philosophy of music education must be carefully
evaluated if we are to succeed.

The General Music Course. A general music course
should provide a broadened base of musical experiences for
all secondary school pupils. General music education as
provided by the general music course is designed for all
students who desire to enjoy the benefits to be derived from
all forms of musical study.

Where the general music course has been imaginatively
tried, it has been proved that all individuals will respond to
some form of musical experience. Vocal and rhythmic responses are undoubtedly basic manifestations of musical sound
and movement. There basic media of music expression have
made song and dance two of the more powerful forces of artistic communication.

Such a concept of a general music course would not

delimit the breadth and depth of its content, but would encourage musical experiences of a degree consistent with the
ability of the people who are to be educated. The key to the
success of any such program is the understanding that it
brings.

The listening course should not become a substitute
for a general music course. A good general music course
should serve as a core around which the entire secondary
music curriculum is constructed. General music emphasizes
varied experiences in music. It should include listening,
singing, instrumental playing, rhythmic experiences and theoretical study.

Knuth has emphasized the great common purposes of
general music for the general high school student. He
stresses the importance of such a program when he says,

> At first one is often led to think that the typical
> music program for the average high school con-
> sists of choral and instrumental activities. Often,
> the instrumental activities are limited to band and
> marching band without any string or orchestra pro-
> gram. However, we do sometimes find the addi-
> tion of string instruction and orchestra or some
> specialized aspect of music theory or music history
> and appreciation for music students. The large
> majority are the forgotten students who may not
> have the talent or skill to take any of these classes.
> It is for this large group of students that the gen-
> eral music class has come into being.[1]

The general music program is for the average student,
as stated by the North Central Association of Colleges and
Secondary Schools. Its 1951 report recommends:

> All schools should develop the music curriculum
> with a view to serving every student. The practice
> of limiting the musical offerings to those requiring
> special interest, skill and accomplishment is not in
> accord with the basic principles of American educa-
> tion, which demand that the school serve the needs
> of all children. Musical experience for the general
> student should be planned to meet the needs of:
>
> (1) The student who may have had no previous mu-
> sical background and needs at his own level of ma-

turity of interest the most elementary of music activities from the point of view of skill required, to give him an immediate enjoyment of participation in music activities, to introduce him to possible participation in more advanced activities, and to develop in him an appreciation of the musical performance he hears.

(2) The student with some interest and background in music, who does not participate in the traditional, established musical performing groups such as band, orchestra or chorus, but who may become an active amateur in music (singing, playing, listening, etc.) in the community if given some school experience through informal, home-room and assembly singing, the general music classes, music club activities, etc.

(3) The student whose chief interest in music is derived through listening to live, recorded and broadcast music. Many of these consumers of music are not at all interested in producing music. It is important that through music appreciation classes they be given an opportunity to develop an intelligent understanding of music, and the ability to enjoy the literature of great music which has become a permanent part of our cultural heritage.[2]

From the foregoing it is clear that the objectives should be to

(a) arouse and develop interest in music;
(b) give further contact with music and some experience in producing it;
(c) give information about music that the well-informed person should have;
(d) provide exploratory experience in singing, listening, and playing;
(e) further desirable musical skills; and
(f) provide opportunities to discover musical skill.[3]

There should be

(a) singing of interesting songs of all classifications, songs with strong melodic or rhythmic appeal are especially desirable;
(b) enough voice training to enable each pupil to use

good tone quality and good diction, and to understand the possibilities in the use of his singing and speaking voice;
      (c) use of attractive illustrative materials of all kinds;
      (d) use of varied techniques in teaching this course,
for demonstrations, discussions, programs by visiting artists
and speakers, class concerts, and class expeditions to places
of musical interest;
      (e) a tie-up of subject matter as far as possible with
the pupils' in-and-out-of-school interests such as topics or
projects which interest them in social studies, English, art,
and modern languages, including music they have heard and
enjoyed in radio, television, concert performances, church,
or motion pictures;
      (f) frequent use of all audio-visual aids and other new
teaching devices including informal instruments--melodic,
harmonic, and rhythmic.[4]

To this list of activities Knuth has added "reading about the
composers, their lives, the times and countries in which
they lived."[5]

     For a comparison, a résumé of the 7th- and 8th-
grade general music program of Binghamton, New York,[6]
reveals the following course content.

1.   Group singing and voice training with attention to
     part singing, breath control, the adolescent voice
     and its change, diction, tone color and interpre-
     tation.
2.   Appreciation, concentrating on music value, taste,
     imagination and a rich cultural background. Pu-
     pils are encouraged also to attend community con-
     certs and to make use of the music library facil-
     ities.
3.   Theory of music, including definition, treble and
     bass staves, symbols, key and meter signatures,
     scales, intervals, simple chords, ear training,
     rhythmic patterns and original material. The
     unit plan is also used: e.g., The Orchestral In-
     struments, Types of Songs, Nationalism in Music,
     American Folk Music, Historical Periods in Mu-
     sic, Contemporary Musicians and Music of the
     State. Each junior high has a grade 9 festival
     chorus as a performing group for assemblies and
     evening concerts. Membership in this last is
     elective and the participant receives 1/4 credit
     for the year applicable towards graduation from

senior high school.   Rehearsals are on school
time.

But more specifically such a general music education
course connotes an all encompassing generalized philosophy
or concept of useful learning.   It is not specialized learning.
It means that all knowledge is good knowledge, if it results
in the functionalism of which we have already spoken.   Music
instruction must not become an artistic veneer, and the keystone in the arch of general music is participation.

Music educators during the current century have been
provided an opportunity which they have as yet failed to seize.
Music educators must not be misled into believing that a pa-
tronized musical art will solve apathetic interest, appreciation, and musical illiteracy.   Emphasis upon performance
during the 17th, 18th, 19th, and 20th centuries created what
Horn calls "a period unsympathetic to music and musicians,
or devoid of discrimination and taste in music, few brilliant
musicians will be developed and little great music written."[7]
He concludes by saying "for that reason, if for no other, the
general education of our children, young people, and adults
in the area of music is of direct and personal concern to every musician and music educator."[8]

Among the recommendations approved by the various
Divisional Conventions of the Music Educators National Conference during 1955, it was cautioned that "we deplore the
tendency to use the general music class as a catch-all.   We
recommend, therefore, that the size of the general music
class be comparable to the size of classes in other subjects."[9]   It was further recommended

> That greater stress be given to the general music
> program on the secondary level so as to continue
> the pattern established in the elementary schools;
> that all students be given the opportunity to explore
> the areas of the history of music, theory, instru-
> mental music, singing, listening, and creative ex-
> perience within that program; that we as educators
> take a new look at this phase of music education
> in the schools.   We also urge the growth of the
> 'assembly sing' as a means of augmenting and en-
> riching the music curriculum.[10]

Barr's committee earlier had recommended that "The general music class should include six broad areas of music ac-

tivity: singing, playing, listening, creative, rhythmic and music reading. "11

Tomorrow will witness some form of further post-high school continuing adult education where men will prepare for better vocational specialization beyond formal high school education. Into this new dream of educational opportunity, will be molded a general education program for all men. If general education implies what its generalization indicates, then the arts must assume their role in preparing individuals for a broadened culture which will be able to assume its rightful role in its coexistance with other school subjects.

Scheduling and Accrediting Courses. General music courses are a partial solution to the desire to conduct junior and senior high school music courses on a regularly sched-uled classroom basis. These courses should meet a mini-mum of three and preferably five times a week. Credit should be proportional to the number of meetings held each week and the amount of preparation required outside of class. There is no reason why daily classes could not be main-tained. Class size should be consistent with regular aca-demic class sizes. Success is more likely to attend the in-structor's efforts, if a carefully organized course of study is used and an imaginative and broadly trained musician con-ducts the class. The finest musicians should be assigned to teach these courses.

There have been occasions when the general music course has been hampered because:

1. There is a woeful lack of imaginative develop-ment of general music courses. Many music teachers are interested in developing performing organizations rather than broad diversified pro-grams of music education. The aura about per-formance must not overshadow the importance of knowing how to construct imaginative general mu-sic course activities for the average individual.

2. Teacher training programs have too often been guided by performing musicians whose interests center about performance.

3. There is some evidence that a popular philosophy of American music education favors the commer-cialized values of music rather than its basic

cultural contributions.

4.   There is a lack of competent teachers and of
     adequate budget for general music courses.   In
     many school systems the addition of these courses
     would necessitate additional teaching staff.

Obviously, these obstacles to the development of a
strong general music program in secondary schools place
a great responsibility upon institutions of higher learning.
It is to their leadership that we must eventually look for a
solution to many general music course problems.   General
music education has a more practical meaning today than it
ever had.   Today, music education must be designed for every student if we are to provide him with an opportunity to
enjoy and enlarge his knowledge of music.

The Envisioned Program.   Experience in dealing with
teen-agers in the junior high school music programs indicates
conclusively that their success depends upon:

1) A challenging singing program that is fun-oriented
as well as one that provides learning opportunities.
2) Programs that do not waste student time; achievement is the supreme objective.
3) A singing program of quality.   Students are the
first consideration; standards must be attained.
4) Performance involvement.
5) Good classroom organization.
6) Singing light music that has teen-age identification.
7) Singing quantities of good vocal literature; it should
be vibrant literature.   Work on unison, two and three part
songs.   Part-singing requires much practice and perfection
of vocal techniques.   Rounds and canons are good starters.
They aid in the development of appreciation for choral singing.   Don't forget those folk songs!
8) Having a minimum understanding of vocal techniques.
9) Imaginative classroom activities.   Performance
goes a long way toward maintaining student interest.   Fun,
joy, and music learning must be coupled with teen identification if success is to attend the singing program.
10) The teacher's maintaining a good rapport with
the students. [12]

Suggested Program Possibilities.   There are many
areas of music study that should prove challenging to junior

and senior high school students. General music as a course
has a great future and could easily become a basic course
content consideration for all music programs. In secondary
schools the course is usually offered on an elective basis for
two 45- or 50-minute periods per week; five periods would
be more acceptable. Five periods permit the following:

MWF   Lecture and/or Academic-Theoretical
                        Concentration*

TTh   Functional Involvement-Participative**

---

*Academic-Theoretical Concentration	**Functional Involvement-Participative
Ear Training	Junior High Band
Musical Form	Junior High Orchestra
Music Reading	Instrumental--Solo-Ensemble
Rudiments of Music	Junior High Girls' Glee Club
Musical Theory	Junior High Boys' Glee Club
American Music	Junior High Mixed Chorus
Appreciation of Music	Song-Singing
Contemporary Music	Vocal--Solo-Ensemble
Folk Music	Autoharp
History of Music	Banjo
Instruments of the Orchestra	Guitar
Jazz	Piano
	Recorder

[The above may be titles for course offerings or units of instruction. It is not uncommon to offer units of instruction
for a period of nine or 18 weeks.]

The MWF and TTh arrangement may be altered to fit instructional convenience. The Cleveland Course of Study[13]
sets forth a general music program with its attendant offerings that meets the Ohio State requirement which states that
music be taught through the eighth grade. It recommends a
class size of 30-40 pupils, with a maximum of 60. A course
of study should contain a statement of objectives. (Paren-
thetically, there are enough statements of objectives. The
important consideration is what is happening to the child?
Pages of objectives are worthless unless they are put into
action.)

Lesson Plans.[14] It is essential that the teacher have a well-organized, written teaching plan for each class if the ultimate goals are to be achieved. There are two phases to be considered, the whole unit plan and each daily lesson within that plan.

Suggested topics for the unit plan:

Music in Recreation
The Making of Instruments
America at Work
Music in Our Town (current events)
Music of the People
Music of Various Nations
Accoustical Principles of Instruments
How a Composer Works
You and Your Voice
Ancient Music and Instruments
Dance Forms in Music
Music in Our Lives
Music is Sound
Music and the Spirit of Our Time
Careers in Music
Modern Sounds: Hi-Fi vs. Stereo; AM vs. FM Radio

It is vitally important that the teacher have clearly in mind at the beginning of every class the answers to these two questions:

What is to be done today? (the daily lesson)
How does this fit into the larger plan for the unit or semester?

The plan for the daily lesson should include the following:

a.   Objectives
b.   Methods of motivation
c.   Procedures
d.   Follow-up and evaluation of the lesson.

LESSON PLAN FOR A GENERAL MUSIC CLASS
(Meeting twice a week for 30 minutes each)

The heart of the lesson should involve as many students as possible. A busy student doesn't have time to get into trouble.

1. If a rhythm lesson is being taught, make sure the students know the rhythm patterns before distributing rhythm instruments. If the rhythm accompaniments become louder than the singing, then their purpose as an accompaniment is defeated.
2. If harmony parts are being worked out, have the whole class learn all parts in their own octave to prevent discipline problems.
3. In order to dismiss on time, use the last few minutes of the period to either review previous lessons, or sing familiar songs while the books are being collected.
4. A "song bag" is better than having the class choose songs. Have them put their requests in this "bag" and draw one or two out when time permits.

Dismiss in an orderly fashion (row at a time, sections, etc.). Remember the bell is for the teacher and not the students. Many of them jump up as soon as the bell sounds if you let them. Set a definite pattern for dismissal and adhere to it early in the school year.

Courses of Study. The general music class is not just a singing class. It must include a balanced variety of activities which are based on and extend the child's previous musical experience. In the elementary school, music activities are organized around a five point program which includes singing, listening, rhythmic activities, playing and creating.

In planning lessons for junior high school general music classes, it is wise to keep these five points in mind, together with the special or specific needs which the individual school presents. Following is an outline of materials presented to 4th, 5th, and 6th grade music classes. This should be used as the foundation for planning 7th and 8th grade general music activities.

GRADE IV
1. Recognition of orchestral instruments by sight and sound.
2. Use of bells to motivate the learning of the letter names of the treble clef.
3. Learning to recognize, name, and understand musical signs, symbols and other note values.
4. Recognition of beat, accent and rhythm pattern.
5. Meter signatures $\frac{2}{4}$, $\frac{3}{4}$, and $\frac{4}{4}$.

6. Simple Song Form (AABA, ABAB', etc.).
7. Rounds, ostinato, and dialogue songs as preparation
    for two part singing.
8. Recognition of major and minor tonalities.
9. Descants and simple part songs.
10. Correlation with units.

GRADE V

1. Study of keys, key signatures and scales to 4 sharps
    and 4 flats.
2. Two part singing.
3. Study of major chord, using letters and numbers and
    relating to sight singing.
4. Use of autoharp in connection with chord study.
5. Introduction of 6/8 meter.
6. Creative project--original songs for Composer's Day
    broadcast.

GRADE VI

1. Conducting Patterns: 2-, 3-, and 4-part meter.
2. Use of autoharp to accompany songs.
3. Songs with a low part to interest boys.
4. Syncopation--hearing, clapping, playing, singing and
    writing.
5. Creative use of instruments for special effects--tam-
    bourines, maracas, claves, castanets, etc.
6. Minor keys and chords (difference between major and
    minor--hear, see, play on bells or piano, sing).
7. Dance types, their rhythms and time signatures.

Junior High School Music Activities

SINGING

Objectives
a. Build a repertoire of songs of various types.
    (Keep a record of songs learned by each class.)
b. Develop an understanding of the elements of
    good singing.
    1. Good tone quality
    2. Correct breathing
    3. Proper phrasing
    4. Clear diction
    5. Effective interpretation
c. Continue to develop sight reading in treble and
    bass clef.
d. Learn music symbols, such as notes, dynamic

          markings, signatures, etc. (Use of flannel
          board is helpful.)
    e.   Develop a music vocabulary.
    f.   Develop the ability to recognize voice classifi-
        cation.

LISTENING

1. Objectives
    a. To acquaint pupils with worth-while music.
    b. To stimulate an interest in listening to good
        music outside the classroom.
    c. To recognize a variety of musical forms.
    d. To increase musical understandings.
    e. To develop good listening habits, musical dis-
        crimination and taste.

2. Suggested Units for Listening Lessons
    a. Student interest in the music of an individual
        composer.
    b. Music from a particular historical period.
    c. Student interest in nationality backgrounds.
    d. Music and composers of modern times.
    e. American music--folk music, popular music,
        serious music--and how each has grown sep-
        arately and together.
    f. Correlation with art and literature.
    g. Theme music of popular radio and television
        programs.
    h. Instruments of the orchestra.
    i. Preparation for attendance at children's con-
        certs.
    j. Current musical events.

RHYTHMIC ACTIVITIES

1. Objectives
    a. To give the child an opportunity to experience
        rhythm through a physical response.
    b. To provide opportunities for participation for
        the non-singer as well as the singer.
    c. To help children realize how rhythm and tempo
        are related to mood.

2. Suggested Activities

    a. Conducting

  b. Folk dances
  c. Square dances
  d. Use rhythm patterns taken from a song for clapping, tapping and playing rhythm instruments.
  e. Recognizing and naming two and three part meters.
  f. Use recordings and songs to illustrate the relation of rhythm and mood.

PLAYING

1. Objectives
   a. To stimulate activities for the non-singer and the singer.
   b. To enhance the beauty of a musical performance.

2. Suggested Instruments for Use
   a. Piano
   b. Tone Bells--use to build and play scales and simple chords
   c. Autoharp
   d. Fretted instruments
   e. Rhythm instruments
   f. Recorders and flutophones

CREATING

1. Objectives
   a. To discover creative talent and to provide opportunities for its outlet.
   b. To correlate music with visual arts and creative writing.

2. Suggested Activities
   a. Composing melodies.
   b. Creating accompaniments using piano, autoharp, bells and rhythm instruments.
   c. Creating harmony through singing.
   d. Interpretive dancing.
   e. Dramatic performances.
   f. Drawings.
   g. Making instruments.

Because music may be used in conjunction with every subject in the curriculum, it is potentially a unifying subject. In this role music, rather than losing its identity and significance, assumes new authority and makes more sense to the pupil, as it becomes part of the fabric of everyday life. [Andrews and Leeder.]

The teacher should be aware of and utilize the areas of correlation listed below.

IN SCHOOL

1. Curriculum correlation

    a. Inter-relationship with other subject matter fields, such as English, Social Studies, Science, Mathematics, Languages, Art, Physical Education and Dramatics. (Use maps and illustrative material.)

    b. Within the music department, such as the demonstration of instruments by members of the band and orchestra, and cooperation in the preparation and presentation of programs.

2. Commemoration of special events or days.

HOME AND COMMUNITY

1. P.T.A. Programs
2. Open House, Parents' Night, etc.
3. Musicals to which parents and friends are invited
4. Christmas caroling
5. Severance Hall concerts
6. Encouragement of student participation in church and community musical groups.

CITY

1. Radio, television, movies
2. Recitals, concerts and operas
3. Newspaper and magazine articles
4. Exhibits (art museum and libraries)

Evaluation and Grading

RECOMMENDATIONS

1. Inform students of the bases for grading at the be-

ginning of the term and refer to them frequently there-
after.

2. The teacher needs to have tangible justification for the
grade given, such as objective tests, reports, note-
books, etc.

3. Give credit to those who do extra assignments and
make extra assignments readily available. This ap-
plies particularly to those who are having serious
voice problems.

4. Consult with the administration as to preferred grading
system for general music classes in your school. It
has been suggested that grades be given in general
music at the end of the second marking period so that
teachers have a better opportunity to get to know their
students who meet just twice a week.

FACTORS IN GRADING

1. General intelligence level of group
2. Outside assignments (research and art projects, note-
books, current events)
3. Participation in class (singing, class discussion, etc.)
4. Musical ability as related to performance
5. Test grades
6. Attendance

Special Groups. Students who possess unusual musical ability must encounter challenges and opportunities
greater than those possible in the general music classes.
One or more of the following special groups should be provided to answer that need: Boys' Chorus, Girls' Chorus,
Mixed Chorus, Vocal Ensembles. The selection of choral
activities for each school rests with the administration and
the teacher involved. It is desirable to allow at least 10
periods per week in the teacher's schedule for special groups.

In addition to the primary function of these special
groups, which is to provide challenging experiences for outstanding students, there are other very important values.
The fine musical performances of which they are capable
form an invaluable agency for building school morale and for
maintaining good community relationships. Another equally
important value lies in the boost to teacher morale which
comes from the satisfaction derived in working with these
special groups.

ELECTIVE GROUPS

1. Elective groups are special groups, usually Boys' Chorus and Girls' Chorus, which qualified 7th and 8th grade students may elect in place of general music.

2. Qualified students are those who possess unusual ability and interest, those for whom the general music class presents inadequate challenges.

3. The music office will supply the names of students who have participated in elementary school choirs. These students should be guided into elective groups.

4. Teachers will note students in general music classes who should be guided into elective groups.

5. Teachers will need to plan carefully for these classes, using music of the highest caliber, stressing fundamentals of choral technique, and keeping in mind that these classes must provide significant social and musical experiences.

6. Very large classes are apt to be unwieldy. A maximum of 60 is suggested.

SELECTIVE GROUPS

1. Each school should provide at least one group, preferably a mixed chorus, which offers the greatest challenge possible to selected groups of 8th and 9th grade students.

2. Students should be selected on the basis of unusual ability and interest as displayed in general music classes or in elective groups.

3. Performances for the school and the community will provide effective motivation.

4. Performances must be of a quality that will help to raise the level of music appreciation in the school and the community.

5. All facets of these groups: music performance, behavior, appearance, and organization, must be of a

quality that will foster school pride.

6. Public performances and the preparation for them can
    be used to stimulate community interest in the school.

STUDENT ORGANIZATION

1. A student organization presents an ideal situation for
    the practice of student self-government.

2. It is desirable for the teacher to guide pupils in elect-
    ing officers who will provide leadership and who will
    assume responsibility.

3. Section leaders in each choral group help to lighten
    the load of the teacher and will develop early respon-
    sible leadership.

REHEARSALS

1. Rehearsals should be carefully planned and organized.
    Stress such fundamental factors as intonation, dynam-
    ics, good tone quality, breath control, phrasing, blend
    and balance, diction, musicianship.

2. Work out rehearsal techniques that do not require the
    various voice sections to sit idle for many minutes
    at a time. For example: Sopranos sing along with
    the Tenors and Altos sing along with the Basses.

3. Build a repertoire suitable for public performance.

4. Provide a set of folders for each performing group
    and assign these folders to individuals. Keep only
    current repertoire in the folders.

5. Give student accompanists the opportunity to practice
    new numbers before they are presented to the class.

6. If facilities are available, sectional rehearsals are
    invaluable to your group as a whole.

       <u>Ann Arbor, Mich., Music Curriculum.</u> The Ann Ar-
bor, 7th-grade general music curriculum for 1964 reasonably
suggests:

       Generally speaking, no two people agree on the

meaning of 'general music' except that it is a poor
name to use. What we imply is 'music in the general education of the child' where music is taught
as an academic discipline. Through such a course
we hope to promote musical growth in each child
through different musical experiences which are
geared to the interests, needs and the abilities of
the child. [15]

The Ann Arbor general music course reveals by implication
or statement some commonly accepted course expectancies:

1)   General music is usually either required to be taken
     one year in either the 7th or 8th grades and some-
     times both. In Ann Arbor general music is offered
     three times one week and two times the next week.

2)   The above minimum requirement may be satisfied by
     taking general music in either of the above grades as
     a select chorus, or membership in band or orchestra.

3)   The general music course is usually offered a mini-
     mum of two 45-minute periods per week.

4)   Any variance in individual musical ability is deter-
     mined by administrating tests for the purpose of de-
     termining individual innate competency and acquired
     performance ability in music.

5)   In practice, most non-instrumentalists elect sev-
     enth grade general music, thus fulfilling their
     last obligatory contact with music. Many are
     not likely to pursue music upon an elective ba-
     sis. They often become lost to the music de-
     partment for the remainder of the junior-senior
     high school years.

6)   Often by the 8th grade and certainly by the 9th grade,
     a student starting out in a 7th-grade music experience
     may become either a "non-selected" general music
     student or an instrumentalist or selected vocalist who
     indicates an interest in further music study (e.g.,
     band, orchestra, or choir).

7)   Successful general music teachers are those who have
     been especially trained for teaching the course. Band,
     orchestra, and vocal teachers who are often converted

to teaching general music courses are not certain to insure success to the program.

8) General music programs should not become a continuation of the elementary music vocal program; more singing or record listening should not constitute the program of studies. A desirable course should functionally involve students in as many aspects of music as possible.

9) The general music program must be first and foremost a program taught for pupil enjoyment. Curiously enough, pleasurable experiences must sometimes be taught. It is the musical neophyte getting his feet wet at the cultural shrine of music!

A Wide-Ranging Music Program. The following indicates the wide range of musical experiences that may be pursued. It remains the teacher's judgment to develop a program that involves the students' interests. Naturally, the comprehensive nature of the program would be modified according to student needs. Whether singing, listening, or playing, the teacher must build the general music program about needs and interests.

SINGING

Why? For enjoyment. For increased skill in handling musical notation of pitch and rhythm. For growing awareness of form in music. For developing functional repertoire of songs. For personal involvement in the techniques of music (e.g., harmony vs. counterpoint). For realization of the potential of one's own singing voice (e.g., vocal range in reference to compass of songs).

How? Through unison song of widely varying types: Familiar songs (such as "All Through the Night," "I've Been Workin' on the Railroad," "Finiculi, Finicula"); Songs for pure recreation (folk songs, songs of armed services, nonsense songs); and Songs selected for beauty of expression (e.g., "The Minstrel Boy," "Where'er You Walk"). Through part songs--the ideal activity in light of differentiation in vocal ranges: Songs with harmonic orientation (Chant on scale tones 5-6, Harmonize in thirds and sixths, Experience fundamental harmonic relationships I, IV, V, I); and Songs contrapuntally conceived (Rounds, canons, descants) which stir an awareness of balance, interdependence, rhythmic interplay of parts.

Through reading in unison and in parts-- repetitive melodies moving along chord and scale patterns of particular value in early stages. Through singing with vitality--attention to melodic shape and proper phrasing to call forth proper breathing and correct support. Through conducting-- standard conductor's patterns to draw attention to metrical framework, other rhythmic aspects. Through criticism-- develop class-established criteria for placing songs in class repertoire. Through chanting--clap and chant (pulse and rhythm) in manner suggested by Hindemith in Elementary Training for Musicians.

Why? For enjoyment: manipulating instruments, diversification in sound, the pleasure of gross movement. For a better understanding of pitch notation--the spatial representation of pitch provided by instruments, and the one-to-one correlation between a tone produced by an instrument and its position on the staff. For increasing variety in singing through accompaniment (melodic, harmonic, rhythmic).

For a growing awareness of harmonic and rhythmic concepts and a developing sense of ensemble--simultaneously played pitches are more distinct, and therefore better heard, than simultaneously sung pitches; the physical movement necessary to play a rhythmic pattern makes the experience more concrete than singing the same pattern. For a more complete involvement of the student, who is often more willing to play an instrument than to sing because of the less personal nature of playing; also, the independence of instrumental parts yield independence of activity.

How? Through use of a variety of instruments: melodic--bells, metallophone, recorder, piano; harmonic-- piano, ukulele, guitar, autoharp; rhythmic--drums, claves, castanets, cymbals, maracas, hands and feet. Through adding accompaniment to singing--rhythmic accompaniment, support for harmony part. Through independent instrumental compositions--rhythmic round; round played on melodic instruments (e.g., "Are You Sleeping?," "Row, Row, Row Your Boat," "Old Abram Brown"); melodic-harmonic-rhythmic construction of one's own devising, in the manner of percussion marches in Music in Our Life, Music in Our Times (Silver Burdett), using student-composed examples as well as pre-existing pieces.

LISTENING

Why? For enjoyment--the pure sensuous enjoyment of organized sound; the intellectual enjoyment through analytical listening. The ideal: to be able to hear all there is to be heard in a musical composition--the relationship of the parts to one another and to the whole. For an increased involvement in the specifics of composition: color--instrumentation and orchestration; forms--unity-variety dichotomy solved in various ways; style--evolving an historical framework.

For a growing awareness of artistic principles--how and when to stop: cadence; how to keep moving: add interest (e.g., change key, weaken cadence, change color, deceive by a wrong note or chord); how to make it stick together--unity (e.g., the first movement of Beethoven's Fifth Symphony) and repetition (e.g., Leroy Anderson's Irish Suite); how to avoid boredom--variety, and contrast. Keep in mind a combination of the principles above: balance (symmetrical-asymmetrical). For experiencing a wider variety of music than that possible through only student or teacher performances. For establishing a norm for student activities--the teacher's performance, or a recorded version, to be learned by class. And, finally, for realizing appropriate concert etiquette.

How? Through listening for the role of melody in composition--the dynamic content of melody (shape and pace for example); melody as a structural determinant (e.g., theme and variation, song form); the pull of tonality (e.g., the fourth movement of Mendelssohn's "Reformation" using the familiar melody with a strong drive toward the tonic-- arrival at the tonic is delayed or blurred until the end of the movement). Through observing the role of harmony--a single tune harmonized in various ways (e.g., the fourth movement of Beethoven's Eroica, where simple tonic and dominant harmonization gives way to a rather lush harmonization in a later variation, and chorale melodies set in various ways by predecessors of Bach and by Bach himself). Through the dynamic nature of the dominant seventh chord in tonal framework (e.g., the introduction to the first movement of Beethoven's Symphony No. 1: simple chord sequences at piano); and harmonic flux (e.g., the slowly changing harmonies in Barber's "Adagio for Strings."

Through recognizing the role of rhythm--rhythmic

wholeness is demanded: $\frac{3}{4}$ ♩♩|♩♩|♩♩♩| is represented as
complete, but class performance will add a down beat of
fourth measure; rhythm is the driving force of music (begin
one-fourth of the way through the first movement of Bartók's
Music for Strings, Percussion and Celesta, and the effect
is nebulous; then, play it from the beginning and the rhythmic character of the melody becomes apparent and clarifies
the remainder); rhythm is a stylistic determinant--a regular
rhythmic pulse is common to Baroque, Classical and Romantic periods, and an irregular pulse is especially notable in
modern music as well as in pre-Baroque.   Through listening
for color--orchestration for an overall effect (the orchestra
has gained a primacy since 1750) and look at the concerto
principle, and the string quartet, which are "colored" for an
overall effect; instrumentation for a specific effect, using the
natural connotations of various instruments (e.g., horn,
flute); there is humor through unexpected color, and drama
in an abrupt change in color.   Through the identification of
orchestral instruments--Britten's Young Person's Guide to
the Orchestra (film available), Wheeler-Beckett's album,
Instruments of the Orchestra, Leroy Anderson's "Irish Suite,"
Ravel's "Bolero," and Grofé's "Grand Canyon Suite"; recommended is a classroom demonstration of instruments: by the
general music teacher where he is proficient, by student
teachers if they are well rehearsed, and by students when
available.

      Through noting the role of dynamics--its relation to
orchestration, the idea of climax, the sense of movement
possible with a single sustained tone or chord, and the element of surprise (sforzando, subito).   Through the recognition of forms as various solutions to unity, variety, and
duality--first, the fewest different melodic ideas: fugue,
theme and variations, song form; then the "expanding frontiers": rondo, and first-movement form; third, the complete
works based on single extramusical idea: tone poem, and
overture; and, finally, the complete works built of opposing
types: suite, sonata, symphony, concerto, quartet, opera,
oratorio, and musical (Broadway).   Through an awareness
of stylistic development--the history of music in sound; the
role of social and political history (courtly patronage, public
support, the artist in a totalitarian society); in the effects of
invention and improvements in instruments: the beginnings
of the modern string family in Cremona, Italy, the progress
of the clavichord through the harpsichord to the pianoforte to
satisfy ever larger arena (Cristofori's hammer mechanism,
1709), the revolution in brass instruments caused by keys,

the proliferation of percussion instruments since the invasion
of Latin American music, and electronic music making (tape
recorder, sound studio, the computer); and the alternate as-
cendancies of homophony and polyphony.[16]

* * * * *

Erie, Penn., General Music Course of Study, Grades
7 & 8. The school district of the city of Erie has stated
that

> The primary purpose of a course in General Music
> at the Junior High level is to educate the young
> person so that he may become a more perceptive,
> informed, and active citizen where matters of an
> aesthetic nature are concerned. This implies a
> dual responsibility toward the arts and toward the
> student.

It is suggested that there must

> ... emerge value patterns that embrace the culture
> of his sub-groups, his nation, western civilization
> and the world. The study of music as an art must
> always remain central--its historical, illustrative,
> or anecdotal value must take second place.[17]

OBJECTIVES OF THE COURSE*

1. To develop aesthetic sensitivity.
2. To cultivate independent musical judgment.
3. To explore the nature of the related arts.
4. To explore the creative process.
5. To develop an awareness of music in social context.

The philosophy of instruction underlying the Erie general music course suggests using the term "cognitive" to the
structure of a piece of music and all the techniques and organizational skills that go with it. Similarly, it also seems
proper to use the term "affective" to the interpretation of a
work on the sensuous or expressive level. The sensuous,
formal, technical, and expressive points of view form an

---

*Paraphrased and condensed from "An Instructional Guide
for a Course in the Arts in the Secondary Schools," prepared by the Fine Arts Division, Department of Education,
Commonwealth of Pennsylvania.

"episode" of experience which has far-reaching implications
for teaching and learning. It is suggested that the episode
has three stages:

"1. INITIAL CONTEMPLATION of a piece of music.
    Largely affective or feeling-based. Respondent does
    not wish to discuss or analyze. Responses are sub-
    jective.
"2. ANALYSIS through comparison. Respondent attempts
    to become more objective. Wants to recognize and
    name the qualities to which he is responding. Stu-
    dent needs a field of comparison--teacher may find
    it useful to present structured pairs of works or a
    series of multiple choices.

    "As he learns to isolate various elements of the
    piece of music, he finds the need for vocabulary,
    growing from an urge to share his perceptions with
    others and to seek help where his own perceptions
    are inadequate. Comparisons lead to further com-
    parisons, and the whole complex world of music be-
    gins to open up.
"3. SYNTHESIS. The episode is not complete without an
    attempt to restructure the original experience. Put-
    ting the elements back together, now enriched in
    both thought and feeling through association with
    other works, results in a new experience, often-
    times quite different from the original experience."[18]

    Obviously, this three-stage episode is artificial and
over-simplified. In reality there may be no clear definitions
between the sections.

    The main work of the classroom takes place in stage
2. It is here that the teacher can exercise some direction
and control by the selection of works furnishing a musical
vocabulary, and setting up a dialogue that will deal with
concepts and principles most in need of clarification. Here
the teacher can "steer" the class by structuring his choices
toward differences (or similarities) in purpose, style, in
form, or in any other aspect of an aesthetic experience.

    Nine units are presented in grades 7 and 8, and the
teacher is asked to teach those units which best apply to
his particular class. Presented here in full will be Unit 1,
"The Historical Approach." The other (suggested) units are:

Jazz
Music of the Black Man--Africa and the United States
Creative
    (Class prepares tapes on the following: timbre, rhythm,
    form, harmony, etc.)
Earliest Oriental and Hebrew Music
Music in America
Music in Our Community
Autoharp and Classroom Instruments
    (creative approach, with song-singing)
Recording Industry Today

        In order to provide for individual differences and tal-
ents, the outline is divided as follows: basic requirements
and challenge experiences.

                Unit I: The Historical Approach

RECORDS/SUPPLEMENTARY MATERIALS
        Music 100--An Introduction to Music History, by
            Brown & Troth, New York: American Book Co.,
            1967.

        Three long-play records
        46 worksheets for students
        75 colored slides
        Teachers Guide

        Reader's Digest Albums, as follows:
            Festival of Light Classical Music
            Music of the World's Great Composers

        Additional records, films, film strips, slides, ref-
        erence books, as listed in outline.

TEXTBOOKS
        All About Music, by Swift & Musser, Rockville Cen-
            tre, N.Y.:   Belwin, 1960.
        People And Music, by McGehee & Nelson, Boston:
            Allyn & Bacon, 1963.
        Basic Music Theory, Chicago: Neil A. Kjos Music
            Co., (c) 1970.
        Making Music Your Own, Morristown, N.J.:   Silver
            Burdett Co., (c) 1968 (for Grades 7 & 8).

REFERENCE WORKS

> Art & Music in the Humanities, by De Long, Egner,
> & Thomas, New York: Prentice-Hall, 1966.
> Encyclopedia of Art, by Munro, New York: Golden
> Press, 1963.

Basic Requirements	Challenge Experiences

PRIMITIVE, ANCIENT, AND PRE-BAROQUE PERIODS

Basic Requirements	Challenge Experiences

Listen to Side 1, in Music 100, and discuss thoroughly
  Primitive Music
  Greek Music
  Early Church Music
  Organum
  Troubadours
  Lute
  Clavichord
  Harpsichord
  Polyphony
  Palestrina
	Record--History of Music In Sound--Oxford University Press, vols. 1 & 2.

	Record--Masterpieces of Music Before 1750, by Parrish & Ohl, New York: W. W. Norton Company.
Show slides 1-15, in proper context, using explanatory material in Teacher's Guide	Correlate with primitive and ancient Art, Architecture, Earliest Writings & History--start a file of interesting pictures
	Find a record of early aboriginal dance music
	Start a vocabulary list for students' notebook

MUSIC OF THE BAROQUE PERIOD

Baroque Period remembered
for its elaborate and ornate
designs in art and in music

Introduce this unit with the
record: The Swingle Singers
Going Baroque--Philips, PHS-
600-126 or PHM-200-126

Listen to Side 2, Bands 1-6, in Music 100 and discuss thoroughly	Record--Bach Organ Favorites.

Basic Requirements   Challenge Experiences

Beginning of concert music
as we know it today

Bach   Record--Bach Toccata &
  music writing by rules   Fugue in D minor--Marie
  polyphony   Clair Alain--Musical Herit-
  fugue   age Society, Carnegie Hall,
  subject   N.Y.
  answer
  exposition   Record--Bach Orchestral
  personal life--large family   Suite
    great volume of music
    writing before widespread   Pipe Organ
    use of printing press   take field trip
                                         record several of best
Record--Little Fugue in G   church organs on tape
minor--Philadelphia Or-   contrast with electronic
chestra--ML 5065   organ
                                         vocabulary: pedal, manual,
Record--Bach Organ Favor-   stops, cipher
ites

Film Strip--"Life of Bach"

Handel   Messiah--"Overture,"
  Oratorio   "Aria," "Recitative,"
  Chorus & Orchestra   "Chorus"--play best ex-
  Personal life--great ac-   ample of each
    ceptance in England

Record--Basic Choruses,
from the Messiah

Record--Handel's Messiah
Excerpts

Film Strip--"Life of Handel"

Vivaldi   Record--Vivaldi, The Four
  concerto grosso   Seasons, Archive Produc-
  hundreds of concerti and   tions--ARC 73141
    sonatas for various in-
    struments   Additional suggestions of
                                       fine baroque music: (Time-
                                       Life Series), The Story of

Basic Requirements   Challenge Experiences

Record--Four Bassoon Con-
certi--Vox--10740

Great Music--"The Baroque
Period"

Show Slides 16-23 in proper
context, using explanatory
material in Teacher's Guide

Bring a recorder to class
and demonstrate it

Record--......

How long a list of baroque
composers can you make?
Here's a start:
    Gabrieli
    Monteverdi

Keep working on an ex-
tended vocabulary list

MUSIC OF THE CLASSICAL PERIOD

Listen to Side 2, Bands 7-15,
in Music 100, and discuss
thoroughly:
    Classical Period stressed
      elements of balance,
      form, design in music,
      art & architecture
    Opera, a drama set to mu-
      sic became one of major
      forms during Classical
      Period
    Gluck--opera
    Haydn--symphony--wrote
      125 symphonies--intro-
      duced minuet movement
      in symphony

Show class some examples
of classical art & architec-
ture clearly illustrating balance, form, design, &
rhythm. Suggest Encyclo-
pedia of Art, Munro, New
York: Golden Press, 1963.

    Mozart--concerto & opera,
      light, graceful, full of
      frills, introduced clari-
      net to orchestra, per-
      sonal life very colorful,
      early death

Record--"Lacrymosa" and
"Dies Irae" from Mozart's
Requiem Mass

Record--The Magic Flute--
learn to recognize some of
this music

Basic Requirements	Challenge Experiences
Beethoven--Symphonies, sonatas, concerti, chamber music, choral works	Report--Life and Times of Haydn, Mozart, & Beethoven (3 colorful composers)
His compositions bridge gap between the classical emphasis on forms & restraint & the romantic emphasis on freedom & emotion	Record--Beethoven's Ninth Symphony--play the choral section--unusual in a symphony
Originality, power, emotion, strength	Record--"Moonlight Sonata" Record--"Overture"-- "Leonore No. 3" Record--"Coriolanus Overture" (program music)
Contemporary of Napoleon	
Show slides 24-33 in proper context, using explanatory material in Teacher's Guide	Keep working on an extended vocabulary list

MUSIC OF THE ROMANTIC PERIOD

Listen to Side 3, Bands 1-5, in Music 100, & discuss thoroughly:
  The term "romantic"--based on chivalry, adventure, supernatural, stories about folk material--emphasis on imagination & emotions

A study of music of the "Romantic" period must indelibly convey the impression that this music broke away from the hard & fast rules of harmony and counterpoint and became more daring & melodic

Romantic Period starts early 1800's

Imagination, ingenuity, lyricism and beautiful melody is the watchword of the romantic period

Paganini--famous violinist
Rossini--set standards of Italian opera
Mendelssohn--pianist, oratorio
Chopin--poet of the piano
Liszt--great piano virtuoso
Gounod--oratorios & masses

Make a fetish of finding as many beautiful melodies as you can--here are a few suggestions:
  Intermezzo--Cavalleria

Basic Requirements	Challenge Experiences
Verdi--great Italian operas	Rusticana, Mascagni.
Wagner--great German operas (difference between Italian & German opera?)	"The Swan," Saint Saens "On Wings of Song," Mendelssohn
J. Strauss--waltz king	Nutcracker Suite, Tschai- kowsky
Stephen Foster--American popular songs	Second Mov't--Symphony No. 5, Tschaikowsky
Brahms--romantic classicist	Last Mov't--New World Symphony, Dvorak
Tschaikowsky--beautiful melodies	"One Fine Day"--Madame Butterfly, Puccini
Mussorgsky--nationalistic style	"Solvejg's Song," Grieg (sing it)
Bizet--opera "Carmen"	
Leoncavalla--"Pagliacci"	
Grieg--beautiful song-like melodies	How many more can you find?
Dvorak--"New World Sym- phony"	
Sibelius--tone poems	Record--"Swan of Tuonela"-- plaintive (longest English horn solo)

Show Slides 34-59 in proper context, using the material found in the Teacher's Guide

See Unit Evaluation at end of Romantic Period, p. 48 on Teacher's Guide for Music 100

Listen to Side 5, in Music 100, Bands 5-8

Keep working on an ex- tended vocabulary list

The new sounds of the 20th century

Composers who bridged the gap between 19th-century romanticism and contempo- rary music
  Ravel
  Debussy
  de Falla

Record & Filmstrip-- "Sorcerer's Apprentice"
Record & Filmstrip-- "Danse Macabre"
Record & Filmstrip-- "The Moldau"

New importance of rhythm

Ravel's "Bolero" is the longest crescendo in all music

What is the meter signature of a bolero? Would music with a similar rhythm, in 2/4 meter, be a bolero?

Basic Requirements	Challenge Experiences

Debussy's "whole tone" scale
  Prelude to the Afternoon
  of a Faun
  Clair de Lune
  La Mer (The Sea)
	Be able to play a whole tone scale on the piano. Can you write one?
	
	By experimenting at the keyboard, can you find or play another whole tone scale in another key?

This is IMPRESSIONISM--vague, ethereal--you have to "dream in" in the meaning of it. Often, the title will start you on the right track	How much impressionistic art can you find? Bring it to class--can you describe the qualities of this art?
de Falla--"Ritual Fire Dance" strong rhythmic feeling, colorful harmonies	Record--The Three-Cornered Hat, by de Falla

20th-Century musical terms:

  Atonality--music without key feeling

Ostinato--short bits of melody repeated over and over again	What is "neoclassicism"--new classic style

  Dissonance--clashing harmonies

(Play illustrations in Teacher's Guide, pp. 55 & 56)

| Stravinsky--pagan rhythms, clashing harmonies, brilliant orchestrations | Write short biography of Stravinsky (lived in California many years, recently deceased) |
| Record--"The Firebird" (ostinato)
Record--"Petruchka" (polytonality) (This is program music, tell the story) | Record--"Rite of Spring"--composed way back in 1913 - is it "modern" music? (This is program music, too--find the story) |

Basic Requirements	Challenge Experiences
	This is Polytonality This is EXPRESSIONISM, as opposed to Impressionism
Schönberg--atonality his specialty--father of the "twelve-tone row"	Can you find any biographical material on Schönberg? If so, bring it to class.
Explain the tone row--write a couple of them in class by selecting the 12 tones to be used. Number them, 1 thru 12. Now mix up the numbers to build a new melody.	Record--Der Mondfleck, by Schönberg
Will you ever find a satisfying 12-tone row? Have you found one in what is considered "good" music?	Bring in examples of contemporary art & architecture

In General Music in grades 7 & 8 we need not go into the mechanics of contemporary music too deeply. The children should, however, have a certain amount of exposure to it, so they may gain an appreciation of things contemporary.

Show Slides 60-63, in their proper context

CONTEMPORARY TECHNIQUES IN OPERATIC AND ORCHESTRAL MUSIC

Listen to Side 6, in Music 100, Bands 1-6

Menotti--"The Medium"
   Briefly review opera as
   a musical form

   Uses 12-tone row to describe a dramatic scene

Basic Requirements

Gershwin--"Porgy and Bess"
Introduction of the Jazz
medium

Shostakovich--Symphony No. 1
He gives the classical
symphony a modern dress
by using percussion in-
struments prominently,
by using the piano and
very involved rhythms,
moderate dissonances,
and a larger orchestra
with a fuller sound

Villa Lobos--"The Little
Train of Caipira"
Play this without com-
ment--ask students what
this music describes--
can they hear the train?

Very famous Brazilian
composer

Copland--"Rodeo"

Play this without comment,
too. Does the class hear
the "cowboy" flavor?

Play "Rodeo" in its en-
tirety

Foss--Echoi
This is "chance" music.
What is "chance" music?

Could we experiment with
it?

Lukas Foss is presently

Challenge Experiences

Records--Have fun playing
"Rhapsody in Blue" and
"American in Paris"

Play other Copland works

Probably America's most
distinguished composer

Find biographical material
on Aaron Copland--leave
something impressive in
the minds of our students
for this great man

Basic Requirements   Challenge Experiences

the conductor & music
director of the Brooklyn
Philharmonic

Show Slides 60-75 in proper
context

_____

    Maumee, Ohio, General Music Course of Study, Jun-
ior High School. The content of any course of study provides
only a suggested guide of activities to be pursued for study
and will not guarantee learning; learning is the only measure
of its success. The instructional staff must relate the content to the child. The teacher may have factual knowledge
to be made available to the child, but he must have the capacity to put into practice relationships between the phenomena
of knowing and learning and the how of that learning. It is
the pupil that needs to learn what the teacher has found worthy to be known. What the child needs to learn is what the
teacher has to know.[19]

GENERAL MUSIC

1. Required of all pupils for two 45-minute periods per
    week (some exceptions).

2. Variety of musical activities include:

    a. Singing, using a wide range of materials.
    b. Listening, recordings, radio, television, live con-
        certs.
    c. Music reading, explanation, development and use
        of music symbols.
    d. Instrumental exploration (study and perform) from
        recreational (song flutes, autoharp, guitar, etc.)
        to standard band and orchestral instruments.
    e. Rhythmic activities--folk dancing.
    f. Investigation of the place of music in our society.
        This includes music history and composers.

3. General procedures:

    a. Learn general and individual interests and needs
        by:

class discussion;
use of inventory form;
use of tests for accumulated knowledge and
    innate abilities;
use of anecdotal forms;
study of accumulative records;
discussion with former teachers and parents;
observation during out-of-class and out-of-
    school activities.

b. Organization of learnings around central themes
(units or centers of interest), established by
teacher-pupil planning.

c. Compilation of a basic song list.

d. Compilation of a basic listening repertoire.

e. Plan for both talented and limited pupils:
large group activities for all;
small group projects to help develop individual
    needs of the more talented students;
development of proper attitudes and knowledge
    to enable the limited, non-performing pupils
    to become intelligent music consumers.

f. Use of accumulative record form, covering all
musical activities of each pupil throughout the
junior high school years (one card per pupil).

g. Use of progress report forms for pupil evaluation.

4. Basic music materials:

a. Song book texts (one copy per pupil)--7th Grade:
"Singing Juniors"--Ginn and Company;
"Book Seven" (Birchard Music Series)--Summy;
"Sing Out"--Birchard;
"Music Sounds Afar"--Follett;
"Music In Our Life"--Silver Burdett Company.
Eighth Grade:
"Singing Teenagers"--Ginn and Company;
"Book Eight" (Birchard Music Series)--Summy;
"Proudly We Sing"--Follett;
"Let Music Ring"--Birchard.
Both Grades: "Joyful Singing," "Singing Ameri-
ca," "Twice 55 Brown Book."

b. Music workbook texts (one copy per pupil):
7th grade--"Living With Music," Volume II--
    Richardson and English--(M. Witmark and
    Sons);
8th grade--"Living With Music," Volume II--
    Richardson and English--(M. Witmark and
    Sons);

Both grades--"Music in the Making"--best--
(Summy, Birchard).

c. Instruments (recreational or social)

Percussion (for rhythmic work), drums, maracas, castanets, gourds, etc.;

Melodic and chordal--set of song flutes, quartet of recorders (soprano, alto, tenor and
bass), harmonicas, ocarinas, ukelele, guitar and autoharps (several, if possible).

d. Library of books: reference books: dictionaries
and encyclopedias, folk and national music,
history and appreciation, opera, biography,
things to do, music as a career, music periodicals.

e. Recordings:

(1) Voice types (soprano, contralto, tenor,
baritone, bass);

(2) Choral illustrations (vocal combinations);

(3) Instrumental illustrations--single instruments of four classes (strings, woodwinds, brasses and percussion);

(4) Instrumental combinations--from small ensembles to full orchestra and band;

(5) Music form illustrations--opera, symphone,
suite, overture, fugue, ballet, marches,
rondo, theme with variation;

(6) Periods of music composition--early church
music, preclassical music (baroque),
classical music, romantic music, art
songs, impressionistic music, modern
music.

f. Pictures, prints and photographs--for further illustration, explanation and coordination of the
arts. (Films for the same purpose are obtainable in profusion, but should be rented only.)

g. Recording and play-back equipment--tape recorder
deck, 3-speed manual turntable with tone-arm,
amplified and pre-amp speakers.

h. Room furniture--movable chairs, with tablet arms,
work table, blackboard with painted staffs, bulletin boards, piano (studio size), wall maps (of
world), globe, and ample storage space.

i. Source Books:

Andrews and Leeder: Guiding Junior High
School Pupils in Music Experiences. New
York: Prentice-Hall, 1953.

Ernst, Snyder and Zimmerman: A Manual for
Teachers, Books 7 and 8, (Birchard Music
Series), Evanston, Ill.: Summy, Birchard,
1958.

Pitts: Music Integration in the Junior High
School, Birchard, 1935.

Curriculum Guide: General Music in Grades 7
and 8, Baltimore, Md.: Anne Arundel Co.,
1958.

Music for Children and Youth. Highland Park
Public Schools, Dallas, Texas, 1958.

5. Specific aims in junior high school music:

   a. Continue the development of music skills.
   b. Provide a singing program of unison and part
      songs.
   c. Recognize the importance of changing voices.
   d. Provide a variety of instrumental music experi-
      ences to include social instruments.
   e. Develop a discriminating taste through a well-
      organized listening program.
   f. Provide opportunities for creative self-expression
      in all areas of the music program.
   g. Stress the importance of our musical heritage and
      its effect on present-day culture.
   h. Offer challenging experiences for gifted children
      through participation in solo, choral and instru-
      mental ensembles.
   i. Understand the adolescent in relation to his mu-
      sical development.

BAND

1. Enrollment--Students from grades 7, 8, and 9.

2. Rehearsals--Two 45-minute rehearsals per week.

3. Objectives--
   a. Present behavior patterns which are necessary
      to participate in an instrumental group.
   b. To play, with musical taste, music of junior
      high school level.
   c. Encourage group participation in a music activity.
   d. Discover and promote talented students in their
      respective instruments.
   e. Promote music as worthy cause of leisure time.

ORCHESTRA

1. Enrollment--Students from grades 7, 8, and 9.

2. Rehearsals--Two 45-minute rehearsals per week.

3. Objectives:
   a. Develop the student artistically.
   b. Develop the music aptitude of the student.
   c. Fulfill a desire the student may have to play a string instrument.
   d. Develop a student socially.

State of Pennsylvania Music Course of Study, Grades 7, 8, and 9.[20] Objectives are to:

recognize basic forms in music;

promote understanding of chordal progressions and structure;

develop the understanding and skill in making two-, three-, and four-part harmony;

study, in greater depth, the relationship of music and science;

study increasingly difficult melodic movement;

develop the singing voice with particular emphasis on the changing voice;

learn the characteristics of the types of music;

develop critical thinking and evaluation of music;

learn the purposes of music;

review instruments of the band and orchestra;

learn to use the social and recreational instruments (e.g., Latin American, African);

learn to make value judgments in determining good music;

understand how composers use instruments for various musical effects;

develop judgment in selecting and buying recordings and record playing equipment;

review and develop the knowledge of musical notation;

obtain knowledge of current music affairs;

recognize voice types;

acquire knowledge of vocal and instrumental literature;

understand the vocational and avocational aspects of the music program; and

understand the individual performer and his media of performance.

A general music program should: Provide pleasurable

music experiences for all children. Provide experiences
which will eventuate in carry-over community musical organizations; church choir, civic bands, chorus, orchestra,
etc. Provide opportunities for broadened cultural experiences and intellectual growth--give life a pleasurable and
significant meaning. Provide unlimited opportunities for instruction in singing, music reading, theoretical study, rhythmic expression, creative vocal and instrumental expression,
instrumental study, and music appreciation. Provide functional opportunities for complete involvement in music through
all media of musical expression; musical skills must be developed if music is to become a permanent quest for realization of individual happiness. Provide correlative opportunities with every aspect of the academic curriculum.

SUGGESTED UNITS: GRADE 7

1. Percussion Instruments.

2. Instruments of the Band and Orchestra.

3. Music I Know.
   An orientation unit: pupils will share musical experiences they have had before coming to junior high
   school.

4. The Significance of Rhythm in Music. Consider the fol-
   lowing questions:
   What is the meaning of rhythm?
   What is the nature of rhythm? What examples of
      rhythm are there in nature?
   How is rhythm a basic element in music?
   How do composers use rhythm? What is the effect
      upon the listener?
   Are rhythms and styles of music related?
   What does rhythm have to do with tempo?
   What is syncopation? How has it been used in seri-
      ous music? In popular music?

   In arriving at answers to these questions, pupils should:
      play, sing, notate, and create rhythmic patterns;
      isolate rhythmic patterns in song texts and analyze
         their effects upon the songs;
      listen for the rhythmic patterns in recordings;
      learn to use drumsticks as well as other classroom
         instruments;
      report upon observations in out-of-school listening;

build a repertoire of songs and add to their knowledge
and understanding of recordings.

5. The Nature of Music (Elements of Music).

6. Styles in Music.

7. How Music Is Produced (Vocal).

8. Dancing and Music.

GRADE 8

1. Choral Music.
   Opera
   Oratorio

2. Form in Music.

3. Keyboard Instruments Through the Years.

4. Shapes in Music.
   This unit can be effective in helping pupils to direct
   their listening by concentrating attention on short and
   frequently familiar themes; then listening for their
   recurrence or the introduction of contrasting themes.
   A great wealth of material is available and should
   include vocal as well as instrumental music.   For
   example:

   Two-part (AB) Form
      Yankee Doodle
      Brahms' "Cradle Song"
      Minuet from Don Giovanni--Mozart

   Three-part (ABA) Form
      All Through the Night
      Believe Me If All Those Endearing Young Charms
      Show use in "popular" music by playing such
         examples as: "Over the Rainbow, " "Time
         on My Hands, " and "'Till There Was You."

   Five-part Form (extension of three-part form)
      "March, " Love for Three Oranges--Prokofieff
      "Spinning Song"--Mendelssohn

Song Form with Trio
Minuet from "Surprise" Symphony--Haydn
Minuet from "Haffner" Symphony--Mozart

"Group of Parts" Form
"Invitation to the Waltz"--Weber
"Tales from the Vienna Woods"--J. Strauss
"Waltz of the Flowers"--Tschaikowsky

5. Ceremonies and Celebrations in Music.

6. Current Events in Music.

7. Pennsylvania Music and Musicians.

8. History of American Music.

GRADE 9

1. Twentieth Century Music.

2. Tips on Tables (Discs and Tapes).

3. Electronics in Music.

4. Music Makers for the Future (Careers in Music).

5. What Is Jazz?

6. Romanticism in Music.

7. Nationalism in Music.

8. Impressionism in Music.

9. Background Music.

10. Art and Music.

11. Tone Painting in Music.

Plainedge Public Schools, Bethpage, N.Y., General
Music Course. Plainedge public schools employ curriculum
guide lines for junior high school general music which it is
hoped will "find the interest, develop the talent, and bring
to each child a program which will stimulate growth with
music, appreciation of music, and bring about understanding

of what music can contribute to the sheer joy of living."[21] Such objectives, commendable as they may be, can only be attained through the efforts of dedicated administration and teacher services. However, teacher services can be greatly enhanced if their efforts can be reinforced with basic instructional needs.

The Plainedge general music program employs the unit of instruction concept in its structure. The suggested areas for study are as follows:

OUTLINE OF COURSE OFFERINGS

1. Elementary Level

   a) Elementary Vocal--general music appreciation offering.
   b) Recorder--pre-band and pre-orchestra instrument: one half-hour lesson per week.
   c) Instrumental instruction on all band and orchestra instruments--average one 2-hour lesson per week.
   d) Band participation--two 40-minute periods per week.
   e) String Ensemble--two 40-minute periods per week.
   f) Chorus--two 40-minute periods per week.

2. Junior High Level

   a) General music classes--two to three periods a week.
   b) Instrumental instruction on all band and orchestra instruments--one lesson per week on rotating schedule.
   c) Band--three to five periods per week.
   d) Orchestra or string ensemble--two to three periods per week.
   e) Chorus--two to three periods per week.
   f) Special groups (stage bands, choraleers)--one period per week.

3. Senior High Level

   a) Music appreciation offering--five periods per week.
   b) Instrumental instruction on all band and orchestra instruments--one period per week on rotating schedule.
   c) Band--five periods per week.
   d) Stage band--average one period per week.
   e) Marching band--two or three times a week during marching seasons.

    f) Twirling--two periods per week.
    g) String ensemble--five periods a week.
    h) Choir--five periods a week.
    i) Madrigal group--average once a week.
    j) Folk-singing group--once a week.
    k) Theory--five periods a week, or a special class of
        one period a week.
    l) Humanities--five periods a week.

4. District-Wide Music Program

    a) Elementary Chorus.
    b) Elementary Band.
    c) Elementary Orchestra.
    d) Junior Chorus.
    e) Junior/Senior High Band.
    f) Junior/Senior High Orchestra.

5. General Aims and Objectives

    a) Awareness.
    b) Use of leisure time.
    c) Avocations.
    d) Vocations (careers).
    e) Cultural enrichment.
    f) Discriminating taste.
    g) Active participation.
    h) School spirit.
    i) Part of everyday living and community life.

AIMS AND OBJECTIVES (Junior High)

1. To provide opportunities for young people to participate
in musical activities rather than experience them vicari-
ously.

2. To provide youngsters with an appreciation of their musical heritage and an understanding of the music in our
modern world.

3. To provide an awareness and foster sensitivity to sound,
rhythm, lyric poetry, form and style in music through
a study of its history and development.

4. To provide a rudimentary knowledge of the elements of
music that can be utilized on a practical level.

5. To provide youngsters with ample opportunities for developing into responsive and responsible audiences through their experiencing recorded and live perform- ances of musical works and artists deemed to have lasting value and interest for them.

6. To hopefully provide opportunities and demonstrate areas in which music can enrich and augment the learnings going on in other areas of the total curricu- lum through cooperatively developed team teaching proj- ects.

7. To provide integrated experiences with the other arts-- sculpture, painting, graphics, ballet, literature, poetry, and drama--and to show music's relationship to the newer arts of cinema, television, and other electronic media.

8. To utilize and be aware of music's impact on modern youngsters outside the school setting and capitalize on this influence for implementing the general music class's objectives and goals.

9. To provide convincing and meaningful demonstration of music's value, position and status in the world outside the classroom, the school and the immediate community.

10. To recognize the differences in youngsters of unequal talents, abilities, and intelligence as they come to class and to tailor our course offerings so as to keep them meaningful and interesting.

CURRICULUM GUIDELINES (Grade 7)

Reference Text:
"Making Music Your Own"
Silver Burdett, Books 7 & 8

Unit I. The Elements of Music

A. Sounds--Music's Raw Materials (pp. 1-2).
    1. Environmental sounds,
    2. Street cries.
B. Description Through Music (pp. 3-4):
    Selected recordings.
C. Rhythm (p. 6):
    1. Build up a rhythm band-stration in class through elementary notation (p. 100),

 2. Explain the terms: beat, tempo, meter.
 D. Melody:
 Union of pitch and rhythm patterns (pp. 11-12).
 E. Harmony:
  1. Blending of tones, elementary chording (pp. 13-15),
  2. Dissonance and consonance.

Unit II. Instruments Used in Music

 A. Introduction to Families of Instruments (pp. 28-35):
  1. Strings,
  2. Woodwinds,
  3. Brass,
  4. Percussion,
  5. Keyboard and Electronic.
 B. Strings (pp. 88-92):
  1. Sub-families--viols; fretted; harp-like; exotic;
  2. Characteristics of string sounds;
  3. Technical characteristics: vibrato, spiccato, pizzicato, double-stops, etc.;
  4. Live and recorded demonstrations;
  5. Study of string ensembles (quartets, trios, string orchestra, etc.).
 C. Woodwinds (pp. 94-95):
  1. Three types of woodwinds--
   a. Non-reed,
   b. Single reed,
   c. Double reed;
  2. Live and recorded demonstrations of each;
  3. Woodwind ensembles (quintets, etc.).
 D. Brass (pp. 94-95):
  1. Characteristics of each,
  2. Live and recorded demonstrations,
  3. Brass ensembles (quintets, etc.).
 E. Percussion (pp. 97-101):
  1. Description of percussion section in orchestra and band,
  2. Live and recorded examples of individual and group percussion instruments,
  3. Differentiate as to "tuned" and "untuned";
  4. Percussion ensembles (Example--"Ionisation" by Edgard Varèse).
 F. Keyboard and Electronics:
  1. Piano, harpsichord (pp. 84-87)--
   a. Historical background and famous pianists,
   b. Characteristic sounds of each;

　　　2.　Organ--
　　　　　a.　Its uses in church, orchestra and as a solo
　　　　　　　instrument,
　　　　　b.　Recorded examples;
　　　3.　Accordion, concertina, and other "squeeze-boxes";
　　　4.　Electronics--
　　　　　a.　Electronic tone filtering (pp. 23-24),
　　　　　b.　Building and overtone series,
　　　　　c.　Some details about the Moog synthesizer.
　G.　Instrumental Ensembles:
　　　1.　What is an orchestra?
　　　2.　What is a band?
　　　3.　What is the function of a conductor?
　　　4.　Study "A Young Person's Guide to the Orchestra"
　　　　　by Benjamin Britten; Use of theme, variations and
　　　　　fugue;
　　　5.　Demonstration of concert band sound "American
　　　　　Salute" by Morton Gould.
　H.　Team teaching between teachers of chorus, band, or-
　　　chestra, as well as arts, literature (plays and poems),
　　　phys. ed. (eurhythmics), general science (properties
　　　of sound transmission), and others.

　　　　　　CURRICULUM GUIDELINES (Grade 8)

　　　　　　　　Reference Text:
　　　　　　　　"Making Music Your Own"
　　　　　　　　Silver Burdett, Books 7 & 8

Unit I.　The Elements and Development of American Jazz*
　　　　　(pp. 18-29)

　A.　Elements of Jazz:
　　　1.　Syncopation--
　　　　　a.　Definition and examples of,
　　　　　b.　Classroom rhythm activities with syncopation;
　　　2.　Blue Notes--
　　　　　Same procedures as above;
　　　3.　Timbre--
　　　　　Same as above.
　B.　Early Jazz Styles:
　　　1.　Ragtime, Dixieland, blues,
　　　2.　Recorded examples of each.
　C.　Later Jazz Styles:
　　　1.　Boogie-Woogie, be-bop, cool jazz, progressive,

―――――――――
*used concurrently with "Jazz," Folkways Records, vols. 1-6.

    2.   Recorded examples of each,
    3.   The big band era and the era of swing,
    4.   Recorded examples and popular songs of these
        eras.
  D. Improvisation as a Tool in Jazz:
      Use procedures as in Book 8 (pp. 20-21).
  E. The Birth and Rise of Rock and Roll:
    1.   First phase (1955-1960)--
        Presley, Ricky Nelson,
        Country, hymn, and jazz combined in folk styles,
        Emphasis on single star with guitar;
    2.   Second phase (1962-present)--
        The Rise of the Rock Group (British Imports),
        (The Beatles, Dave Clark Five, etc.);
    3.   The new "folk" rock--
        Rock as a "social commentator," its use in
          protest songs, civil rights songs, and the new
          anti-war sentiment,
        Exponents of "folk" rock:
        Peter, Paul and Mary
        Bob Dylan
        Simon and Garfunkel
        Joan Baez, etc.

     Cincinnati Public School General Music Course. Pupils in the Cincinnati public schools have the opportunity to enjoy and participate in music throughout all grades from kindergarten through the 12th grade. Junior high school pupils in their schools are required to study music for one year; this year being spent in general or instrumental music. The remaining music experiences in junior and senior high school are selected on an elective basis. The junior high school program offers elective opportunities in choir, general music, band, or orchestra. More broadened opportunities are available in senior high school. They include boys' glee club, girls' glee club, mixed chorus, choir, music appreciation, music theory and harmony, junior orchestra, orchestra, and junior band or band.

     Elective music is available in grades 9 through 12 which carries credit toward graduation; the supervisor may approve the application of college level work toward high school graduation.

     The general music course emphasizes five areas of study: 1) melody, 2) harmony, 3) tempo, 4) rhythm, and 5) dynamics. Preliminary to their study would be a review

of basic understandings relative to the keyboard, the clef
signs, the chromatic signs, note and rest values, and pitch
relationships relative to scale degrees, and chromatics in
major and minor modes.

Melody.   Melodic discussion would include many aspects of scales (Major and Minor) and the influence of chromatics, tonal tendencies, and intervals and clef study.

Harmony.   Harmonic study would include chording
and a study of tonality.

Tempo.   This includes a study of dynamics and nuances within a general understanding of tempo.

Rhythm.   A practical and individual relevancy to a
child's background and understanding is very important.
Technical learning and its mastery must be reinforced by
relevant applications.   Rhythm must be experienced, therefore the individual must become personally involved through
his personal expression of it.   A variety of rhythmic activities are suggested for a general music program in grades 7
and 8.

Dynamics.   Suggested study and interpretation of dynamics and nuances includes such topics as: 1) forceful
changes in tempi, 2) concern for metronomic accuracy, 3)
use of appropriate tempi, 4) demonstration by teacher of appropriate conductoral movements and baton extensity, 5) ju-
dicious usage of dynamics and tempi meanings, and the employment of the necessary media to demonstrate all aspects
of dynamics, tempi and nuances.[22]

Techniques for Running Music Courses.   General music courses are frequently sought after by students seeking
a "snap" course.   The academic challenge of these courses
is sometimes criticized for being devoid of scholarship.   Offering credit for the course is an attractive recruitment gim-
mick, although the credit is not generally recognized for college entrance.   Frequently, students who have not been successful academically or who have registered no interest in
extra-academic offerings are "signed-up" for general music
courses.   Then too, students who are in need of an elective
music course are usually urged to take a general music
course.   Too often the course is but a duplication and continuation of a given school system's anemic elementary music program. Boredom from lack of musical challenge often

causes the uninterested student to drop the course. Course drop-outs occasionally run as high as 50 per cent during a given semester in inner city schools.

Frequently classes are too large. Instructional success depends upon small teacher-pupil ratios. Lecture sections can be larger. Enrollments beyond 35 limit the amount of individualized instruction. A chorus class cannot be considered a general music course!

Also, sometimes the equipment is inadequate and insufficient in kind (piano, guitar, banjo, autoharp, etc.). Teaching materials are usually inadequate and classes are often conducted in non-musical lecture environments (band, choir, and orchestra rooms).

General music classes are generally more successfully taught when the unit or area of instructional subject matter is devoted to a wide spectrum of interesting creative activities. The general music teacher must be imaginative, resourceful, and able to adjust her instructional techniques to each student. Every student should find ample opportunities for becoming involved.

No unit of work should require that every student participate in the same activity. The teacher should let every student express interest areas of study which are appealing to him. Student involvement is more likely to stimulate better learning. The teacher should coordinate all interests toward a common objective. Such an approach always appeals to individual differences.

If a unit is to appeal to students with limited musical background it must not include lengthy meaningless objectives and euphemisms which do not get students actively involved in music. It must provide units for study conceived by the students and include programs which are constructed around student interests. Teacher-student coordinated effort should aid in developing the focusses for unit learning. And also it must eliminate undue amounts of discussion and include more functional musical experiences. Some of the specific instructional areas might include:

Keyboard skills	Mexican-American music
Orchestra instruments	Afro-American music
Films	Puerto-Rican music
Tapes	Country/Western music

Film strips	Rudiments of music
Folk songs	African/Caribbean drum music
Ethnic music	Guitar and banjo playing.

Unit Evaluation. Each unit of study should be evaluated by the following criteria: 1) Did the children become ethnically, functionally, and culturally identified with the music? 2) Did the theoretical and functional participative aspects of music study provide sufficient academic stature for their course work? 3) Were the organizational details of the unit successfully administered? 4) Did the unit incorporate a well-rounded program of music studies?

Frequently elementary and junior high school music programs are too loosely coordinated and organized. These programs must help children to experience joyful music. Musical enjoyment breeds participation and a desire to further continue experiencing music.

Sample Unit. Let us venture into an 8th-grade room which was enjoying a music lesson mid-way in a four-week unit on Stephen Foster. The room was seething with activity. Apparently, groups of students had been assigned to various phases of the project, the prime objective being to bring together for study purposes many important aspects of Foster's life and musical creativity. Simultaneously, the following activities were being pursued for bringing about a realization of the project called "Fosteriana": 1) In one section of the room some of the singers were practicing around the piano. They were rehearsing "Old Black Joe." 2) A group of students were busy making scenery to become a part of the stage properties when the project was to be presented before the entire elementary school student body. 3) Another group of students were making costumes to be worn by the principle soloists. 4) In an adjacent room the soloist who was to sing "Old Black Joe" was being rehearsed by a music teacher. 5) Outside of the classroom a boy and a girl were in the process of painting a mural on the wall of some of the events in the life of Foster. This mural when finished was approximately 40 feet long. 6) There were some other students working on the script that was to be used in connection with the presentation of the performance.

Now, it is not to be construed that this is necessarily a music lesson. It is a unit, or project. It indicates a variation to the often witnessed stereotyped and even monotonous music lesson. Naturally, prior to witnessing this

project in action, there had been many preparatory lessons
in attaining what was about to be realized--a performance.
Such a project takes considerable instructional time, especially when there are but one or two rehearsals per week.   A
special advantage in pursuing a unit of work is that talented
individuals can be devoting outside work to their particular
assigned task.

What we saw was a room in which music, art, dra-
matics, stage design, and its craftsmanship were finding creative expression.   Most important was the opportunity for expressed imagination according to individual interests.   When
the performance of the project took place it is reasonable to
assume that every individual was vitally appreciative of the
part he played in bringing about its consummation.   We believe this illustration serves as an excellent example of creativity at its functional best.

Notes

1.   Knuth, William E.   "General Music for the General
     High School Student."   California Journal of Second-
     ary Education, 30: No. 4 (April, 1955).

2.   "Music Education in the Secondary Schools."   Reprinted
     from the Music Education Source Book, Music Educa-
     tors National Conference.   (Washington, D.C.:   Mu-
     sic Educators National Conference, 1951), 5.

3.   "The Function of Music in the Secondary-School Curric-
     ulum."   Reprint edition of The Bulletin (November
     1952) of the National Association of Secondary-School
     Principals, a department of the National Education
     Association.   Prepared by the Committee(s) on Music
     in the Senior (and Junior) High School Curriculum.
     Chicago: Music Educators National Conference, 1952,
     21.

4.   Ibid., 21-22.

5.   Knuth, William E.   "General Music For the General
     High School Student."   op. cit., 224-225.

6.   Letter from Thomas J. Clune, Director of Vocal Music
     City School District, Binghamton, New York, Febru-
     ary 6, 1958.

7. Horn, Francis H. "Music for Everyone," Music Educa-
    tors Journal, 42: No. 4 (February-March, 1956),
    27.

8. Ibid., 27.

9. "We Recommend; Excerpts from the Resolutions Adopted
    at the 1955 Division Conventions of the Music Educa-
    tors National Conference," Music Educators Journal,
    42: No. 1 (September-October, 1955), 20.

10. Ibid.

11. Barr, E. Lawrence. "Music Teaching in the Secondary
    Schools," Music Educators Journal, 41: No. 2
    (November-December, 1954), 38.

12. Bradley, Jane Wickson. "Eighth Grade Singing; Is it
    Fun? Music Educators Journal, 51: No. 6 (June-
    July, 1965), 49, 50, 52.

13. "A Teachers' Guide for Junior High School Vocal Mu-
    sic." Cleveland: Division of Music, Cleveland Pub-
    lic Schools, 1966, 7, 10-11, 14, 17, 21-26, 33, 39,
    40. Permission of excerpted material granted for
    use by the Music Division, Cleveland Public Schools,
    Paul W. Briggs, Superintendent. The supervisor of
    Junior High Vocal Music is Helen N. Socolofsky.

14. Ibid., 10, 11, 14.

15. "Seventh Grade General Curriculum Guide." Ann Ar-
    bor, Mich.: Ann Arbor Public Schools, 1964, 5-9.
    Guide developed by Peter Johnson, Catherine Ann
    Cook, and Thomas B. Johnson. Used with the per-
    mission of the Ann Arbor Public Schools, Lew J.
    Wallace, coordinator of music.

16. Ibid., "Seventh Grade General Music Curriculum Guide."

17. "General Music 7 & 8. The School District of the City
    of Erie, Pa." A Working Paper, 1970-71, 1-14.
    Permission to use granted by Carl J. Peterson,
    coordinator, Department of Music Education, Erie,
    Pa.

18. Ibid., 15.

19. "General Music Course of Study, Junior High School."
    Maumee, Ohio: Maumee Public Schools, 1971, 12-
    15. Permission to use granted by J. H. Morin,
    Chairman, Department of Music.

20. "Music Curriculum Services, No. 15." Harrisburg,
    Pa.: Commonwealth of Pennsylvania Department of
    Public Instruction, 1963, 15-17. Permission granted
    by Pennsylvania State Department of Education, Rus-
    sell P. Getz, coordinator of fine arts.

21. "General Music Aims and Objectives--Course of Study,
    1970-1971." Bethpage, N.Y.: Plainedge Public
    Schools, 2-5, 9-10. Permission to use granted by
    Anthony J. Messina, district director of music.

22. "Vocal Music," Curriculum Bulletin 60. Grades 7-12.
    Cincinnati Public Schools, 1967, 125-140.

CHAPTER IX: THE SENIOR HIGH SCHOOL

Music has established a permanent place for itself in the curriculum of the secondary school, because music can aid in the cultural development of the individual. Critics of school music point to the lack of the carry-over of music into adult living.

While mass music education does not guarantee the continued exploration of each individual's abilities, there is evidence that education can upgrade the intellectual level of the average person.

The perfectionist concept of music education which characterized much school music education during the period 1925-1941 seemingly emphasized performance at the expense of music education for every individual regardless of his talent. This perfectionist concept was more common among secondary than elementary school music educators. Winning a contest was sometimes more important than building a good music program for every individual in the school system. However, during this same period there were some music educators who were convinced that the contest idea, as then conceived was educationally wrong. These educators believed in attainment based on growth--attainment for individuals in proportion to their ability. Since the inauguration of the Frank A. Beach rating plan (the "Kansas Plan": superior-- I, excellent--II, good--III, average--IV, and below average-- V) for adjudicating contests, a great expansion of the competition-festival idea has taken place.

The great success of competitive sports may be largely attributed to the pleasure the individual derives from being able to display specialized skill. In music, impeccable performance is often emphasized at the expense of pleasure from the participation itself.

Our philosophy of individual and mass music education emphasizes the importance of excellent training for the gifted individual. This stress on training individual differences creates greater opportunity for both the gifted and the

211

less gifted because each is provided opportunity to experience
music in proportion to his ability. A music program must
be relaxing and creatively satisfying. Relaxation is induced
by enjoyment and opportunity for freedom of expression.
American music educators have available the talent, equipment, and financial resources to develop intelligently conceived programs of music education.

Functions of a Secondary School Music Program.
There are three major considerations in the formulation of
the secondary school music program: 1) a curriculum that
makes the individual the center of concern; 2) opportunity for
individual achievement; and 3) permission for each individual
to express his innate musical ability.

The challenge to secondary music education is to develop a positive all-inclusive program for every child. Wilson[1] visualizes for us this program for the secondary school
when she suggests 11 significant aims:

1. To increase the enjoyment of present musical experi-
    ences.
2. To stimulate the desire for more and richer musical
    experiences.
3. To foster a sensitivity to the beauty of music.
4. To increase a sense of power in understanding music
    and in realizing its essential meaning.
5. To increase a sense of familiarity with music and
    thereby prevent the development of an inferiority feel-
    ing in regard to this art.
6. To promote a freedom of response, both intellectual
    and emotional, to the aesthetic content of music.
7. To increase the desire for good, sincere, and artistic
    music and a distaste for poor music.
8. To develop a sensitivity to tone color, both in har-
    mony and instrumentation.
9. To foster habits of listening to music so that recogni-
    tion of specific features will become automatic and not
    interfere with the response to the inherent beauty of
    the music.
10. To arouse intellectual curiosity concerning music, the
    way it is made, the people who make it, and the sig-
    nificant characteristics of various styles and types of
    music.
11. To promote growth of knowledge concerning composers,
    performers, instruments, types of voices, etc.

These aims have been amplified by the Committee(s) on Music in the Senior (and Junior) High School Curriculum of the Music Educators National Conference.[2] They are as follows:

1. Music education gives young people the opportunity to find a richer life through music, to guide students into a better understanding of, and love for music, to teach the pupil through music. It emphasizes the values of human living. It assists in developing an integrated person who may take his rightful place in the world in which he lives. Music may be his career, his hobby, his recreation, or simply another experience in his life.

2. Music education offers activities and studies which tend to develop the social aspects of life. Group activities in music in both junior and senior high schools offer some of the most effective ways of developing cooperation, discipline, personal initiative, individual responsibility, and fellowship.

3. Music education contributes to the health of the student through the development of correct posture, rhythmical deep breathing, voice hygiene, and other social habits. It also contributes to the mental and emotional health which is known to respond to the stimulus of music.

4. Music education aims to develop good work habits. It demands and encourages discipline.

5. Music education aims to develop wholesome ideals of conduct.

6. Music education contributes to the development of citizenship by helping to produce an integrated personality; by giving students an opportunity to experience the democratic way of life which music groups demand; by teaching love of country, pride in its achievements, knowledge of its history, dedication to its improvement, hope for its future, and neighborly regard for the people of other lands through their music.

7. Music education contributes to home life by encouraging the pupils to take their music to their homes.

8. Music education aims to contribute to recreation and to the fun of living.

9. Music education aims to discover talent. In discovering an art, the pupil comes to discover himself also.

10. Music education in the secondary schools affords a foundation for vocational training for all pupils whose interest and aptitude warrant their preparation for a professional career in some phase of music.

The broad functions of the program would be of considerable help. These have been expressed by Barr:

> The great responsibility of the Junior and Senior High School music program is to provide enjoyable musical experiences and to foster cultural growth through: (1) thorough reexploration of the broad area of music itself; (2) relating music to the cultural experiences within other subject areas; (3) allowing music to play a leading role in the creative and social development of the individual student.[3]

This program would necessitate scheduling general music in addition to the elective performance and theory music program throughout the school year. General music should be required two or more periods weekly in grades 7 and 8, and should be offered at least on an elective basis in grades 9 through 12.

Also needed would be provision for integrative experiences within and in addition to the singing, listening, playing experiences of the general music class. This includes the recognition of music's place in daily living, its importance in the cultural history of all peoples, and its emotional impact upon the individual.

And finally, scheduling extensive elective performance opportunities for the musically interested and gifted would be necessary. For many students the activities of elective choral and instrumental groups are the most challenging and satisfying experiences in their school lives--experiences which later carry over directly and indirectly into adult living. Activity groups of this type should meet frequently and be open to as many young people as possible.[4]

The Junior and Senior High School Music Program. The administrator and music educator will do well to evaluate the following suggested organizational considerations in planning the junior-senior high school programs designed for the non-organized, non-specialist teacher, the organized specialist, and the organized program for larger schools. No attempt is made to discuss the number of class periods per day, the amount of credit, nor the facilities that may be available to implement the suggestions.

NON-ORGANIZED NON-SPECIALIST: Many fine programs have developed from activities in schools which have no organized music and music teachers who are not specialists.

1. They can include recreational singing suitable to the needs and local background of the pupils, keeping in mind the broader cultural and aesthetic aspects of music.

2. They can encourage pupils toward individual growth and performance both in and out of school. The person directing the music activities should (a) furnish performance outlets; (b) assume leadership in working with interested pupils; (c) encourage other teachers and adults to participate in working informally with groups and individuals; (d) bring outside musicians to help in school programs if necessary and possible; (e) promote group listening to records and to radio and television; (f) use motion pictures; (g) encourage attendance at local music events.

ORGANIZED SPECIALIST (Small School): A proportionately large percentage of the entire student body must be encouraged to enroll in music groups if these groups are to be successful.

1. It will be necessary to secure the interest of the pupils in music. The personal promotion of music by the teacher with the assistance of the principal through school assemblies is the best way to reach all the pupils. Then it is advisable to arrange for personal contact by the teacher with each individual pupil to discover his interests, his abilities, his time limitations and to attempt to fit the program to the teacher load, the rooms and equipment available, the entire school program as well as the needs of the pupils.

2. A required general music course to discover ability, aptitudes, and interests is a good beginning in planning a music program. Subsequently, only first-year and new pupils need be required to take the course. In small schools, this general course may include other arts, thereby extending its usefulness as an exploratory course.

3. The minimum activities to assure participation and to allow for development in such a program should be (a) assembly singing for all the pupils; (b) instrumental and choral performance groups; (c) general music appreciation classes for the pupils who do not wish to be in the performance groups or who are not able to be included in those groups.

4. In order to sustain a music program, the teaching must be inspiring and good, and material must be suitable to the ability and interests of the group, and music should be recognized by the principal as an essential part of the entire school program.

5. Since performance motivates a music program both for the performers and for the listeners, performances which grow out of class procedure should be provided to enrich the musical experiences of the music groups, of the other pupils in the school and of the community.

ORGANIZED SPECIALIST (Large School): Assuming an adequate staff of music teachers, a sufficient number of music classrooms, adequate equipment and material, and a flexible enough program schedule, a good program can be developed along several lines:

1. A general music course, which qualifies for its value for general educational purposes as well as for its orientation in the field of the arts, should be offered to all pupils regardless of previous experience in music. This course may be required in the 9th or 10th grade. It can be the backbone of the music education program.

2. Assembly music which employs well-developed assembly singing toward the end of participation for all and which also uses the various performing groups and individuals to bring interesting and rich

musical experiences to the entire school is an asset to the school, the student body, and most assuredly to the music education program. There is no better way to interest pupils in a music program than by planning for all pupils to become a part of the existing program either in the capacity of performers or listeners. Thus the assembly program can be a vital part, in any school, of the over-all music program. However, the assembly program must be a good one planned for the needs and local background of the pupils--one in which the development toward the appreciation of the best which music has to offer is kept in mind.

3. Performing groups may be set up on a broader base to reach all who are interested in singing or playing. These groups should have the opportunity for advancement by levels so that the pupils in the school can pace themselves by others of equal ability and experience. The more sections available in a school program, the easier it is to make a satisfactory individual program. The following observations may be helpful in planning a music education program: (a) school groups, large and small, should be available to suit the experiences of any pupil who wishes to enroll; (b) instrumental groups, from the smallest ensemble to the symphony orchestra and concert band, should be provided; (c) choruses, choirs, glee clubs, and small vocal ensembles should be available; (d) combination of instrumental and choral groups in performance should be encouraged; (e) high standards of performance should be maintained; (f) solo performance should be encouraged.

4. Music appreciation classes should be offered to pupils because a large number of these boys and girls will be the listeners, the audience, the patrons, the consumers of music throughout their lives. These classes should be enrichment courses, opening the door to musical experiences and, through music, to human experience and human relations.

5. Theory, harmony, and composition courses may be offered to particularly interested and talented pupils. These should be elective courses, which may

not appeal to the average boy or girl as much as
music appreciation and performance courses, but
should be required of music majors.

6. Individual and group lessons in piano, orchestral
    and band instruments, and voice are desirable ei-
    ther from private teachers properly approved by
    school authorities or in school.

7. Music clubs which are means of motivating per-
    formance or music study are excellent extracurric-
    ular activities.

Areas of Instruction. Out of the many aims and
broader functions of secondary music education there have
developed some larger areas of instruction which have come
to be fundamental in constructing junior and senior high
school music curricula.

Recommendations proposed by the Music Educators
National Conference at the request of the North Central Association of Colleges and Secondary Schools, and adopted in
1951, outlined the following instructional program in music
for secondary schools.

JUNIOR HIGH SCHOOL

(1) General Music Course: open to all students regardless of previous musical experience. A course offering
a variety of musical activities such as playing, singing, listening, reading music, creative activity, etc.

(2) Vocal Music: boys' and girls' glee clubs, chorus
or choir, small vocal ensembles, assembly singing for all
students.

(3) Instrumental Music: orchestra, band, small instrumental ensembles, class instrumental instruction, wind,
string and keyboard, for beginners and more advanced students, applied music study for credit available in grade 9.

(4) Special Electives in Music: in some junior high
schools there is need for special elective classes in music
appreciation and in music theory, especially in grade 9.

SENIOR HIGH SCHOOL

(1) Vocal Music: boys' and girls' glee clubs, chorus,

choir, small vocal ensembles, voice classes, applied music
credit for private lessons. Some of the large choral groups
selective and others open for election by any interested student, unless the school is too small to allow for more than
one group.

(2) General Music: open to all students, regardless
of previous musical experience. A course similar to that
described above under junior high school, but adjusted in its
content to senior high school interests and needs.

(3) Instrumental Music: orchestra, band, small ensembles, class instrumental instruction, wind, string, percussion and keyboard for beginning and advanced students,
dance band. Orchestra and band should be divided into beginning and advanced sections, or first and second groups,
if the enrollment warrants such division.

(4) Elective Course Offerings: music theory, music
appreciation, music history. Many high schools find it feasible to offer several years of instruction in each of these
fields. [5]

FOR ALL STUDENTS

(1) Assembly Programs: music programs with singing by all the students, the appearance of school musical organizations, and the appearance of outside artists.

(2) Recitals and Concerts: student performers.

(3) Educational Concerts.

(4) Music Clubs: clubs devoted to those interested in
certain phases of music study or related areas--Record Collectors' Club, Conducting Club, Folk Dance Club, Recorder
Club, etc. [6]

School and music administrators should broaden the
secondary school curriculum to include a general music program. They must set forth a philosophy of general music
education that will provide functional music studies for every
secondary school child. The individual must learn those
tools which will give him the power of rediscovering music
as a functional medium for his personal use and enjoyment.

General Objectives of High School Vocal Music. 1. To

provide satisfying musical experiences conducive to student
growth in music theory, techniques, appreciation, creativity
and general excellence in performance both within and without the school, in the church and home, in the community,
and in competitive and cooperative activities between schools
and communities for all enrolled students according to their
ability, talent and prior orientation; 2. to develop discrimina-
tory taste in students concerning music as an art form; and
3. to meet the needs of the individual student and to help
him to achieve the limits of his capacity, mentally, spir-
itually and emotionally.

Also, 4. to cause music, other forms of art and related subjects of the school curriculum to become more
meaningful through intelligent correlation and integration;
5. to foster the growth of democratic principles; 6. to establish further a desire for musical expression, esthetic as
well as functional, which will continue through the years as
an asset to the community in which the student may make
his future home; and 7. to aid in setting the stage for a
well-balanced, ordered and emotionally stable life through
music in later years. [7]

VOCAL MUSIC ACTIVITIES

Small Groups	Large Groups	Classes
Solos	Mixed Choruses	General Music
Duets	A Cappella Choirs	History/Apprecia-
Trios	Boys' and Girls'	tion
Quartets	Glee Clubs	Elementary Theory
Sextettes	Madrigal Groups	Sight-Singing
Triple Trios	Select Perform-	Ear Training
Other Ensembles.	ance Groups,	Vocal Training
	Cantatas, Oper-	Conducting
	ettas, etc.	Composition/Ar-
		ranging.

High school students especially college preparatory
students, who are enrolled in the vocal music program
should achieve the highest development of skills, techniques
and performance experiences commensurate with their readiness and emotional maturity. They should be familiarized
with the fundamentals of theory, history and appreciation,
sight-singing and ear training, good vocal production and
have some acquaintance with the piano.

Suggested Scheduling[7]

HIGH SCHOOL VOCAL MUSIC

A minimum of two to five 45-minute periods weekly for mixed chorus or a cappella choir.

A minimum of one to two 45-minute periods weekly for glee clubs.

A minimum of one 45-minute period weekly for ensembles and other small vocal groups.

Added class activities may be scheduled at the discretion of the supervisor and executive head of the school.

HIGH SCHOOL INSTRUMENTAL MUSIC

A minimum of two to five 45-minute periods weekly for orchestra and/or band.

A minimum of one 45-minute period weekly for solos and/or ensembles.

A minimum of one 45-minute period weekly for instrumental choirs, special performance groups and novelty organizations.

A minimum of one 45-minute period weekly for string orchestra.

Added class activities may be scheduled at the discretion of the music instructor and executive head of the school.

Scheduling[7] requires the cooperative effort of the school administration and the music staff. The great expansion of academic and extracurricular activities has thrust upon both those responsible for arranging schedules and the student himself the problem of choosing those subjects which will provide the best possible education. Providing a broadened music education program has been made somewhat difficult because of the tendency to reduce the number of class periods in the school day from seven or eight, to five or six. As the number of class periods per day decreases, the problems associated with scheduling classes increases.

Scheduling Problems in a Small High School. The size of the student body predetermines the amount of talent that will be available for the major music organizations. In the small school the talented student must be used in many organizations. This dependence upon a few students for the success of many organizations does not always lead to happy student-teacher relations, and competition for the same talented few develops.

High School Vocal Music Chart[7]

OBJECTIVES	ACTIVITIES	MATERIALS	EVALUATIONS
To make music a wholesome, vital, sharing experience between students and their classmates, and community and the home and church.	High school mixed chorus, a cappella choir and glee clubs; vocal ensembles and solos.	Choice octavo music, secular and sacred, accompanied and unaccompanied. Seasonal literature and music selected for special events.	Is there a planned program for the year whereby the various vocal groups may be heard outside of school as well as in important school functions?
To acquaint students with the great music literature of all time, developing a keener sense of discrimination and evaluative appreciation of the esthetic appeal of the art for later years.	General music classes, history and appreciation classes. Mixed chorus and a cappella choir, ensembles and solos.	Selected octavo music. Cantatas and oratorios of the masters. Good contemporary literature, sacred and secular. Music from noted operas and operettas.	Are the students aware of the great and lasting values of good music? Do they indicate broadening horizons in the appreciation of all music literature?
To extend and improve the students' ability to perform music of greater difficulty, with corresponding increases in the knowledge and command of vocal and choral tech-niques, music theory and	High school mixed chorus, a cappella choir and glee clubs; ensembles and solos.	Progressive introduction of music of a higher degree of difficulty, both harmonic and contrapuntal in form. Motets, madrigals, chorales, folk songs in addition to mate-rials mentioned above.	Is vocal independence assured? Is the performance level artistic, accurate and inspired? Are the students capable of sight reading? Are they cognizant of music signs, terms and artistry?

...ented, and to encourage the average student to participate to his fullest capacity.	theory, history and appreciation, and voice classes on the high school level. General music classes.	plies; selected supplementary texts and compilations of song material suitable for class instruction.	and filled?
To pave the way for continued growth in music.	As listed above.	As listed above.	Is interest in and love of music firmly implanted in the lives of the students?
To correlate and integrate vocal and instrumental music literature with allied subjects in the school curriculum, both in the singing and listening activities of the students.	General music classes; history and appreciation classes.	Audio-visual aids; planned unit-project studies in conjunction with associated subjects of the curriculum.	Do the students discern the contribution of music to the history of Man, and the history of Man's contribution to musical literature?
To heighten motivation by competitive and cooperative events between schools and communities.	County, district and state competitions and festivals.	As listed above. Selections from official lists for competitions and festivals.	Are students encouraged to greater effort by contact with others of similar interests?
To inspire better group consciousness, cooperation, tolerance and social attitudes through music.	As listed above.	As listed above.	Is there a defined unity of purpose, a sense of fairness, a display of equal opportunity for all?

Scheduling is easier when cooperative administrative and faculty action results in an understanding of each other's problems. The creation of an activities council is usually helpful in bringing this about. The council can work out a master schedule to reduce conflicts.

A music program constructed within a five or six class period day is constantly vying with other offerings for schedule time and for a sufficient number of students in order to assure a measure of success. Those students who desire to carry five academic subjects obviously do not have time during the regular school day to participate in many extra-curricular music offerings. When a student must stay after school or attend evening music classes he is being penalized by the extension of the school day. The dominant force insuring enrollment in music activities is the functional character of music study and the strong personality of the music educator. Moreover, experience shows that after-school music courses in the smaller high schools may become professionally frustrating and disappointing. The part time student's chance for music study is equalized, if he may secure music instruction during the regularly scheduled school day.

School systems which transport a considerable portion of their student body find that when the bus leaves, all children, including those interested in music, are required to leave the school building at one time. In the small school system, the limited number of students, the hauling of students from widespread areas, and the tendency to reduce the class day have done much to affect the growth and quality of school music.

Leeder and Haynie[8] suggest that there are some important considerations in scheduling music courses for the small high school (100-350 students):

1. Students should indicate desired courses well in advance of the opening of school each year. Preliminary registration can be planned at the close of each school year to determine what courses students intend to take the following school year.

2. The principal should have the names of all music students before individual schedules are made.

3. Schools which have to alternate courses from year to

year, such as physics and chemistry or geometry and
trigonometry, should keep the schedule stable, so that
students can make definite plans well in advance.

4. The major music courses, such as band, orchestra,
   and chorus, should not be scheduled to conflict with
   any one-section classes. For example, the band
   should not be scheduled the second period if a one-
   sectioned required English course is offered at the
   same time.

5. Do not overlook the possibility that before-school and
   after-school time for certain music activities, Operettas, festival programs, and special ensembles might
   require rehearsal time which cannot be scheduled during the regular school day.

6. By special arrangement between the principal and the
   music director, individual students can often be scheduled for private lessons or extra help during study
   hall periods.

It is clear that the student carrying a full academic
load and who registers for participation in major music organizations may have little time for general music courses.

Lickey believes that he has a partial solution to the
problem of scheduling a music program in a small or mid-
dle-sized high school. He offers helpful suggestions for
principals and music directors who desire an effective program with a minimum of scheduling conflicts. It is believed
that each student should be able to secure, if he desires, a
variety of music experiences. Consideration is given to student interests in band, chorus, glee club, and orchestra.

Let the orchestra alternate with band the same period
every other day. First semester, during the football season,
let band meet three periods a week and orchestra twice; second semester, during the concert season, let orchestra meet
three times and band twice. Give the orchestra indoor
events such as plays and commencement. Give the band
outdoor events and its share of indoor concerts.

We find that the majority of players want to be in
both organizations. String players can quickly learn to double on band instruments and the surplus band players on
strings. This plan gives students a broader participation

with little loss of quality in their band or orchestra.

Mixed chorus can be scheduled in the remaining two and one-half periods per week. As many as three sections of girls' glee club and two sections of boys' glee club may then be staggered during other periods. In this way it is possible for a pupil to belong to any three of the four major organizations--band, orchestra, chorus, or glee club.[9]

"If school-bus schedules will permit, chorus can meet before school, making all four groups available. A course in fundamentals also may be scheduled like any other elective academic course."[10]

The ramifications of Lickey's suggestions include four "simple" points:

1.   Keep the orchestra, band, and chorus periods free of one-section classes as far as possible. Place in these periods only those one-section classes that seem to draw few musicians (as shop or agriculture).
2.   Obtain from the music director the names of music pupils before making individual schedules.
3.   Keep the schedule stable from year to year for a wider choice. For example, if speech and physics are the same period, a pupil could take speech the eleventh year and physics the twelfth.
4.   Ensembles can sometimes be scheduled in the same day, if members belong to the same class. Most ensembles, however, must get together after school hours. We have what we call neighborhood ensembles.

Lickey concludes that "it takes a director and principal who want a balanced program."[11]   Rafferty and Michael draw the same conclusion by stating that

> The principal and the music staff must agree as
> to the total school program and plan ways of pro-
> viding those extensive and varied opportunities in
> the daily schedule that will make the program ef-
> fective.[12]

Scheduling music courses in the large senior high school is somewhat easier because: (1) the large high school permits multiple sections of academic courses and the student is thereby permitted a choice of class periods; (2) a wide variety of music courses may be offered because of the

increase in the flexibility of the class schedules; (3) the
larger high school will usually employ more music teachers,
thereby permitting greater freedom in scheduling.

If the principal of the high school and the music staff
conceive a varied program of music course and organizational
offerings all for the students, it is possible in a large high
school to schedule a reasonably satisfactory program. However, it is imperative that there be agreement on basic objectives and a plan for achieving them during the regular
school day.

> Arranging a satisfactory schedule is a major test
> of administrative competence, demanding a great
> deal of time and effort and the cooperation of the
> staff. The scheduling of music classes and activities requires particular skill because of the large
> percent of the student-body involved, and because
> music is usually elective. [13]

Credits in Music. [7] High school students enrolled and
actively participating in musical organizations and classes
under the direct supervision of the school music instructor
are eligible for credit. They are permitted to use a maximum of two units of credit toward graduation. Fractional
credits earned by students may be combined to meet state
requirements.

Any organization or class which meets five days per
week without formal outside assignments will credit the student with a maximum of one-half unit.
Any organization or class which meets five days per
week with the inclusion of outside preparation daily will credit the student with a maximum of one unit.
Any organization or class which meets at least two or
three days per week will credit the student with a maximum
of one-quarter unit, providing that no outside assignments
are given by the instructor.
Any organization or class which meets three days per
week with outside assignments will credit the student with a
maximum of one-half unit.
Any organization or class which meets one day per
week with or without assignments will credit the student with
one-eighth unit.

NOTE: no units of credit contributing to the student's
graduation can be earned by attending instructional meetings

outside of school hours or during the summer months. However, unexcused absence from evening or out-of-school hours performances and activities may be reflected in the final awarding of units of credit.

The General High School Assembly. One of the most important assignments of the school music director is the general school assembly programs. Assemblies can serve to integrate the school program. All forms of classroom teaching experiments could be brought to the attention of the entire assemblage. These programs should broaden student interests.

The assembly sing is one area of music that encourages total student participation. He who directs the sing must see to it that the students enjoy the experience. He must have a voice of good quality, and know how to elicit results in the shortest possible time. His selection of songs and the devices he uses for gaining student interest must intrigue the assemblage into participation.

Those who conduct the assembly sing usually employ many methods for conveying to the audience the music and words of the songs. Seating conditions and the extent of the organizational procedures used in conducting these sings very often predetermine whether or not song books, song sheets, or song-word slides would be effective. The choice of the songs will largely determine whether or not visual aids are to be used.

Among the many techniques that help to achieve success of assembly sings is the use of the individuals, small ensembles, or large musical organizations. They can help to bring variety to the program. The major objective is audience singing and activities that involve many students; student participation must be emphasized.

Private Study for High School Credit. Private music study under the instruction of a teacher not employed by the Board of Education is common. Effective administration of this phase of a student's music study is essential if he is to receive credit for work done outside the high school. Among the many considerations, the following need scrutiny for the purpose of determining integrity of instruction:

1. Is the teacher sufficiently qualified to justify credit for the instruction that is offered?

2. Does the teacher maintain standards of achievement that command both pupil respect and interest?

3. Does the teacher attempt to maintain a professional liaison between himself and the school music department he serves?

4. Does the school's music department attempt to
encourage its students to pursue music study with private
music teachers in their community?

5. Does the school music department maintain control over such instructional considerations as: length of lesson period, number of lessons, the size of classes (as instrumental or piano classes), the minimum number of lessons taught per week, the number of recital appearances per
school year, and whether or not the student participates in
school music organizations. School music departments need
the services of all those students who by the magnitude of
their talent will be able to make a contribution to their organizations. If private instruction means siphoning off the
better student musicians for private music study, then it can
possibly become a detriment to the department's organization.

6. Is the private music teacher interested in promoting both the professional and school music point of view
in his professional relations with the student?

7. Does the private music teacher cooperate with
school music department functions?   There must be good
professional rapport in order to strengthen each other's
work.

Gaining music credit for courses taught by private
teachers appeared on the scene after 1925. The State Department of Education of Louisiana stated in 1937:

> ... any student receiving music instruction under
> a teacher not regularly employed by the school
> board may receive high school credit for this in-
> struction under the rules and regulations stipulated
> herein. These rules are set up temporarily, pend-
> ing the arrival of the time when all music teachers
> will have met the full requirements for a state mu-
> sic teacher's certificate. [14]

CONDITIONS

1. During the first month of the semester for which

credit is requested the private music teacher will secure two application blanks from the office of the high
school principal. The teacher will then fill in the
blanks for each student describing his course of study,
leave one copy of the course with the principal and
forward one copy with the sum of $1.00 to an exam-
iner selected from a list which is in the hands of the
high school principal. The examiner in turn inspects
the course of study and returns it with suggestions if
necessary, to the private music teacher.

2. At the end of the semester the student will appear
    before the examiner and, upon payment of a $1.00
    fee, will receive an examination.

3. The examiner then does or does not recommend that
    the student receive the credit upon the basis of his
    examination. The examiner forwards one copy of his
    report to the high school principal and one copy to
    the Music Division of the State Department of Educa-
    tion. Necessary blanks for reporting results of this
    examination may be secured by writing the Music Di-
    vision of the State Department of Education.

4. The pupil must take a minimum of one-half hour les-
    son weekly and devote a specified amount of time
    daily to practice. The total number of minutes thus
    spent determines the amount of credit. The following
    example is worked on a basis of 400 minutes per week
    for 36 weeks, which would total one unit.

        Minutes of instruction weekly:
        1 times 30 =   30

        Minutes of outside practice weekly:
        5 times 40 = 200
        Total   230

    Dividing 230 by 400 = .57 and, estimating to the
    nearest tenth, credit of 0.6 unit would be awarded
    for Applied Music under the above arrangement.
    (The minimum amount of credit which will be ac-
    cepted for graduation under this plan is 0.2 unit.
    The maximum amount is 3 units.)

5. The student must successfully complete an examina-
    tion at the end of each school semester before credit

for the work may be granted.

6. The place of the examination will be designated by the examiner. If several students in one city or parish are to be examined at the close of a semester, an examiner may go to some convenient central point; if the number of pupils to be examined is small, the pupils will travel to the resident city of the examiner.

From 1937 to 1957 the provisions for granting high school credit for private music study have changed very little. One major change was the use of 300 instead of 400 minutes as a basis for determining one unit of high school credit. The total number of minutes of lesson and practice, and credit unit allotted was as follows:[15]

Total Minutes (Lesson and Practice)	Credit (Unit)
150	.5
180	.6
210	.7
240	.8
270	.9
300	1.0

The State of Louisiana requires the private music teachers to file a copy of intention to study music (pupil) with the high school principal and one copy with the state music examiner. The application form gives student's name, high school, city, number of minutes of study (lesson and practice) per week for 18 weeks, voice or instrument, and unit or grade credit. The detailed nature of the form, with the co-signatures of the private teacher and the examiner, recognizes the administrative and instructional checks to guarantee the intent to pursue serious music study. At the conclusion of the private music study, a final examination report is submitted by the teacher as evidence of successful student achievement.

Private music study needs encouragement from the school music educator if the music program is expected to grow. The Boise, Idaho public schools in their Handbook for Music Teachers state:

All students playing instruments in the bands and orchestras, and those singing in the choirs are en-

couraged to study with a private teacher in order
that they develop correct techniques and improve
their playing and singing. This private study not
only makes every student a more valued member
of the music groups but also, because he learns to
play and sing correctly, enables him to derive a
great deal more enjoyment from the musical experience. [16]

Because nearly all schools provide group rather than
private music instruction, it is exceedingly important that as
many of the young high school musicians as possible study
with private music teachers. School administrative regulations often include specific regulations concerning private music study if it is to take place during the regular school day.
Typical of these are the following.

Regarding School Music Personnel. Faculty are in-
frequently allowed to offer private music instruction on school
property, even outside of school hours. If the music instructor is allowed to teach music the board of education and
the superintendent usually specify the number of lessons that
may be taught. Lessons taught in a school building are more
often permitted in small communities. Permission to give
private music instruction to students in school organizations
is usually given in writing to the teacher. The teacher should
have a statement in writing authorizing her to give such private music instruction. Permission must be obtained from
the proper school authorities for use of the school building
and its facilities.

After-school teaching must not interfere with the music teacher's effectiveness as regular school music teacher.
The music administrator must assume responsibility for securing competent teachers. Regular school music teachers
must be ever aware of any employment unbalances that may
develop between them and the regular academic faculty. Other academic faculty members do not ordinarily have as many
employment opportunities afforded him as a direct result of
his teaching. Music staff members must not abuse the privilege particularly if such teaching should interfere with the
earning power of private music teachers.

Regarding the Private Teacher. The school music
staff should encourage private music study with competent
teachers. In some states private teachers submit to examinations given by some local, state, or national accrediting

body. Music degrees from accredited colleges, or examinations offered by various music teachers' associations are often useful for determining teacher competence. Usually the music department of a school system publishes a list of teachers accredited or approved for private study.[17] Frequently, especially in large school systems, there is a published list of conditions under which a private teacher may be approved for teaching.

Private teachers should be encouraged to cooperate with school music administrators and teachers in promoting music through clinics, workshops, and attendance at school music performances. Private music teachers should become interested in instrumental and vocal classes as a means of stimulating interest in attaining proficiency through private music study. Private music teachers have a responsibility to work with the school music administrator and staff in achieving musicianly goals. The private teacher should attempt to understand what the school music program is attempting to achieve.

A statement of policy was entered into, "to promote cooperation in an understanding of the interrelating fields of music teaching," by the Ohio Music Teachers Association and the Ohio Music Education Association.[18] A portion of the statement says: "As a citizen, the studio teacher shall cooperate in the support of public education, including music instruction at elementary music levels in the schools for the general good of the community."[19] Furthermore, under "Section III, Agreement," the following statements occur:[20]

> It is mutually agreed, between the aforesaid organizations that it is unethical for any music teacher, whether teaching in school or in a private studio:
> (a) To discuss with parents or pupils the work of another teacher in such manner as will injure the professional reputation of any teacher;
> (b) To claim sole credit for the achievement of pupils under separate or co-operative instruction, when such claim shall reflect or imply discredit upon a preceding or cooperating teacher.

> It is the common purpose of music teachers to cooperate:

(a) In raising standards of music instruction;
(b) In promoting interest in active participation in music performance;
(c) In developing wider appreciation of music;
(d) In establishing opportunities for elementary music instruction under the auspices of the school for exploratory purposes;
(e) In encouraging study with private teachers at the end of the period of exploratory instruction;
(f) In extending opportunities for music study to the underprivileged child through scholarships or extension of school instruction in individual instances;
(g) In encouraging regularity of attendance at both school and private lessons, rehearsals, recitals, and performances;
(h) In operating an organized plan for giving credit toward graduation study with recognized studio teachers;
(i) In alleviating the influence and practice of unethical methods of music instruction.

It is obvious from the Code of Ethics set forth by the two professional music teacher groups in Ohio that all music teachers have a responsibility to uphold high standards of professional integrity in their association with school children.   Attention is called to the interrelatedness of the private music teachers' professional responsibilities with those of the music teacher in our public schools.   Conceivably the important function of the school music educator-musician is to provide intensified exploratory experiences in music for youth of elementary and secondary school age.   It is he who seeks the aid of the private music teacher in strengthening the school music program.   What are some of these student-private teacher study regulations and professional considerations?

Regarding the Student.   Private study helps to maintain student interest in music.   Private study aids the school music program by increasing the student's technical proficiency.   Private music study for credit is usually allowed only if the private teacher is approved by the school's administration; also, there are requirements as to minimum study (practice) and eventual growth in performance.   Private music study is usually not allowed during school hours. Private music study often receives a letter grade for achievement; credit may vary from school to school. Private music study may be encouraged through such special inducements as: special music credit, certificates of recognition, and awards. Students usually respond to the challenge of receiving recognition for their work.

The Boise Public Schools stress the importance of maintaining good professional relations with the private teacher. "Teachers should strive in every way to maintain a high type of professional and ethical relationship with these excellent helpers in the community."

> They should feel free to: 1. Let dealers know what they want their students to have in the way of accessories, quality of second hand and new instruments, key or type of instrument, ensemble, solo, and instructional methods, etc. 2. Let dealers know the methods they will be using and not change methods too often. 3. Let dealers know the type of services they [teachers] would like. 4. Let dealers know immediately when something in the way of service, equipment, repair, etc., is unsatisfactory and give them an opportunity to remedy the situation. 5. Let dealers know of new equipment and materials they [teachers] hear of and would like to have available for their students.[21]

> Those associated with the music administrator in teaching music in the Boise public schools are urged not to: 1. Associate themselves with one store and deal with it exclusively. 2. Take a commission from a dealer or sell instruments, accessories, etc. 3. Condemn an instrument or other item sold by a dealer unless the item is decidedly inferior and the dealer has been informed and yet does nothing about it. Dealers usually want to sell any stock items which the teachers want. 4. Fail to let dealers know well in advance that they wish to change methods or type of equipment that must be stocked in advance.[22]

Private Teacher Certification. Such certification is important to the director of music in public schools but parents also find it helpful. An attempt at evaluation of the private music teacher through certification standards is under way in New Mexico. A brochure dealing with certification requirements is being distributed to all members of the New

Mexico Teachers Association. This group deems certification to be designed for three reasons:

    1. For private teachers. (a) To raise teaching
standards in the private studios throughout the state of New
Mexico. (b) To achieve professional status in keeping with
the high ideals of professional teachers of music.
    2. For the public (parents and children): The aim
is to give the assurance of an organization to which they
may turn to receive instruction of the highest professional
standards based on an ethic of professional proficiency.
    3. For the music teaching profession: The aim is
to fortify all branches of music teaching and performance by
strengthening the teaching of music in the private studios.[23]

* * * * *

Twelve Problems to be Resolved
in Secondary School Music Education

    1. Failure to Secure Administrative Support for Sec-
ondary School Music. Very often music educators have become so engrossed in performance, that they have left everyone, including school administrators, uninformed regarding
the problems and needs of school music education. Music
educators frequently fail to recognize the importance of good
administrative relationships for achieving the professional
recognition and support that school music so richly deserves.

    2. Failure to Develop a Comprehensive Music Pro-
gram. A good music program should provide manifold musical opportunities for every student in order that he may
find many opportunities for expressing himself musically. It
also must provide opportunity for the individual to achieve
those artistic ideals which every young musician desires to
attain in the pursuit of a musical career. His greatest satisfactions will accrue from his music experiences when effort is made to relate, in so far as possible, musical endeavor with individual musical development.

    To develop a performing band, choir, or orchestra
does not of itself constitute a well-rounded plan for secondary
music education. A program designed entirely around any
musical organization--band, choir, or orchestra will never
achieve this objective. Many of the smaller secondary
schools devote the major portion of their music programs
to the development of these organizations. These groups

do represent specialization, and such specialization is desirable, but when the program makes no provision for other types of instruction, a large proportion of the student body is neglected.

The general music course is now beginning to receive recognition in high schools and it should become the foundation course about which the entire secondary school music program is constructed. It should provide a variety of music experiences. For every student there should be keyboard opportunities suited to his individual needs and skills; there should be opportunity for playing melodic instruments such as xylophones, autoharps, and instruments of the percussion section of the orchestra; there should be singing of songs including unison and part songs which provide folk and art song experiences; there should be a stimulating listening program which provides interesting explorations in all media of performed music. The breadth and intensity of the general music program should be adjusted to meet the musical interest of each individual. This could be made further advanced by concentrated study of the history of music, sight-singing and ear-training, music theory, instrumental class, voice class, and intensive study of the opera, oratorio, and other music forms. Interest in music might be further increased through the organization of folk dance groups, operetta clubs, and listening groups of many kinds. All of these courses could be designed for both the superior and average musician as well as the individual with limited musical interests.

There have been some major obstacles in realizing this concept of secondary school music. There is a great shortage of competent personnel. Former concepts of secondary school music have been geared primarily to organizational goals (band, choir, orchestra) rather than to educational needs. Organizational programs have taxed available personnel to such an extent that the wide variety of music offerings which have been suggested were not offered. School administrators have often been unwilling to schedule music courses for credit and have discouraged students from studying music other than that provided through organizational participation. And, the current emphasis upon adequate preparation for college entrance requirements has stressed the academic program at the expense of a wider variety of music courses.

3. Need for Adequate Financial Support. Without financial support no music program can be successful. Many

music departments are functioning at a marginal level because
of the lack of money to pay competent personnel and to provide the necessary materials and equipment.

Down through the ages music has always been a pa-
tronized art and there is much evidence that it will continue
to be so. Music educators who are characterized by their
unswerving devotion to musical ideals have often been unreal-
istic and even remiss about the necessity for educating school
administrators and lay leaders concerning the physical and
personnel needs of a good music program. It is the responsibility of the music educator to present music education as
a subject worthy of academic respect. Music administrators
should seek administrative counsel in the intelligent presentation of music budgets in order that they may be interpreted
with effectiveness. Budgets must be planned on a long-term
basis. A five- or ten-year program of needs is more effective than a single-year request that has not been properly
conceived for effective use in the future. A well-planned
budget that sets forth needs and purposes should eventually
secure moral support and financial assistance.

4. Lack of Availability of Qualified Secondary School
Music Teachers. This situation is further aggravated by the
fact that those who enter music teaching are often characterized by lack of musicianship, poor or insufficient training,
and by inability to excite and develop the interest of children
in music. Young musicians of promise, capable and desirous
of helping children to enjoy music for the opportunities it
provides for the exercise of creativity, must be encouraged
to enter school music teaching. The music educator must
in fact be an educator as well as a musician if he is to be
successful at the secondary school level.

5. Unfavorable Academic Emphasis on Secondary
School Music. Local, state, and national accrediting bodies
require that certain basic academic subjects be taught in order that the youth of today become functionally intelligent citizens for tomorrow. Currently, the great stimulus being
given to the sciences may have a tendency to depress further
the support given to music.

6. Failure to Secure Credit for Secondary School
Music Courses. Progress has been made in offering credit
for secondary school music study. Credit for music is usually contingent upon such factors as number of class meetings per week, the amount of required outside preparation,

and whether or not the course is laboratory or recitation or both. A general music course meets on a laboratory basis,

> ... one-half unit for one year's work, consisting
> of daily recitations, when no preparation is re-
> quired outside the classroom. When the class
> meets daily, and outside preparation is required,
> full academic credit should be given which is usu-
> ally one full credit per year. It is recommended
> that the pupil secure more than one-half credit in
> music activities in order to satisfy certain college
> entrance requirements.[24]

Such courses as music appreciation and music history are usually given one unit of credit if classroom recitation and outside preparation are required. Examinations are usually included in the determination of an individual's score in these courses. Organizations such as band, choir, and orchestra are frequently given one-half the amount of credit that is accorded the recitation-preparation music courses. Music credit toward high school graduation is essential, if music courses are to attain the same importance as the academic subjects. Instructional integrity must characterize music teaching at all grade levels. There must be continual evaluation of the breadth and depth of all music instruction. Any music course properly organized and competently taught deserves credit.

7. Inadequate Music Guidance Counselor Services. The gifted as well as the average and even less talented individual should be encouraged to take up the study of music, However, due to scheduling, transportation, home environment, and other relevant circumstances, it is found that occasionally but a small percentage of the secondary school students are registered for the study of music in formal music classes, or participate in performing organizations. Stimulating interest in music participation in secondary school music activities has been and should be the function of the music teacher and the school guidance counselor whenever his services are available.

Guidance and counseling have become an accepted practice in many American secondary schools. However, this type of service has not been too widely applied for the purpose of determining an individual's aptitude for music. Instrumental music teachers have been more active than the choral music teachers in employing guidance services in the

public schools. These music teachers insist that many individuals who have good musical ability have not always been
made aware of the fact, because they have not had adequate
counseling.

Actually, discovering an individual's musical ability
should take place in the elementary grades. In these grades
the teacher will have many opportunities to ascertain the music aptitude and achievement of children. Information about
their aural acuity, rhythmic sensitivity, tonal memory, interpretative ability, and general interest in music will be
constantly brought to the attention of the music teacher.

Guidance and counseling services continue to be important to an individual entering secondary education. Whenever the school provides guidance services, the director of
these services could aid the secondary school music teacher
in ferreting out talent.

The results obtained from any of the following music
aptitude tests should be useful in encouraging those with musical ability or in detering misdirected interest in music
study. 1) Seashore Measures of Musical Talent, 2) Kwal-
wasser-Dykema Music Tests, and more recently 3) Seashore
Measures of Musical Talent (rev. ed. by Seashore, Lewis,
and Saetveit), 4) Gaston Test of Musicality, 5) Tilson-Gretsch
Musical Aptitude Test, 6) Whistler-Thorpe Musical Aptitude
Test, and 7) the Drake Test of Musical Talent. It is strongly urged that the music teacher and pupil compare aptitude
test results with the general musicianship reports which the
teacher may have made of the pupil. The combined evidence
may give the pupil a clue as to whether or not he should
pursue music study.

8. Scheduling Secondary School Music During the
School Day. There is an increasing tendency to condense
the school day into as few as give class periods. The student must take a minimum of four academic courses. In
addition, a physical education requirement uses part of the
fifth class period. Thus music, in these school systems,
must be offered during the fifth class period not consumed
by physical education, or in after-school hours.

There are encouraging signs that school administrators are becoming convinced of the importance of music education, and there is further evidence that they are making
earnest efforts to schedule music in the same manner as the

other academic courses. Naturally, the school systems with the larger enrollments find scheduling on the five-period-day basis somewhat more flexible.

It is pertinent at this point to consider some suggestions and precautions which are helpful in setting up music course and organizational schedules: A. If possible, large musical organizations should be scheduled during the regular school day. Smaller sectional and ensemble organizations could meet after school hours. Regular school scheduling usually assures more continuous practice and guarantees greater attendance. Obviously, there is a close correlation between the amount of regular practice and the quality of performance.

B. The scheduling of all regular and after-school music activities must be well planned in advance of the opening of the school year. This not only aids in minimizing serious schedule conflicts, but it also aids the administration, faculty, and students to budget their school day more intelligently.

C. The problems connected with the scheduling of music courses are usually more easily resolved, because their enrollments are not too large. It is the large organizations as band, choir, and orchestra that need thoughtful scheduling. Then too, there are the activities and performances by these organizations that need to be taken into consideration when schedules are being constructed. Music schedules must be dovetailed intelligently into the calendar for the entire school. When the calendar is completed, it should be made available to all administrative and instructional personnel. This type of cooperative planning usually aids in obtaining a more sympathetic understanding by each department as to what the entire school is attempting to accomplish.

9. Arousing Student Interest in Secondary School Music. The music administrator and teacher cannot expect to build a successful music department without good teachers. This is a never-ending selling job which is best accomplished via intense interest and a superior quality of energetic teaching. The following is one music department's approach to the problem of recruitment.

A. Teachers are encouraged, upon arrangement with their principal and music director, to put on a program-display using instruments and other materials from music dealers as long as no advertising is in evidence.

B.   Teachers should not invite music dealers to come
into the school and promote as this is not permitted by school
board policy. This is also a matter of policy in other phases
of the school program. Dealers and other sales people are
expected to check at the school administration building and
should have a pass from the director of music education pri-
or to contacting a teacher in his classroom.

C.   Teachers are encouraged, upon making the necessary arrangements with the principals involved, to utilize the
very best students and adults in demonstrating instruments
and other phases of the school music program. Playing for
the students, often by the instructor is the very finest recruiting and retention device. Civic and school music programs should also be utilized to develop an ever continuing
interest on the part of the students in the music program.

D.   Teachers are encouraged to use the various test
blanks and results which are available in the music director's
office. The E. Thayer Gaston "Test of Musicality" will be
administered to all 7th- and 8th-grade students as a routine
matter. The C. L. McCreery "Elementary Rhythm and Pitch
Test" is available for use in the elementary grades. It is
recommended that tests be given as recruiting devices rather
than for the elimination of students.

E.   Teachers are reminded that they must have a
healthy three way relationship (Student body, parents, and
principal) if they are to be successful in their program of
recruitment. And 6. Teachers are reminded that they must
gear their enrollment to large class instruction. Private
and semi-private instruction is not considered to be a major
responsibility of the public schools. Individual help when
needed is of course important in music as in the case of any
other school subject.[25]

From these general and specific suggestions for encouraging participation in music, it is obvious that much depends upon the co-operation of the administrator, teacher,
and parent. Interest in music can be aroused. This can be
accomplished more easily, if the music educator is a performing musician. Then too, as an administrator he must
be conversant with the various techniques for determining an
individual's musicality. Once the musicality of the prospective music student has been established and his interest
aroused, it is as a performing musician that the educator-
teacher can inspire the student through a wide variety of

continuing music experiences to pursue the study of music. Naturally, the study of music at the secondary level encourages many of the more talented students to pursue its study seriously.

10. Continued Over-Emphasis on Virtuosity. It often appears that the music educator's primary efforts are directed toward displaying student talent before the public. This is the situation not so much because the music educator is insincere or is incapable of performing the more important elements of his job, as it is because parents and other members of the community are more responsive to such performances, whether on stage or football field, than by sound classroom teaching. True, musical performance has a great appeal, but its permanent educational values are dependent upon the completeness with which its derived satisfactions appeal to the individual performer. The music educator who allows the tawdry, the insincere, the sensational, and the superficial to influence his musical standards will never achieve permanent and rewarding artistic dividends. It must be emphasized that artistic sincerity will result in personal satisfaction of lasting value. The superior quality of the musical literature chosen, the thoroughness with which it is prepared, and the artistic treatment given to its performance are certain to result in more artistic secondary school music performances.

11. Achieving Good Musical Performance. Good performance is but a refinement of many creative experiences. It is always an outgrowth of music study. Playing an instrument or singing a song may be satisfying to the individual, but additional joy may be derived by performing for others. It would be unusual to find a musical organization that rehearses solely for the benefits to be derived from such an experience. Musicians need to perform because satisfaction through performance furthers their desires for further musical achievement. Musical performance is always a demonstration of achievement. They should challenge each student's innate musical ability. They should provide opportunity for each student to attain greater artistic satisfaction. And they should stress the benefits to be derived by the individual rather than the satisfactions that may accrue to the parent, teacher, or community.

Also, they should contain challenging music literature which is consistent with the student's training and experience at the time of its performance. They should improve the

musical tastes of the performer and the listener. They
should become a medium for developing the social poise and
grace of the individual. And they should be so planned as
to promote school and community growth in musical understanding.

A good performance is always indicative of the fact
that adjustments have been made to learning situations and
that progress has gone beyond the stage of talking and reading about music. The reader about music is never as completely satisfied as is the creator of music. Creativity is a
manifestation of the way music affects the individual. The
creative individual is the active, achieving individual.

12. Selection of Suitable Instructional Materials.
This extremely important aspect of an instructional program
is often overlooked. The adjective good has many connotations when it is applied to listeners and performers of music. The distinguished musician's judgments are based on
highly trained technical skills, whereas the layman may think
that good music is "that which I like." In between these two
extremes are to be found all gradations of the meaning of
what is good music. If good means enjoyment, then we are
forced to accept the layman's appreciative reply. He may
receive real pleasure out of music that is proclaimed trash
by the distinguished musician.

For some musicians, good music may imply the superior technical structure of a composition. But a composition that is quite correct technically may still not be good
music. Consequently, we are forced to suggest that the
technical structure of a composition must be fortified by a
distinctive feeling state--a mood--that which expresses a
significant emotional and intellectual message to the listener.
It is possible to find all types of music for instructional purposes, that possess these attributes.

The challenge in selecting instructional materials is
that the music teacher must consider not only those basic
technical opportunities that a composition provides for learning, but also the inspirational qualities that will contribute
to an individual's artistic maturity. Artistic maturity depends upon many accummulative musical experiences.

No one has been able to define a standard of excellence for music! Consequently music educators must place
the selection of suitable instructional materials in the hands

of musicians and musicians must select those attributes of music which provide for every individual's insight and artistic understanding.

Discussion

1. Describe the organizational considerations involved in establishing a choral program in a school system of approximately 1,200 students; 200 of that number are in the junior and senior high school and the remaining 1,000 are in the elementary school. The high school day is composed of eight forty-five minute periods. All children leave the school at 3:10 P.M.

No equipment is available in the school except a grand piano in the auditorium. A budget must be submitted to the superintendent of schools for the new music program. After you have your program outlined, evaluate it with reference to the following:
A. The entire school vocal teaching program.
B. Physical equipment.
C. Musical equipment.
D. Daily-weekly-rehearsal schedules.
E. A cappella choirs, glee clubs, general chorus, and small vocal ensembles for the high school.
F. Type of music to be purchased.
G. The voice class.
H. The choral program budget.

2. List five portable kinds of music-room furniture for either band or choral rooms.

3. There are many important considerations involved in building music schedules for the large high school. Discuss some of the more onerous ones.

4. What is the name of a good musical aptitude test?

5. What do you mean by applied music study?

6. What is the basic purpose of a general music course?

7. List five of the basic concepts to be found in American music education. Discuss their various merits.

8. Is music education still in a pioneering stage?

9. From what point of view have we failed to develop a strong program of music education?

10. Is it possible to give every child an opportunity to experience music?

11. During the last two decades there has been more emphasis upon elementary rather than upon secondary school

music. Defend whatever position you take in satisfying the implications of this statement.

12. Generally speaking is there a tendency to compromise music standards in a small school system?

13. Is there an increasing tendency to offer music activities during after school hours?

14. Who creates love for music?

15. How can parents serve the high school music teacher?

16. How can the music teacher aid in bringing about good community relations?

17. What de we mean by the following school organization plans: 6-3-3; 8-4?

18. Has there been during the last two decades an increasing tendency to develop performing organizations rather than general music education in our secondary schools?

GENERAL MUSIC EDUCATION

1. Do the schools in your community offer credit for music study?

2. At what grade level would you start your beginning instrumental classes?

3. In organizing a music department for a school system in a city of 10,000 population, what would be the minimum personnel requirements for all instructional levels?

4. What are the merits and demerits of purchasing just one set of music song books?

5. At what grade level would you begin general music courses?

6. What music courses would it be possible to include in a junior high school music program?

7. Would you teach a music appreciation course at the elementary school level? If not such a course, what do you suggest as a course of study in music appreciation?

8. How important are instrumental practice cards in the development of a good band and orchestra program?

9. Would you recommend a certain make of instrument for purchase by a student?

10. Should the music teacher sell instruments to students?

11. Who should run the Band Mothers' Club?

12. How would you go about selling the school music program to the community?

13. How many public appearances should the various music organizations in a school system of 2,000 students (1,275 elementary; 725 junior and senior high school stu-

dents) give during a school year?

14. How would you go about getting the local music teachers to work cooperatively with the school music personnel and its program?

15. Discuss school music teacher's salaries in comparison with those of the private music teachers in your community.

16. What are some of the after-school employment opportunities for the school music teacher? To what extent should he be so employed?

17. What are the purposes of the general school assembly? What part does music play in such an assembly?

18. How would you go about discovering music talent in our public schools?

19. What is the purpose of class piano instruction in the elementary schools? Would you start piano classes in the junior and senior school?

20. What is considered a workable enrollment for voice class? Do you believe in the efficacy of voice classes?

21. Is a cappella choir the ideal singing unit for all school systems?

22. What changes have taken place during the past two decades which indicate to you that there has been an upgrading of the music education profession?

23. How would you check on the function of music in the home life of the child?

24. Is there a conflict between the professional musician's point of view and that of the music educator?

25. What are some of the considerations involved in making out daily-weekly teaching schedules?

Notes

1. Wilson, Margaret Welch. "A Dynamic Music Education Course of Study for High School Students," Education, 69: No. 7 (March, 1949), 447.

2. "The Function of Music in the Secondary-School Curriculum." Reprint of The Bulletin (November, 1952) of the National Association of Secondary School Principals, a department of the National Education Association. Prepared by the committee(s) on music in the Senior (and Junior) High School Curriculum. Chicago: Music Educators National Conference, 1952, 5-7.

3. Barr, E. Lawrence. "Music Teaching in the Secondary

Schools," Music Educators Journal, 41: No. 2 (November-December, 1954), 38.

4. Ibid.

5. "The Function of Music in the Secondary-School Curriculum," op. cit., 13-17.

6. "Music Education in the Secondary Schools." Reprinted from the Music Education Source Book, Washington, D.C.: Music Educators National Conference, 1951, 9.

7. A Curriculum Guide for the Fine Arts. 1st ed. New Philadelphia, Ohio: Tuscarawas County Board of Education; n.d., 20-22, 28-30, 36-38.

8. Leeder, Joseph A. and Haynie, William S. Music Education in the High School. Englewood Cliffs, N.J.: Prentice-Hall, 1958, 217-218.

9. Lickey, Harold L. "Scheduling The Music Program." Music Educators Journal, 41: No. 4 (February-March, 1955), 42.

10. Ibid.

11. Ibid.

12. Rafferty, Sadie M., and Michael, Lloyd S. "Scheduling The Music Program." Music Educators Journal, 41: No. 4 (February-March, 1955), 43.

13. Ibid.

14. State of Louisiana, Department of Education, Circular No. 1123.

15. State of Louisiana, Department of Education, Circular No. 3920, March 30, 1954.

16. Von der Heide, Henry J. Handbook for Music Teachers. Boise, Idaho: Independent School District of Boise City, 1957.

17. Rather than list an approved number of private music teachers, the Boise public schools publish a list of

all voice, string, woodwind, brass, and percussion
teachers. The merits of listing all teachers are obvious. In a small school system such a procedure
should eliminate some of the unhappy professional relations that may develop between the music department of the public schools and community private
teachers. Often it is very difficult to select some
piano teachers (or trumpet, voice, violin, etc.) from
others who are willing to teach and who declare that
they are competent.

18. Von der Heide, op. cit.

19. "Music in American Education." Music Education
Source Book Number Two, ed. by Hazel Nohavec
Morgan. Chicago: Music Educators National Con-
ference, 1955, 318.

20. Ibid.

21. Op. cit., Von der Heide, 9.

22. Ibid., 9.

23. The New Mexico Musician, (January, 1957), Portales:
Eastern New Mexico University, 12.

24. Music Education Source Book Number Two, op. cit.,
161.

25. Von der Heide, op. cit., 1-2.

Bibliography

Barr, E. Lawrence. "Music Teaching in the Secondary
Schools." Music Educators Journal, 42: No. 2 (November-December, 1954).

Hartshorn, William C. "Music in General Education." Music Educators Journal, 42: No. 1 (September-October,
1955).

Horn, Francis H. "Music for Everyone." Music Educators
Journal, 42: No. 4 (February-March, 1956).

Knuth, William E. "General Music for the General High

School Student." California Journal of Secondary Education, 30: No. 4 (April, 1955).

Leeder, Joseph A., and Haynie, William S. Music Education in the High School. (Englewood Cliffs, N.J.: Prentice-Hall, 1958).

Lickey, Harold L. "Scheduling the Music Program." Music Educators Journal, 41: No. 4 (February-March, 1955).

"Music Education in the Secondary Schools." Reprinted from the Music Education Source Book. Washington, D.C.: Music Educators National Conference, 1951.

"Music in American Education." Music Education Source Book Number Two, ed. by Hazel Nohavec Morgan. Chicago: Music Educators National Conference, 1955.

"The Function of Music in the Secondary-School Curriculum." Reprint ed. of The Bulletin of the National Association of Secondary School Principals, a Department of the National Education Association. Chicago: Music Educators National Conference, 1952.

Rafferty, Sadie M., and Michael, Lloyd S. "Scheduling The Music Program." Music Educators Journal, 41: No. 4 (February-March, 1955).

State of Louisiana, Department of Education, Circular No. 1123.

State of Louisiana, Department of Education, Circular No. 3920, March 30, 1954.

The New Mexico Musician (C. M. Stookey, editor). Portales: Eastern New Mexico University, January, 1957.

Von der Heide, Henry J. Handbook For Music Teachers. Boise, Idaho: Independent School District of Boise City, 1957.

"We Recommend." (Excerpts from the resolutions adopted at the 1955 Division Conventions of the Music Educators National Conference.) Music Educators Journal, 42: No. 1 (September-October, 1955).

Wilson, Margaret Welch. "A Dynamic Music Education

Course of Study for High School Students." Education,
69: No. 7, (March, 1949).

Sunderman, Lloyd F. "Music Education in Tomorrow's
Democracy Will Begin to Serve the Child." Educational
Music Magazine, XXVIII: No. 3 (January-February, 1944).

BOOKS HELPFUL TO UNDERSTANDING
OF SECONDARY SCHOOL MUSIC.

Anderson, William Robert. Music as a Career. New York:
Carl Fischer, 1939.

Barr, A. S., Burton, William, and Brueckner, Leo. Supervision. New York: Appleton-Century, 1947.

Brooks, Marian B. and Brown, Harry. Music Education
and the Elementary School. New York: American Book
Co., 1946.

Cain, Noble. Choral Music and Its Practices. New York:
M. Witmark & Sons, 1932.

Christy, Van A. Glee Club and Chorus. New York: G.
Schirmer, 1940.

Davidson, A. T. Choral Conducting. Cambridge, Mass.:
Harvard University Press, 1940.

Davidson, Archibald T. Music Education in America. New
York: Harper and Bros., 1926.

Davis, Ennis. More Than a Pitchpipe. Boston: C. C.
Birchard & Co., 1941.

Dykema, Peter W., and Cundiff, Hanna M. School Music
Handbook. New ed. Evanston, Ill.: Summy-Birchard
Co., 1955.

Dykema, Peter W. and Gehrkens, Karl. The Teaching and
Administration of High School Music. Boston: C. C.
Birchard & Co., 1941.

Fuhr, H. M. Fundamentals of Choral Expression. Lincoln:
University of Nebraska Press, 1934.

Jones, Llewllyn Bruce. Building the Instrumental Music Department. New York: Carl Fischer, 1949.

Krone, Max. Expressive Conducting. Chicago: Neil A.
   Kjos Music Co., 1945.

Kwalwasser, Jacob. Problems in Public School Music. New
   York: Witmark Educational Publications, 1932.

Leonard, Charles. Recreation Through Music. New York:
   A. S. Barnes, 1952.

Leonard, Charles and House, Robert W. Foundations and
   Principles of Music Education. New York: McGraw-Hill,
   1959.

Mathews, Paul Wentworth. You Can Teach Music. New
   York: E. P. Dutton, 1953.

Morgan, Russell V. Music, A Living Power in Education.
   Morristown, N.J.: Silver Burdett Co., 1953.

Morgan, Russell V. and Morgan, Hazel B. Music Education
   in Action. Chicago: Neil A. Kjos Music Co., 1954.

Mursell, James L. Education for Musical Growth. Boston:
   Ginn and Co., 1948.

_____ Human Values in Education. Morristown, N.J.:
   Silver Burdett Co., 1934.

_____ Music Education, Principles and Programs.
   Morristown, N.J.: Silver Burdett Co., 1956.

_____ Music and the Classroom Teacher. New York:
   Silver Burdett Co., 1951.

_____ Music in American Schools. Morristown, N.J.:
   Silver Burdett Co., 1943.

Newman, Elizabeth. How to Teach Music to Children. New
   York: Carl Fischer, 1925.

Normann, Theodore F. Instrumental Music in the Public
   Schools. Philadelphia: Oliver Ditson Co., 1941.

Rafferty, Sadie and Weigand, J. J. The Function of Music
   in the Secondary-School Curriculum. Chicago: Music

Educators National Conference, 1952.

Snyder, Alice M. Creating Music With Children. New
York: Mills Music Inc., 1957.

Squire, Russell N. Introduction to Music Education. New
York: The Ronald Press, 1952.

Sunderman, Lloyd F. Some Techniques for Choral Success.
Rockville Centre, N.Y.: Belwin, Inc., 1952.

Tooze, Ruth, and Krone, Beatrice P. Literature and Music
as Resources for Social Studies. Englewood Cliffs, N.J.:
Prentice-Hall, 1955.

Umstattd, J. G. Secondary School Teaching. Boston: Ginn
and Co., 1953.

Van Bodegraven, J., and Wilson, Harry. School Music Conductor. Chicago: Hall & McCreary, 1942.

Ward, Arthur E. Music Education for High Schools. New
York: American Book Co., 1941.

CHAPTER X: SCHOOL MUSIC ADMINISTRATION

The growth of school music since 1900 has been so phenomenal that the position of teacher of vocal music is now variously identified by a large number of titles applying to many broad and even specialized areas of vocal music. The confusion of terminology continues when one attempts to designate administrative, supervisory and teaching duties.

Director of Music. Among the major administrative classifications, the title director of music has very often been used to designate the educator who is responsible for the music education program in a large city school system. This title is more usually associated with a school system that has a large music staff. However, it is possible to find a director of music in a community of 6,500 people who is an administrative director of a school music department, supervises either vocal or instrumental music in the elementary schools, is available as a music consultant to all classroom teachers, and who may actually be teaching vocal or instrumental classes and directing band or chorus.

> Clean-cut differentiations of the work of administrator and of supervisor are rare--whether the school system be large or small and whether the work in music education be divided among many persons or whether it be carried on by a single individual.[1]

The director of music in the large city system is a co-ordinator of all music activities and has limited teaching duties. Any city having a population approaching 100,000 is very likely to employ a director of music. Usually, as the size of the city or school system increases, the amount of his teaching decreases. The organization and administration of such systems vary from community to community and the designations of teaching and administrative staffs differ, as do the work assignments included in any particular position.

Typically, the director of music in large cities is assisted by one or more assistant directors of instrumental or

vocal music. Very often the assisting administrative personnel are designated as supervisory personnel. They assume administrative, coordinating, and limited teaching duties. Since 1838 when music was officially introduced into
the public schools of Boston, the evolution of the administrative concept has passed through the successive stages of
teacher, teacher-supervisor, supervisor, and director of music. As cities became larger, positions of administrative
assistants developed in the enlarging school systems.

With the growth of great metropolitan centers the as-
sistantship concept expanded to include the positions of supervising directors of primary, elementary, junior, and secondary school music. There is widespread use of the supervisor of vocal and supervisor of instrumental title, rather than
that of the supervising director. The following duties indicate some of their responsibilities: 1) as experienced administrators and teachers they work closely with the music
and other teachers; 2) they serve in an advisory capacity to
all teachers teaching music, and are competent to teach music if called upon to do so; 3) as differentiated from directors
of music these assistant directors of music spend more time
with teachers who are actually teaching music; and 4) they
act in an advisory capacity to the director of music and
therefore influence his judgments in the determination of departmental policy.

The early concept of the position of supervisor of music implied teaching duties and administrative responsibilities.
As the size of school systems increased and programs of music education expanded, a new concept of the instructional
and administrative responsibilities of this position developed.

> The new conception--that the principal is primarily
> responsible for the quality of instruction within his
> individual building--makes it essential that some
> program of coordination of duties and authorities
> be worked out. This system, termed line and
> staff, brings up the problem of a supervisor ac-
> cepting responsibility without any authority to carry
> out the desired program. A third procedure, which
> if properly organized promises still better results,
> is the cooperative plan in which the principal and
> supervisor jointly accept responsibility and exercise
> authority. In this case, the supervisor of music
> would have authority in all matters pertaining to
> educational aims, methods, and materials, and the

principal, in addition to administrative responsibilities with respect to rooms, recitation schedules,
and use of equipment would supervise the practice
of teaching within prescribed educational bound-
aries.[2]

In order that instruction may be more effective a music administrator must provide definite well-organized administrative services. These services are concerned with those
basic educational music ideals and instructional techniques
which will aid the teaching staff in attaining success.

Responsibilities of an Administrator. I. The administrator must assist his staff in crystallizing those music educational idealisms which are most likely to insure an effective instructional program. He must envision a broad program of music education. He must believe that music has
an important place in the educational curriculum.

The administrator must constantly be aware of the
great social, intellectual, and spiritual contributions which
music education makes, and how they influence the individual
in school and society. These contributions are undergirded
by those concepts which have become recognized as basic in
attempting to formulate its philosophy. The administrator
must have great concern for exploring the musical interests
of the child. These pupil dynamics must be reinforced by
the administrator's concern for providing the school children
with those understandings that will undergird and assure an
aesthetic and cultural development necessary for enjoying the
Full Life.

II. The administrator must provide for all instructional and educational services, including the construction of
courses of study, the development of appropriate instructional techniques for the improvement of instruction, training the
in-service teacher for more effective instruction, the pro-
curement of instructional materials and equipment, recruitment of a superior instructional faculty, and a happy instructional and learning environment for faculty and student.

The administrator must determine those experiences
which he believes are essential to the development of the individual's musical stature. Will there be instructional emphasis upon the rhythmic, notational, and symbolical aspects
of music study? Will the program demand that the intermediate grade teachers be responsible for the teaching of their

classroom music? Will there be provided a music consultant supervisory service for all elementary school teachers?
Will there be a general music program available for the junior and senior high school students? What will be the teaching load for each music staff member? Will it be necessary
for the band director to devote all of his instructional time
to the preparation of his organizations for school and community functions? Will the administrator honor a well-balanced music program or is he interested in the "show win-
dow" type of education? The music administrator must envision a broad program of musical studies, determining what
can be achieved now and what must be relegated to the future.

     III. Human resources--teaching and non-teaching per-
sonnel--must be coordinated for instructional success. It is
not uncommon to find the president of an academic institution
or a superintendent of schools more favorably disposed toward the athletic program than to music. There are many
situations in which the music administrator and his staff may
become discouraged. The music administrator must help to
alleviate such conditions if he is to develop a successful program.

     The music administrator must obtain funds to operate
a broad program. Budgets very often determine program
success. A strong music program goes far beyond the hiring of competent faculty--there are physical facilities, instruments, instrumental and vocal literature, uniforms, plat-
forms and risers, and other expenses involved in developing
a strong music education program. For these reasons, the
administrator must everlastingly attempt to secure public
support in order to realize his ambitions.

     IV. Plans must be made if goals are to be achieved.
A music program must inevitably be concerned with the best
type of instruction. Faculty participation in the determination of the instructional program must be planned through
cooperation of administration and faculty. The administration must fashion its educational successes around staff participation in faculty meetings, seminars, committees, and
through individual assignments. Interrelated with this staff
participation is the importance of allowing all individuals to
establish organizational techniques which govern participation
in instruction.

     Work-planning, in order to be effective, must ema-
nate from the lowest echelon of staff. It will never succeed

unless expression is permitted at all levels of the instructional and learning process. Growth will be continuous if the participative work-planning program is a continuous experience. Every person associated with the program must eventually experience the satisfaction of knowing that he has contributed something to the success of the learning process.

V. The music administrator and his staff are responsible for a great variety of music instruction. In addition to regular classroom teaching and the training of small ensembles and large musical organizations, many programs are presented for community entertainment during the school year. Faculty members and students frequently appear on programs, thereby bringing about better public relations between school and community. Music as an art form becomes a living force for social enjoyment and cultural development.

MUSIC ACTIVITIES

The following areas of activities indicate the broad scope of the administrator's responsibility in the realm of music activities.

Elementary School

Creative song-singing, rhythmic, and listening activities.

Piano, tonette, song-flute and instrumental classes.

School assembly programs--music furnished by students and augmented by teacher and parent participation.

Elementary school chorus, band, and orchestra.

Operettas.

Parent-Teachers' Association programs wherein elementary school music is included.

Junior High School

Band, choral, and orchestral programs.

The areas suggested for the elementary school are possible in the junior high school, although there is a need for elaboration.

Assembly singing.

Secondary School

Band, choral, and orchestral programs.

Specialized small instrumental, choral and orchestral ensembles.

Solo instrumental and vocal performances by maturing senior high school students.

Instrumental and vocal class instruction.

Assembly singing.

History of music.

Theory and harmony.

Composition.

General music classes.

The suggested areas found at the elementary school level are possible also in senior high school, with great elaboration.

Public Events

Athletic events.
    Bands for football and basketball games.

Community events.
    Patriotic, religious and community.
    Parades.
    Parades (all types).
    Celebrations.

Contests and festivals.

Graduation exercises.
    Baccalaureate and commencement.

All-school music events.
Christmas, Easter, Thanksgiving programs.

All-school regularly scheduled programs.

Exchange concerts with local and neighboring schools.

The following special interest music activities are found upon occasion as variations to the course offerings and organizational activities we have already suggested. These special interest extra-curricular activities often eventuate in study groups or clubs. Among those more popularly found are:

Madrigal groups.
Record collectors' clubs.
Music appreciation clubs.
Barber shop singers.
Bel canto singers (men and women).
Dance band groups.
Composition classes.

VI. The administrator should always discuss with the staff member a proposed instructional schedule. Music staff members should be given an instructional load that is equivalent to that given other academic staff members. It is possible to determine the time required for preparation as it is done for academic courses. The music instructor should not be required to teach the same number of class hours as other staff members and also be expected to produce performing bands, orchestras, and choirs.

The administrator must evaluate the variation in the amount of preparation and instructional time consumed for teaching a piano or vocal lesson on an individual basis as compared with like requirements for teaching a music theory or history of music class that may have enrollments of twenty or more students. Currently, if but one to four students are taught during a class hour, the instructor is given two-thirds of one academic hour credit. Thus, if the instructor taught twenty-four hours of applied music during a week, he would receive sixteen (16) hours of academic teaching load credit. Teaching hour loads of instructional faculty in institutions of higher learning range from twelve (12) to sixteen (16). The music administrator must work out an equation for evaluating all types of music instructional assignments. Frequently, it will be found that an administrator will equate into a faculty member's teaching load those special assignments such as: football band, choir performance, faculty recitals, directing music for convocations and assemblies, school-community choral societies, and specially appointed administrative duties. Staff members over-burdened with unreasonable teaching loads cannot be expected to achieve instructional success.

Publish Teaching Schedules. Regardless of the size of the school system and the number of administrative and music teaching personnel, it is imperative that a daily teaching schedule be made out for every staff member. The chief school administrator, the music administrator, the music faculty, the classroom teachers, and students must know the following facts:

1. The administrator must know where to find his staff during instructional hours.

2. Every music teacher must know what he is expected to teach (prescribed areas of instruction) from day to day.

3. Every in-service teacher who looks to the music administration for instructional assistance must know when and where he may get help.

4. Any instructional schedule must be properly worked out and it should reflect any changes in schedule time, course, or personnel.

The construction of a music teaching schedule usually reveals conflicts that are not anticipated until they are placed on paper. In large school systems, class schedules are very complex because of the interrelated departmental personnel responsibilities which must be given careful consideration. When an individual's schedule is made, there should simultaneously be constructed a master departmental and institutional schedule. The music administrator and faculty member should review together any schedule that is proposed, because it may reveal instructional conflicts that may be solved in advance of their actual occurrence.

VII. Not only do teachers often lack instructional insight and originality, they are frequently hampered by the lack of those teaching aids that enhance their professional success. Prior to 1914 there was but a limited amount of music instructional materials, in either the vocal or instru-

mental field, that were suitably arranged for elementary and
secondary school teaching. The time is gone when the classroom teacher taught from a single song book. Since 1930
there has been a tremendous increase in the amount of instructional materials available for teaching music. So it is
the responsibility of the administrator to see that these should
be made ready for reference and for use by the entire teaching staff. In addition to a wide variety of song books, there
are courses of study, recordings, filmstrips, tape recordings, film and sound films, projectors, and many other teaching aids.

The Curriculum Laboratory. No administrator or
faculty member ever ceases looking for instructional materials. A music curriculum laboratory if properly developed
can provide the in-service teacher with an abundance of instructional suggestions and teaching aids. Some of the more
important organizational details in its establishment are: 1)
copies of all music materials available within the school system should be put in the laboratory for every staff member
to study; 2) all music publishers should be informed of the
establishment of the laboratory; indicate the desire for obtaining copies of those teaching aids and materials which
they are willing to make available; 3) the staff members
should be encouraged to submit lists of additional known
teaching materials which it is believed are obtainable; and
4) directors of curriculum in public schools and colleges
should be asked to submit materials which they believe
would be helpful for in-service teachers. As some of the
materials must be purchased it is desirable that the administrator provides a budget for the laboratory.

The music curriculum laboratory must be provided
adequate space and staff to facilitate its use. Space can usually be found for the laboratory. Frequently, a cooperative
study made by the administration and instructional staff will
result in the release of some area for the beginning laboratory. Even an administrative outer office could serve as
temporary quarters. There are storerooms that may be re-
organized for more functional use. If the laboratory is ear-
nestly desired, space will be found.

Within the laboratory should be found all those music
teaching aids which through proper organization will help in
effecting better music instruction. Teaching aids are almost
worthless unless they are organized so as to point up their
use for good teaching. Categories of songs should be cata-

logued and properly cross-referenced in order that teachers
may be apprised of their availability. Recordings are of little worth unless they are properly indexed. There must be
books containing stories about music that will be helpful to
teachers as well as young people. Rhythm band materials
and melody producing instruments should be available, so
that broad individual interests may be tapped. Every aid
usable for music instruction within the school system should
be recorded.

Staffing the laboratory must not be left to chance.
The administrator must provide the needed personnel for organizing and maintaining the laboratory as a teaching service
for all staff members. If it is to be effective, it will require much organization and administrative time. Bulletins,
either mimeographed, dittoed, or printed should be issued
from time to time to acquaint all personnel with new instructional materials. The laboratory must serve instructional
needs or it will fail to be a functional aid for effecting better
music instruction.

Once the laboratory has been organized, there should
be orientation of teachers and administrator to its many
services. Music teachers are constantly searching out materials for instruction. In-service teachers need supplementary aids. Administrators must be aware of the functional
merits of the curriculum laboratory and how its services
may further aid the music staff in bringing about better music instruction.

VIII. Good public relations must be developed. If the
school music program has failed to receive community support, that is often due to failure of the administrator and
the music department to establish the contribution of music
to the aesthetic development of individuals. The effectiveness of the program will be greatly strengthened if the community is informed about the school music program and its
great value to community life.

School support comes from tax-paying citizens, thus
it becomes the responsibility of the music administrator and
his fellow workers to solicit community interest and support
in every phase of the school's music program.

Where in community life will it be possible for the
music administrator to find opportunity to strengthen school-
community associations save through music? Where in the

schools will it be possible to relate the school music program to community life?   Closer study of these questions reveals many ways in which music relationships may be developed between the school and the community: 1) through participation in community choral and instrumental programs; 2) through participation in specialized music activities and performances; 3) by inviting talented parents to participate in school music activities; 4) through co-operation with professional community musicians; and 5) through participation in those agencies interested in promoting the arts.

The philosophies of the board of education, its chief administrator, the music administrator, and the music faculty collectively determine the magnitude of a music program. There should be perspective as to the type and number of music programs that are to be presented by students during a school year.   Obviously, performances are somewhat proportionate to the number of organizations that a music department is able to maintain.   There should be no attempt to exploit students in the behalf of some ambitious school official, music teacher, or interested community layman or agency.

The community can become aware of the school music program through the place it exercises in assisting with PTA meetings through the school year.   Children's groups from the elementary division of a school system can participate by furnishing various types of delightful music programs for school and community clubs.   The rhythm bands, elementary school choral groups, eurhythmic classes, and piano classes all may present school-community assembly programs.   Pageants depicting various phases of American social and political history can include musical selections which help to trace these developments of our culture.   The exploratory opportunities in music are so great that they can run the gamut of musical expression and human experience.

Within any school system there will be found parents of music students, who can make a great contribution to the development of the music department.   These parents can perform valiant service as organizers of band, choral, or orchestral clubs and music organizations.   They may also help with financial drives designed to raise funds for departmental needs.

The music staff that has unified parental support is certain to develop better school-community relations.   The

annual music festival is more certain of success if parent
and community support is co-ordinated. Schools in the
smaller communities are pivotal centers about which much
social and cultural life evolves.

The music administrator should work co-operatively
with professional musicians in each community. He frequently has occasion to employ private music teachers for special
departmental teaching. Then too, members of the school
music staff may express interest in doing some private vocal
or instrumental teaching.

The music administrator must enlist the aid of the
community in realizing the music goals he envisions. Within
each community there are private citizens who are interested
in the promotion and encouragement of music. Service clubs,
councils of churches, study clubs and art societies are among
the forefront in the promotion of culture for the community;
city recreation directors will usually co-operate in worthy
music projects; national organizations, such as the American
Music Council, will give much encouragement through the
press. The American Association of Piano Manufacturers
will cooperate in worthy music activities.

School musicians may also become solo performers
and participate in community music organizations. They
will be welcomed for taking part in service clubs, church
choirs, community choral societies, community bands, orchestras, American Guild of Organists, Choirmasters' Guild,
and wherever else they may find cultural and musical satisfaction.

School music education in the small community has
played an important role in the development of outstanding
American music administrators and educators. Among some
of the more distinguished names will be found Will Earhart,
Joseph Maddy, William Revelli, Clarence Gates, Paul Paint-
er, E. C. Moore, Otto Kraushaar, Claude Smith, Paul Yod-
er, Carleton Stewart, and Charles Righter.[3] Good music
administrators and music teachers are the most important
factors in the development of school music programs. It is
not the size of the community that will create within children
an artistic comprehension and appreciation of the power that
music can exert upon maturing musicians. The inspired and
well-trained musician, an apt pupil, and an opportunity for
study will insure learning and instructional successes.

The fruits of music education are more frequently observed and expressed in the cultures of succeeding generations. It is the "children's children" who become a living
expression of those who have given dedicated lives to school
music. Probably no better example of this could be illus-
trated than through the vigorous music program initiated by
Mabelle Glenn in Kansas City, Missouri, during the early
1920's. An editorial upon the occasion of a music festival
honoring the Golden Anniversary of the Music Educators National Conference and dedicated to Miss Glenn, commented
as follows:

MUSIC IN OUR SCHOOLS

> Back of the all-city public school music festival
> last Friday night at the Municipal Auditorium lies
> a story of interest not only to parents but to every
> citizen of the community. How did it happen that
> some 4,000 children of elementary and secondary
> school age could be brought to the concert pitch
> reflected in that performance?

> Obviously there was no element of chance here.
> The massed choruses were not thrown together by
> youngsters who just happened to like to sing. These
> were voices carefully selected from a much larger
> number of students and diligently trained. The or-
> chestras and band did not develop because a few
> children wanted to play various musical instruments
> in their spare time. Such organizations are only
> the end result of intensive group rehearsal, backed
> by long hours of individual practice.

> What produced this youthful enthusiasm? The story
> goes back to the early 1920's, when Miss Mabelle
> Glenn was appointed director of public school music
> here. Her skill and vision transformed the teaching
> of music from the kindergarten to the senior year
> in high school. What had been routinely treated as
> a minor phase of education gradually became an ex-
> citing personal experience. Miss Glenn brought
> children into touch with great music finely performed
> by symphony orchestras, at first imported and then
> resident.

> That was for the inspiration of high standards. But
> she also believed that 'the best listeners are those

who have made a little music themselves.' And
so came about those memorable performances in
old Convention Hall, the direct predecessors of
last week's giant concert. The important fact,
however, is that the story goes on. Under Robert
Milton, with invaluable support from the present
superintendent of schools and a sympathetic Board
of Education, the activity Miss Glenn started is
being steadily expanded.

When Superintendent James Hazlett paid tribute to
Miss Glenn and spoke of the importance of music
in a well-rounded education, he was not indulging
in platitudes. The quality of the ensuing festival
dramatically bore out his words. Here were children in the process of adding a new dimension to
their adult lives through a vital school program. 4

IX. Every music education program needs continual
evaluation. If professional vigor is to characterize the program, there must be a continuing process of evaluating the
mechanics of course construction, the personnel needed and
the effectiveness with which the instruction results in student
achievement. The music administrator interested in determining the effectiveness of his program will ask many searching questions.

1. To what extent have individuals participated in the
school music program? Has the individual grown musically?
Is there over-emphasis on organizational development (band,
choir, and orchestra) at the expense of opportunity for the
less endowed individual? Has the administration encouraged
an area of music study to the utter neglect of the general
education of the individual? Are the students actually finding
music a creative opportunity for personal enjoyment?

2. Are the talented music students provided a high
quality of specialized instruction which will insure the type
of training which is commensurate with their ability? Our
philosophy which encourages general music education courses
does not indicate a lack of interest in the talented individual.
True democracy of musical opportunity should connote educational opportunities in proportion to endowment. Distinctive
genius in music could not be served effectively in modern
civilization unless the mediocre student (average) is permitted
to achieve substance and stability for his talents. As in all
these criteria there should be evidence of growth.

3. Is music co-ordinated with the academic program? Do the music courses aid in enhancing intellectual experience in the arts? Do they aid in providing a diversity of course offerings for the cultural development of the individual?

4. Has the music administration been instrumental in securing academic recognition for the worthwhileness of music as an integral part of cultural education? Has the administration secured respect for the quality of course instruction being offered in the general and professional music education courses?

5. Is the music program overloaded with course content which is duplicated by other courses?

6. Is there too great a stress upon applied music instruction at the expense of good general music courses for well-balanced growth in musical understanding? Does the music program offer a sufficient variety of courses in order to attract the greatest number of students?

7. Are the envisioned musical achievements the product of joint thinking on the part of the administration and the staff? Are the musical standards high for individuals of distinctive talent as well as realistic for all who participate in the program of general music education?

8. Does the school music program carry over into community life? Has the administration solicited and encouraged community support for a strong school music program? Has the administration made the community aware of the opportunities which school music provides its students? Are there community music projects, musical organization, and civic music enterprises of professional and amateur stature?

9. Are there faculty discussions for the improvement of instructional techniques? Is there a constant faculty evaluation of the music education program for determining its effectiveness? Are there experiments in the use of new instructional techniques? Have special faculty meetings been devoted to an evaluation of music courses? Has the faculty become measurement minded?

10. Has the music administrator continually fought for additional budget in order to meet the needs of an ever-expanding music education program? Are staff requirements

commensurate to the needs of the envisioned program? Is the program so impoverished through the lack of physical equipment that good results are impossible in spite of faculty competency?

These questions in no way indicate the comprehensive scope of the considerations involved in determining the effectiveness of a good music program. A searching evaluation raises questions about the competency of the faculty, the comprehensiveness of the instructional program, and the effectiveness with which it is transmitted to the learner. The degree to which attainment of learning has been achieved is in the final analysis a true measure of effective administration.

Conclusion. Music administration is a concentric dynamic field of endeavor which continually challenges the administrator and his staff. The development of a strong music program should thrust administrative considerations upon both the administrator and the individual music staff member. The music administrator must guide the educational program with calmness, firmness, and good judgment; he must bring about a coalescence of constructive educational ideas from many sources--the staff, the students, the parents, and the public; he must attempt to refine all ideas for the common objective, which is contributing to the cultural development of all members of society; he must recognize that the administration can function more effectively if there is both individual and group thinking; he must help individuals derive satisfactions from teaching experiences in music which will result in a pleasant teaching environment; he must bring about the creation of work-plans for the organization of many multiple music activities; he must make a determined effort to evaluate programs of music education; he must be able to coordinate all human and material resources for effecting a maximum result; he must create strong school-community relations for aiding in the development of the music program and finally he must attempt to attain prestige for the job well done.

The proportion of classroom teachers who are competent to conduct a music program without professional assistance is small.

It is necessary to provide for the effective conduct of a classroom music program. This is achieved by making available the services of a well-trained director of music,

supervisor, consultant, or specialist. Anyone of these professionals becomes an expert assistant to those teachers to
whom he is assigned. They provide aid in lesson planning,
secure desirable instructional materials, coordinate instructional programs between the classroom teacher and higher
administrative authority, and supply the vision for a music
program which will be satisfying to teacher and pupil. Thus,
with professional assistance, a greater proportion of the
classroom teachers become more effective in conducting a
music program.

Continuing teacher shortages necessitate professional
help in the conduct of classroom music by the in-service
teacher. Elementary school teachers are employed because
of their broad training and competency to teach, and not because they are equally versatile in teaching every subject in
the curriculum. Music requires special competence that is
not possessed by all individuals.

Classroom teacher inexperience in teaching music requires much demonstration teaching. In spite of the concept
of the self-contained classroom this need will remain. The
considerable teacher turnover further emphasizes the continuing need for effective administrative, supervisory, and
instructional programs for implementing music instruction.
The new teacher will always need help.

The need for consultative assistance increases with
the size of the school system.

Supervisory Functions. Some of the more important
supervisory functions are visitations, consultations, administration and staff meetings, evaluation of instruction, and
administrative directives and bulletins.

Visitation: A. Unannounced

Most teachers do not enjoy an unannounced visit from
the supervisor. For the inexperienced teacher this type of
visit may be very disconcerting. There are classroom
teachers who have encouraged their students to ignore frequent classroom entry interruptions and therefore may not
be unduly disturbed by such type of visits.

The unannounced visit permits the supervisor to ob-
serve a classroom operating under normal conditions. It is
imperative that teachers be observed under natural class-

room conditions. There are teachers who prefer to know
when they are to be observed. Others may be just as disturbed whether the supervisory visit is announced or unannounced.

B. Announced Visit

Usually the inexperienced teacher desires this type of
visit. The supervisor should instill within all teachers the
feeling that helpfulness rather than criticism is the purpose
of visitations. This attitude must be established if the supervisor is to be effective.

C. Visitation by Appointment

These visitations emphasize the need for calling upon
the supervisor for professional advice and instructional assistance. This is the purpose of supervision for the improvement of instruction.

Consultation

The supervisor is the professional musician who should
be ever ready to assist the classroom teacher in becoming a
better teacher. At these conferences instructional materials,
techniques for effective instructional presentation, and curriculum content problems should receive detailed consideration.
The consultation should always stress the importance of doing
everything possible to assist the classroom teacher in teaching music. Consultations may be conducted in the teacher's
classroom or in the supervisor's office. The supervisor
should maintain office hours for such purposes.

Administrative and Staff Meetings

The supervisor of music should employ administrative
and staff meetings to co-ordinate instructional effort. Musical idealisms can be more ideally achieved when the administration and instructional personnel work together for the
purpose of realizing common instructional goals. Occasionally, these meetings have resulted in staff workshops. At
these workshops, the staff members may become participants
in the learning of music.

Evaluation of Instruction

The supervisor of music is charged with responsibility

for the evaluation of instruction. He must attempt to determine pupil accomplishment in relation to projected music and aesthetic objectives. He must be able to offer diagnostic opinion and remedial suggestions. Some of the paramount considerations in the evaluation of instruction are:

are instructional supplies and equipment adequate for achieving projected goals?

does the teacher stimulate a desire for musical learning?

does the teacher appear to be wholly incompetent to resolve the instructional techniques necessary for achieving instructional success?

does the teacher fail to recognize the "totalness" of an all-consuming musical experience? Is there too much emphasis upon one category (syllables, song singing, appreciation, rhythm band, operettas, etc.) of musical experience?

is the teacher antagonistic toward teaching music?

The supervisor of music must be a highly trained professional musician, who is imaginatively capable of aiding the in-service teacher in more fully realizing her innate teaching gifts.

Administrative Directives and Bulletins

Music departments in many school systems are understaffed. Therefore, it is frequently impossible to make the number of desired visitations. The supervisor of music through the aid of administrative directives and bulletins is able to keep his teaching assistants and all associated music instructional personnel informed about matters related to professional and musical considerations. These media of transmittal serve to convey the following professional and instructional information:

information concerned with personnel welfare--Salary, Housing, Hospitalization, Social Security, etc.;

information relative to administrative policy;

information regarding all meetings that directly or indirectly affect instruction and personnel welfare;

information regarding professional activities. Interesting comments about staff members could be included if they appear to be of interest to the administrative and instructional personnel;

publications, newspaper items, and personnel suggestions for professional improvement should find release through bulletins.

It is recommended that these directives and bulletins be numbered and punched for loose leaf notebook entry. They are more convenient if they are of standard letter size.

From the foregoing discussions it is easy to discern that a supervisory program can become an effective instrument for in-service education. All supervisor-teacher cooperative actions for the strengthening of an educational program should result in pupil growth in musical understanding.

Supervision is the most important service that can be offered the in-service teacher. A coordinated music program is more likely to evolve. A well organized supervisory program can do much to insure instructional success.

The terms music consultant and music specialist have been bandied about by administrators who advocate the self-contained classroom principle. These two administrative positions offer professional advisory service which is available to all those in-service classroom teachers who are required or expected to teach their vocal music, or if there is inadequate supervisory staff to meet the music teaching demands of the school system. Some progressive school administrators insist upon their classroom teachers being competent to teach all subjects in the curriculum. It is believed that the in-service teacher is better qualified to understand the needs of the students because of her daily association with them. The consultant or specialist should be available to assist in strengthening the music program whenever the classroom teacher feels she needs professional advice. Thus, these two are elementary school music specialists; they are available at all times for professional advice and actual teaching.

The consultant or specialist should project a coordinated program of music for the elementary school grades. They would guide the development of a strong elementary school music program. Under their leadership it would be possible to develop a program by which the in-service teachers should eventually be able to learn how to become effective classroom teachers of music. They assume leadership for a music program. They are conversant with new methods and materials and the underlying educational principles involved in their use.[5] The consultant should be qualified

and immediately available to act as an adviser in the selection
of equipment, such as pianos and audio-visual aids.[6]   The
consultant should also act as a liaison person in the preparation of performing groups for interschool programs, and
should maintain public relations through the press, radio,
television, festivals, community sings, and civic organizations.   He should establish contact with other educational organizations, such as the Association for Supervision and Curriculum Development.[7]

     In the larger school systems special music teachers
are employed principally for teaching in the elementary grades.
These may be in addition to a large group of travelling supervisors.   They are selected because they are superior musicians and teachers.   Their entire teaching assignment may
be devoted to the instruction of theory, chorus, band, orchestra, and vocal and instrumental classes of all types. In
the instrumental field they may teach upper brasses, lower
brasses, single reeds, double reeds, violin classes, or percussion instruments.   In the vocal field they could be teaching at any grade level.   At the junior and senior high level
they may offer voice instruction.   Instrumentally they would
normally start teaching in the fourth and fifth grades.   The
important consideration is that they are teachers and their
administrative duties are at a minimum.

     State Supervisor of Music.   During the second quarter
of the 20th century there has been developed a gradual acceptance of the need for a state supervisor or music education co-ordinator.   The task of articulating and integrating
such a program is fretted with great responsibilities.   Hoffman states that

> ... this one position, properly set up and managed,
> can evaluate, guide, promote and co-ordinate all
> phases of desirable musical activity in the state.
> The office of the state supervisor co-operates with
> local, county, state and federal agencies in their
> continuing efforts to enrich the lives of all our
> people.[8]

> At the present time only eighteen states have es-
> tablished a state supervisory position in music.
> Since this program must necessarily be the product
> of action by the State legislature, the reason for
> the small number of state music supervisors is
> fairly obvious.   It is a comparatively simple pro-

cess to sell a bargain package to an individual, but
it demands a tremendous advertising campaign to
convince the people of an entire state that one
small state job can pay them dividends a hundred-
fold. In North Carolina it took ten years of behind-
the-scenes pressure to set up this supervisory program, which was finally put into law in 1949; some
interested persons claim that it actually took nearer
twice twenty years. [9]

What are the characteristics or functions of the position state supervisor of music on a county, district, and
statewide basis?

This position usually connotes administrative, advisory, and coordinating duties. There must be a formulation
of policy for a statewide program of music education, for all
its citizens. In order to attain this goal the supervisor of
music must become involved in "a full-time program of vis-
itation, consultation, and the development of resource bulletins for teachers, but it should not stop there. That is only
a fraction of the need. There are myriad other cries for
help which cannot be ignored." [10]

The need for in-service training in the music field is
particularly urgent since most general supervisors feel completely inadequate to help their teachers in the specialized
areas of music. Schools which do not have a music specialist in some rural areas this means 70 per cent of the
schools--find that their only help in music comes from the
office of the state supervisor.

There is need for occasional "trouble-shooting" as an
administrator asks for help in developing a schedule for the
music program, or in co-ordinating his needs and facilities
with an existing local situation.

There must be the development of a state course of
study covering all phases of music education, and periodic
writing of bulletins which serve both the administrator and
the teacher as guides and supplementary material in a constantly changing situation.

There is a constant "mail-order" business coming to
the supervisor's desk. This essential service makes the office a clearing house for the immediate problems of music
specialists, classroom teachers, school administrators,

P.T.A.'s, and a host of others interested in music from
many angles.[11]

In a limited way some states provide intinerant instrumental and vocal teachers, through co-operative county,
district, and state action, those who are actually teachers
of music, but who are inadvertantly called supervisors of
music. Usually a state has but one supervisor of music; a
few have three or four.

Arnold E. Hoffman in a service inventory has more
recently stated the more specific duties performed by him
and his three consultants.[12]

Service Inventory[13]

1. Division: Department of Public Instruction.

    Service: advisor in music education and consultants.

2. Professional staff: one supervisor; three consultants.

3. The function of this department:

    a. The in-service training of teachers in the area
       of music education.

    b. The offering of aid in the establishment and de-
       velopment of organized school music programs.

    c. The assisting of superintendents, principals, gen-
       eral supervisors, and music teachers in the eval-
       uation of existing music programs in the light of
       current educational concepts.

    d. The introduction to teacher training institutions
       concepts of current practice and needs which will
       determine course offerings and course content in
       an effort to produce teachers who are able to
       work effectively in the schools of North Carolina.

    e. The acquainting of the community with the aims
       and procedures of a good school music program.

    f. The organization and administration of phases of
       music education in home demonstration clubs in
       North Carolina.

4. Funds are derived from the general allotment to the Department of Public Instruction.

5. No funds are administered by this department.

6. Services rendered:

    a. Organization and administration of local school programs.

    b. Aid to the classroom teacher in developing skills and musical understanding which she may use in regular classroom work.

    c. Work with general supervisors and music specialists in an effort to coordinate music and general education.

    d. Orientation of college administrators and music faculty concerning current practices in the public schools.

    e. Assistance in evaluating materials at hand, and provide, through bulletins, needed materials, not immediately available.

    f. Cooperation with local, state, and national professional organizations.

7. The services of the staff are implemented by the following procedures:

    a. By holding teacher workshops on an administrative unit basis.

    b. By doing demonstration teaching in classrooms.

    c. By having conferences with administrators, general supervisors, music specialists, and classroom teachers.

    d. By visiting colleges in an effort to coordinate inservice needs with college course content.

        1. Hold meetings with the music faculty.
        2. Talk with methods classes to brief them concerning the profession and the services of

this department to teachers in service.

e.   By helping in the evaluation of schools as members of evaluation committees.

f.   By holding area workshops with home demonstration club leaders who in turn give leadership to local clubs.

g.   By providing consultant service for professional meetings on state and local levels.

h.   By working closely with the general supervisor with all the above procedures related to the school.

8.   This department works closely with the following organizations: N.C.E.A., N.E.A., N.C.M.E.A., M.E.N.C., P.T.A., N.A.S.C.D., A.C.E.   Teacher training institutions, national survey groups, N.C. State Symphony, Grass Roots Opera Company.

9.   Clubs and adult activity interests:

Home Demonstration Clubs, 4-H Clubs, and Boy Scouts, N.C. Federation of Music Clubs.

10.   This department affects instruction in the following ways:

a.   Develops concepts and techniques of the classroom teacher in the music area.

b.   Coordinates the efforts of the music specialist, classroom teacher, and general supervisor concerning music and the general curriculum.

c.   Determines future instructional practices through an evaluation of existing music programs.

d.   Encourages the teacher to use music to stimulate the creative impulses of children through associating music with bodily movement, painting and vocal expression.

e.   Influences instruction by the use of music as recreation, music as a conditioning force in the classroom, and by enriching basic classroom activity through music.

11. The policies for operating this service are determined by the Department of Public Instruction and the composite thinking of the music staff.

The delineation of these administrative, instructional, and coordinative duties performed by a state supervisor of music indicates the importance of the position. It can be ascertained that there is a great need for state-wide coordination of all music activities. With his assistant music consultants, Hoffman has also pointed up additional advisory, cooperative, and public relation opportunities which his position provides and sometimes demands. He maintains that, "This one position (State Supervisor), properly set up and managed, can evaluate, guide, promote and co-ordinate all phases of desirable musical activity in the State."[14]

No state supervisor can think in terms of a minimum concept of music education for the few. He must envision for all members of the society for whom and to whom he is responsible a comprehensive concept of music education. For any state it is easily perceived that the responsibilities of the position are seemingly overwhelming and limitless in opportunity.

Discussion

1. Who was the chief music administrative officer in the last high school you attended?

2. Who would be the chief music administrative officer in a school system where there are two music teachers?

3. Name five areas of responsibility which are usually assumed by a music administrator.

4. Name five titular designations used to identify school administrative and teaching position organizational classifications.

5. Do you have a director of music as administrative head of your local public or parochial schools? If not, what is his title and what are his administrative responsibilities?

6. Contrast the duties of the music supervisor with those of a music specialist.

7. Do elementary in-service teachers need supervisory assistance? Describe the nature and extent of this assistance.

8.   Describe the educational functions assumed by supervisors of music.

9.   Do you favor the announced or the unannounced supervisory visit?

10.   What administrative importance would you attach to staff meetings?   How frequently do you think they should be held or under what circumstances?

11.   Why is evaluation of instruction a continuing process?

12.   Generally speaking, why has the music curricula at the secondary school level been so narrowly limited?

13.   What is the basic difference between the elementary and the secondary school curricula?

14.   Is it true that as the size of the school system increases instruction becomes more formalized?

15.   How would a curriculum laboratory aid in the development of your professional growth?

16.   What are some of the community responsibilities of the music administrator?

Notes

1.   "Music Supervision and Administration in the Schools." Music Education Research Council, Bulletin No. 18. Chicago: Music Educators National Conference, 1949, 5.

2.   Ibid., 9.

3.   Ward, Sylvan D.   "A Tribute To The Small Town Musician," Music Educators Journal, 43: No. 6 (June-July, 1957), 26, 28.

4.   "Music In Our Schools." Kansas City Times, May 13, 1957 (editorial). [Also in: Music Educators Journal, (June-July, 1957), 32.]

5.   Music In American Schools.   Music Education Source Book Number Two.   ed. by Hazel Nohavec Morgan. Chicago: Music Educators National Conference, 1955, 35.

6.   Ibid., 36.

7.   Ibid.

8. Hoffman, Arnold E. "What Does State Music Super-
    vision Mean?" Education, 76: No. 7 (March, 1956),
    436-439.

9. Ibid.

10. Ibid.

11. Ibid.

12. Submitted in 1957 by Dr. Arnold E. Hoffman, State
    Supervisor of Music, State of North Carolina.

13. Arnold Hoffman, privately printed administrative direc-
    tive, 1957.

14. Hoffman, Arnold E., "What Does State Music Super-
    vision Mean?" Education, 76: No. 7 (March, 1956),
    436.

Related Articles by the Author

"Early Methods of Popularizing Music Education," The Jour-
    nal of Musicology, 3: No. 1 (Summer, 1941), 60-66.

"Music Education for Tomorrow's Democracy," Education,
    64: No. 3 (November, 1943), 133-135.

"The Music Program in Teacher-Education Institutions,"
    The Elementary School Journal, 43: No. 5 (January,
    1943), 290-297.

"Problems in Graduate Teacher Education," The Southwestern
    Musician, 17: No. 4 (December, 1950), 4-27.

"Supervisional and Instructional Aspects of Early American
    Music Education," Educational Administration and Super-
    vision, 37: No. 6 (October, 1951), 337-354.

"Great Issues in Music Education," Education, 74: No. 1
    (September, 1953), 3-10.

CHAPTER XI: CHALLENGES AHEAD IN MUSIC EDUCATION

Music education has made great progress, but the heroic tasks of the past are in need of further work. There are yet to be established countless thousands of musical organizations. In many hundreds of communities the elementary music program is very largely a cursory one, while the teachers spend inordinate amounts of time preparing their secondary school performing organizations, although many schools employ a director of bands and choral music. But music needs budgeting or progress will be very slow. The expansion of any program is dependent upon sufficient amounts of human and material resources. There are numerous areas of the music profession that need continued pioneering and re-evaluation.

Music teaching is not a "bag of tricks." More skills are needed than just an ability to play or sing well. People accepting such nonsense believe in a concept which states that "anyone can be a teacher." An individual does not qualify for a position for which he served merely an apprenticeship in the college classroom. No degree or certificate in teacher education guarantees that the individual has other than probable academic qualification. The only way this can be improved is through a continuing fight for the type of selective teacher training programs which are in keeping with the professional needs.

True, there are methods of teaching academic subjects, but students are numbed by repetitious ideas which dove-tail all the areas incorporated under the heading of "methods." Too often, methods for teaching music have the student befogged. Preparation for music supervision and the teaching of music is very similar whether the individual is interested in primary, intermediate, or junior or senior high school teaching. Even though a curriculum is entitled "vocal supervision" it does not qualify a person to teach that subject at all grade levels.

Teacher Preparation. The musician of distinctive ability frequently turns professional; the disappointed turn

282

toward private teaching, or if they have found out the truth about the realities confronting such a career, they may pursue a college degree and resign themselves to school teaching. Their degree becomes an insurance policy against a type of professional hopelessness.

The present status of a number of our music teachers is that they are members of a large white-collared class who find themselves slowly, but surely being eradicated as a middle class. They are realizing that their monetary rewards are not always in keeping with their professional training and ability. Often they make less than skilled laborers. Teachers must share blame for the weakness of their position brought about partially by their own complacency.

Criteria for the selection of music teachers still remains in an infantile state. Often the major emphasis is placed upon performance rather than upon the candidate's ability for teaching boys and girls. A determining factor in the selection of school music teaching as a career, has been the awareness that it is both professionally and monetarily a source of vocational satisfaction. Dispositionally not every professional musician is qualified to teach music in our schools. Some individuals who are by training but not by temperament suited to teaching should pursue another profession. Although the student may have been in the upper quartile of his high school class, that in itself does not guarantee teaching success; especially is this true of the music teacher whose aptitude for imparting knowledge is combined with a very specialized performance skill.

The initial baptism to teaching is sometimes overwhelming and almost shocking. The young teacher is faced with "far-out" human problems that are not exactly part of the instructional process. They may have a bearing on child welfare and esprit de corps but certainly are not a part of the actual dissemination of knowledge.

The teacher was hired to teach, but often is required as well to be part-time psychiatrist, permanent psychologist, administrator and disciplinarian; he must handle boy and girl moral problems, be protector of child safety, be schoolroom nurse and first aid caretaker, attempt to understand each child in relationship to his heredity and home environment, sympathetically support local community projects, purchase those teaching materials or artifacts not supplied by the Board of Education, instill commendable qualities of citizen-

ship and patriotism, be subjected to all forms of insolence
and contemptible conduct, attempt to pacify and understand
parental-child problems, instill qualities of commendable
character, and evaluate and determine appropriate biracial
actions and stances in regard to racial problems. The music teacher, as any other, may receive anonymous letters,
have insurance to protect self against possible lawsuits, lose
the lunch period because of the time needed to help resolve
problems, attend staff and departmental meetings, have complete and sole responsibility for the children assigned to him,
be subjected to verbal and sometimes physical attacks, prepare to teach two or more different subjects each day, give
tests for the evaluation of instruction, make out reports to
the administration and sometimes to the parents, be expected
to attend one or more P.T.A. meetings each semester or
year, be responsible periodically for playground duty, possibly eat with his homeroom students, walk his children to
special instructional rooms, conduct parent-teacher conferences with the avowed purpose of securing potential help and
understanding, prepare and correct tests, and most of all,
to present inspired and challenging lessons which appeal to
children who could be physically handicapped, emotionally
disturbed, intellectually disinterested, or otherwise very difficult to reach. Teachers have numerous problems that
must be resolved daily.

   Teacher Training. The general music teacher should
be trained competently. Thorough preparation should include
1) the basic structural elements of music and the ability to
analyze them; 2) an intensive course in form and analysis;
3) an intensive study of the instruments of the orchestra; 4)
ability to use the solo voice and have a knowledgeable understanding of all basic vocal forms; 5) an elementary understanding of the legitimate theatre; 6) a study of the major instrumental forms; 7) the ability to perform acceptably on the
guitar, banjo, recorder, or piano; 8) a study of the arts and
their interrelationship with the humanities; 9) a language facility (speaking knowledge) common to the type of school
where a teaching position is desired; 10) a study of sociology
as related to the teaching position; 11) familiarity with teacher-training curricula which allow for greater flexibility of
studies. 12) The candidate studying to pursue a major in
general music studies should be a scholarly musician. A
comprehensive and functional command of all arts and their
relationship to music should be the individual's goal. 13)
Candidates for ghetto and inner-city teaching should preferably have lived in those socio-economic districts. In addition,

extensive observation and practice teaching must take place
in those areas in which the individual desires to teach.

Teacher training curriculums in music are not adequately geared to the job of preparing teachers for school
teaching. One of the most common conflicts is that of the
competitive nature existing between applied music and professional teacher training courses in music. For a long
time the need has been stressed for more applied music
courses and in some instances apparent deemphasis upon
practicums and in-service participation and practice teaching
in the actual teaching of music. Professional in-service
courses are often relegated to secondary considerations.
With the possible exception of the amount of semester hour
credit offered for specific courses, little progress has been
made in the number of courses designed for music teaching
situations. At the high school level there has been a de-
crease in the classroom approach to music teaching, except
where intelligently planned and coordinated courses in general music have been offered. Few are the school systems
where the theoretical study of music has been expanded by
the inclusion of theory, appreciation, history of music, and
extensive singing opportunities for the entire student body.

A weakness in music teacher education is the omnibus
character of music teacher education curricula. Great care
should be given to the nature of undergraduate requirements.
Too many courses are incorporated which are excessive for
the "job here and now." Although this is an exaggeration,
it is the comment most often levelled at teacher training in
music. Students are saturated with theory and impractical
untried ideas which lack serviceability for teaching needs.
Many methods course teachers have not taught music in
either the elementary or secondary school. The student in
assuming a practice teaching assignment is befuddled by all
of this, because he finds that much of the "old theory" or
"Ivory Tower" philosophy will not function in the every day
situation.

Stop and evaluate the courses incorporated into teaching training programs. The "how" of teaching is rarely applied to what should be taught. There are college faculties
adorned with those who have failed as school teachers and
have secured advanced degrees in order to guarantee their
collegiate teaching position against the erosions of reality--
many are not and have not been successful teachers.

The elementary and secondary school music program can be strengthened by an in-service thoroughly coordinated training program in the "how" of teaching music. Because of the lack of supervisional staff school music programs, much is remiss in this respect. School systems with small enrollments have difficulty in providing more than one or two vocal or instrumental teachers. Therefore a school system with such limited staff cannot afford the luxury of extensive in-service training programs. Supervisors in these school systems are often overloaded with large organization training activities. More than likely the schools with limited supervisory staff, derive greater satisfaction in training organizations whose personnel have attained a respectable degree of musical proficiency. Let us not discount the values to be derived from in-service training programs. An effective elementary school teacher with help can become if so disposed, an excellent classroom teacher of music. Certainly the many aspects of music study should provide some open doors of musical interest for him.

Encouraging results have already been obtained in the field of music therapy. Regardless of the nature of the institution served, expectations of those who have experimented with it have been more than fulfilled. Nowadays, some collegiate institutions such as Michigan State University have instituted courses teaching how to employ music therapy for many types of institutionalized individuals. Recognition of the need for the effective use of music therapy by those people who are responsible for hospitalized cases is rapidly increasing. When the experimentation gets beyond the empirical stages, more objective evidence will be available for study and evaluation.

There continues to be a definite stalemate in the music course requirements for preparing the individual better who is going to be a classroom teacher of music. Generally, the accepted two-to-three semester hour courses have been at best varied by reducing the six semester hours to three courses of two hours each; schools offering quarter hour credits would little change this requirement.

In surveying music major requirements for the baccalaureate degree, it was found that as few as 32 and as many as 90 semesters of academic work credit were required to prepare music teachers for teaching music in schools. Too often there is little differentiation made between the preparation and the in-service training programs of the elementary

and secondary school music teacher. Differentiation in the
curricula of the concert performer (applied music) and the
music educator (school music teacher) is not distinct enough.
Theoretical and applied music overbalances the professional
courses which give practical preparation for teaching school
music. The student is often inadequately supervised and not
wholeheartedly believed in by a majority of faculty; performing faculty have not had actual school music teaching experience; performers have as their major interest technical facility.

> Music Education and Adult Living. Does school mu-
sic carry over into the adult life of the American community? What happens to the choral singer upon graduation from
high school? What does the secondary and collegiate band
and orchestra player do with that expensive instrument his
parents purchased? School music must justify the thesis
that it makes living a more enjoyable experience.

If music can be justified as serving a functional experience in the life of school youth, that functionalism cannot cease upon graduation. If it does, then music has
failed; it has not taken hold of the individual. Whatever becomes part of man is certain to find expression. In a society characterized by much materialism, the tempo of
"just living" undoubtedly does much to consume man's free
time for the pursuit of the arts.

The question is, "What happens to the millions of
school musicians who graduate from secondary and collegiate
schools during every ten year period? What happens to the
hundreds of thousands of fine band and choral musicians upon graduation from high school? It is apparent that if a
small portion of these musicians were to pursue music avocationally in adult life, our nation would see great musical
activity. We are not alone in this concern. Rea states that

> While it is the hope of every sincere instrumen-
> tal music teacher that each of his students will
> gain enough in appreciation of music and other
> benefits to justify the time, effort, and expense
> of his training, the fact of the matter is that far
> too many students learn after graduation that
> their 'music education' was little more than a
> superficial, glorified extra-curricular activity.

The time has arrived for the instrumental music

teacher to give some serious thought to this matter. Some teachers are actually 'under fire' to
justify a budget for expensive instruments, uniforms, music, etc., for a program which to all
appearance has little or no carry-over into adult
life. The more subtle values of training in music which make for a richer and fuller life are
not very obvious to the average layman. For that
matter, the carry-over values of music, over and
above actual performance, are not easily ex-
plained to a parent who has a $200 instrument
lying idle around the house. To such a parent,
the statement that, 'Participation has led to appreciation' may only bring the reply of, 'How and
to what extent?' We as music teachers had better analyze the situation in an effort to determine
why our former students no longer play their instruments, and what, if anything, we can do to
remedy this. [1]

Rea further suggests six simple rules which he believes will help to solve participation after graduation:

1. Train every pupil in such a way as to lead him to
   musical independence.
2. Give every pupil small group experience.
3. Teach every instrumentalist who plays a transposition
   instrument to read from piano music.
4. Encourage every pupil to develop the faculty of playing
   by ear.
5. Give every player the largest possible variety of musical experience.
6. Accept the responsibility to promote the organization
   of groups which will offer an opportunity for adult
   participation. [2]

Undoubtedly the instrumental concern of Rea reflects the integrity of music educators for the profession they espouse.
But there are evidences in many areas that carry-over has
taken place.

In addition to the many professional vocal and instrumental organizations throughout America, the civic orchestras in Idaho Falls and Pocatello, [3] Idaho, opera workshop in
Lancaster, Pennsylvania, [4] and the Paterson Junior Philharmonic Orchestra of Paterson, New Jersey, indicate that music is abroad among the lay peoples in this land of ours.

The Paterson experiment is for youth 12 to 18 years old.
The Greater Paterson Philharmonic Society provides the service free to the children.[5] The Lancaster experiment provides its participants with

> ... the opportunity to sing in opera [which] has
> been presented in this locality by the Lancaster
> Opera Workshop. Although Lancaster, whose
> population is over 63 thousand, is headquarters
> for the group, the members actually live any-
> where within a 30-mile radius of the city. Of
> the 35 members of the workshop, only three in
> addition to myself are music teachers.[6]

These manifestations of carry-over music activity are typically healthy signs of its potential. This type of functional
organized activity should be the epitome of music education's
realization--music education for the entire community of men
for living.

Music for the masses has been successfully tried in
America. We have made some handsome strides in many
lay music appreciation and participation activities. Recent
figures (1969) indicate the significant advances that have been
achieved:

"Ten years ago, 22 million musical instruments were
owned in the United States. The current total: 37 million."

"Ten years ago, the nation counted nearly 30 million amateur musicians. Today, the figure is up to nearly 44
million."

"The number of persons playing each type of instrument
includes 23.5 million at the piano; 11 million at the guitar; 4.7 million at the organ; 800,000 at the accordion;
2.1 million at string instruments; four million at brass
instruments; and 4.2 million at woodwinds."

"The nation also has 1.1 million drummers, one million
harmonica players, and two million who play such things
as the banjo, mandolin, zither, bongo drums. In addition, nearly one million play the recorder, and half a
million plink along on the ukulele."

"The sound of music is loudest in public and parochial

schools. These now support around 70,000 large music
groups, including an estimated 51,000 marching and concert bands, 7,500 elementary, junior high and high
school orchestras, and 11,500 stage bands."[7]

Notes

1.   Rea, Ralph C. "Participation After Graduation." Mu-
     sic Educators Journal, 42:6 (June-July, 1956), 58-59.

2.   Ibid.

3.   Wilson, A. Verne. "The State of Music Education,"
     Music Educators Journal, 42:6 (June-July, 1956), 40.

4.   Tome, Sidney Ann. "Vocal 'Carry-Over' via Opera
     Workshop," Music Educators Journal, 40:4 (February-
     March, 1954), 70.

5.   Hass, Arthur. "Correlating School and Community Mu-
     sic," Music Educators Journal, 40:5 (April-May,
     1954), 71.

6.   Ibid., p. 70.

7.   "The Editor's Notes." The School Music News, 32:6
     (February, 1969), 25.

Appendix A

MUSIC EDUCATION WILL SERVE TOMORROW'S CHILDREN*

If The Administrator ...

.... believes that music is a socializing force for welding the maturing emotions of children into a constructive and purposeful mold for the good life.

.... insists that every known means be employed for giving music its rightly deserved emphasis in the school's program of studies.

.... insists that the music program be scheduled during the school day.

.... evaluates musical achievement not in terms of showmanship, but in terms of the per capita growth in the knowledge that living with good music will insure greater adult appreciation for it.

.... interprets music as an educational enterprise and not as a medium for school popularity or self-aggrandizement.

.... believes that music solidifies community emotions, idealisms, and relations.

.... is interested in solidifying community opinion behind a well-balanced music program.

.... is meticulous in securing a music teacher who is suffused with the idea that functional music makes for better school living.

.... visits his music teachers and becomes sensitive to their problems.

.... expects that music become a happy, functional, emotional, and intellectual experience for all children.

291

.... believes that music plays a vital role in education for dynamic citizenship.

If The Music Educator ...

.... emphasizes the need for exploring the musical interests of the child.

.... recognizes that his first obligation is to teach the child; music is just the medium to be used.

.... insists that techniques and methods are flexibly subservient to the child.

.... is more than just a musician; he must be a highly qualified teacher-musician.

.... maintains the idealism that enjoyable music opportunities for children subordinates all other objectives.

.... employs song materials which are suited to the intellectual, emotional, physiological, and psychological development of the child.

.... makes it possible for the child to become acquainted with all forms of classical, romantic, contemporary music.

.... provides the opportunity for each child to express himself creatively through all forms of musical experience.

.... insists that the music program be offered during the regular school day; a physically exhausted child should not be expected to produce music satisfactorily after-school hours.

.... welcomes research in music education as a necessary adjunct to the proper understanding and development of a school music program.

.... acknowledges that fact that although not all children are inordinately musical, although most of them enjoy music because it is a strong medium for socialization.

.... emphasizes the community sing for all youth; this is a phase or an activity in American music education that

has been woefully neglected; this will aid in bringing
massive song media into the schoolroom.

.... is avante-garde of those groups who attempt to curtail
the music program; the more vigorous the music program, the more difficult will it be to shake its foundations built on service, participation, worthy use of leisure time, and a worthwhile investiture of man's endowment.

.... vigorously supports a program of adult music.

.... uses all musical organizations for attaining musical opportunities for tomorrow's children.

If The Child ...

.... is led through music to enjoy the good life.

.... experiences music as a dynamic continuing process
from childhood through adult life.

.... finds in music an outlet for his creativeness through
the media of vocal and instrumental music.

.... learns songs because they are definitely related to his
enjoyment in experiencing a happy living environment.

.... enjoys modern music media because it is related to his
growth in order to experience growth in music.

.... understands that even mediocrity of musical effort is
encouraged.

.... can become part of a musical program where there is
much emphasis upon informal music.

.... can enjoy music which is taught for its own sake and
not necessarily as a medium for maintaining a happy
school situation in an academic environment.

.... is being fitted with a contemporary musical environment.

.... participates in a music program which is definitely related to home living.

.... enjoys a musical environment which deemphasizes the
music-mathematics of school music of past generations.

.... is led to appreciate the technical aspects of music as
necessary to the refining process so essential to artistic performance.

---

*Sunderman, Lloyd F. "Music Education in Tomorrow's
Democracy," Educational Music Magazine, XXVIII: No. 3
(January-February, 1944), 35, 36.

Appendix B

GENERAL MAXIMS FOR THE TEACHER

1. Never repeat an answer. Demand attention.

2. You are teaching not only music, but everything in the curriculum.

3. Teach the necessary and exclude the exceptional.

4. Use both praise and blame sparingly.

5. Avoid monotony in the lesson.

6. Encourage self-expression.

7. Be sincere but not too serious.

8. The real teacher is one who makes two ideas grow where but one grew before.

9. Good cheer is the twin sister to success in music.

10. Always speak to the pupils as though it were a privilege for them to do things.

11. There is no problem until it develops. Don't anticipate difficulties.

12. Don't encourage mistakes, but don't make the pupils afraid to make them.

13. Have one big objective for each lesson and let the children know what it is.

14. Example is better than precept.

15. Assume that the pupils have common sense. Allow them to develop their reasoning power.

16. Do not tell them things they can discover for themselves.

17. Explain nothing without its application.

18. Always use the positive side of a statement.

19. A powerful teacher is one who does much and talks little.

20. The recipe for perpetual ignorance is to be satisfied with your own opinions and content with your own knowledge.

21. Be a magnet--not a shuttle. Education: "educe, " I draw out.

22. Find the wrong thing and improve it.

23. Come into the room smiling and bring a pleasant atmosphere with you.

24. Be business-like as well as pleasant.

25. Don't take your lessons out of cold storage. Prepare fresh ones.

26. Do more than your duty.

27. A smile is worth a thousand scowls in the classroom.

28. Keep up your enthusiasm. Don't forget that everything is new to the children.

29. A bit of tact is worth a ton of nagging. Variety is the spice of life.

30. Distinguish between essentials and non-essentials.

31. Life is not enriched by selfishness but by joyful service.

32. Be accurate and teach exactness.

33. Don't wear the children out by demanding "fussy" things.

34. Master your materials and routines.

35. Don't mind a disappointment. Keep at it.

36. If measles are contagious, so are melody, rhythm and harmony.

37. Children learn more from other children than from teachers.

38. The most important element in the teacher's native equipment is a discriminating ear.

39. A disinterested child will not try.

40. Children must have an immediate attractive motive offering fairly immediate satisfaction.

41. There must be a large quantity of the right quality of material.

42. Children tend to find meaning in the largness of things.

43. Don't teach: let them learn and guide them in the learning.

44. Don't make promises--make them good. Don't alibi-- try again.

45. Don't dump your woes upon other people. Keep the sad story of your life to yourself.

46. Guard against overteaching.

47. Consider junior high school pupils not as adult infants, but as infant adults.

48. Fit the methods to the pupils and not the pupils to the methods.

49. The habit of attention is the first habit the children should learn in school.

50. Use a conversational voice at all times, pitched low rather than high.

51. When the reason for a device has ceased to exist, the device should be dropped.

52. Emphasize personal responsibility by individual work.

53. Never assume that a pupil does not know.

54. Don't stop to think--think on the run.

55. Always have a reason for everything you do.

56. Keep the sparkle in the children's eyes.

57. Be definite: say exactly what you mean.

58. Take work from the children's viewpoint. Enter into the mind of the child.

59. Say the unexpected thing--keep the class alert.

60. Use humor--but not through sarcasm.

61. Take their efforts seriously. It isn't what you say that counts but the way you say it.

62. Make the children think they can do things. Approach problems from the affirmative side.

63. Admit one mistake if you make it. Never admit two. Never make two.

64. Be sure that the children are working up to one hundred per cent efficiency. Ninety-nine per cent won't do.

65. Diagnose as teachers, the weaknesses of the class.

66. Drill for alertness. Check up by asking questions unexpectedly.

67. Create an interest in the pupils first, by personality and encouragement.

68. Be sure you lend pleasantness and confidence to the class.

69. Be interested and interesting.

70. Be sincere. Personality is no good unless it rings true. Be open and above board and you will have no cause to be afraid.

71. Put a little pep into everything you do and say and look.

72. A grade teacher often needs encouragement rather than censure.

73. To know but one so-called method or system is not to know that one.

74. The supervisor is the best educated who is the most useful. Education is adaptability.

75. The supervisor should be the leading spirit in the musical life of the community.

INDEX